D1558974

CAMBRIDGE COMMENTARIES ON
WRITINGS OF THE JEWISH AND CHRISTIAN WORLD
200 BC TO AD 200
VOLUME 4

Outside the Old Testament

CAMBRIDGE COMMENTARIES ON
WRITINGS OF THE JEWISH AND CHRISTIAN WORLD
200 BC TO AD 200

General Editors:

P. R. ACKROYD

A. R. C. LEANEY

J. W. PACKER

OUTSIDE THE
OLD TESTAMENT

M. DE JONGE

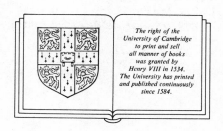

The right of the
University of Cambridge
to print and sell
all manner of books
was granted by
Henry VIII in 1534.
The University has printed
and published continuously
since 1584.

CAMBRIDGE UNIVERSITY PRESS

Cambridge

London   New York   New Rochelle
Melbourne   Sydney

Published by the Press Syndicate of the University of Cambridge
The Pitt Building, Trumpington Street, Cambridge CB2 IRP
32 East 57th Street, New York, NY 10022, USA
10 Stamford Road, Oakleigh, Melbourne 3166, Australia

© Cambridge University Press 1985

First published 1985

Printed in Great Britain by
the University Press, Cambridge

British Library cataloguing in publication data

Outside the Old Testament. – (Cambridge commentaries on
writings of the Jewish and Christian world 200 BC to 200 AD;
v. 4)
1. Apocryphal books (Old Testament) – Criticism, interpretation, etc.
I. Jonge, M. de
29'.91   BS1700

Library of Congress cataloguing in publication data

Main entry under title:
Outside the Old Testament.
(Cambridge commentaries on writings of the Jewish and
Christian world, 200 BC to AD 200; v. 4)
1. Apocryphal books (Old Testament) – Criticism, inter-
pretation, etc. – Addresses, essays, lectures.
I. Jonge, Marinus de, 1925– . II. Series.
BS1700.097   1985 229'.91052   85–5281

ISBN 0 521 24249 5 hard covers
ISBN 0 521 28554 2 paperback

Contents

General Editors' Preface

The three general editors of the Cambridge Bible Commentary series have all, in their teaching, experienced a lack of readily usable texts of the literature which is often called pseudepigrapha but which is more accurately defined as extra-biblical or para-biblical literature. The aim of this new series is to help fill this gap.

The welcome accorded to the Cambridge Bible Commentary has encouraged the editors to follow the same pattern here, except that carefully chosen extracts from the texts, rather than complete books, have normally been provided for comment. The introductory material leads naturally into the text, which itself leads into alternating sections of commentary.

Within the severe limits imposed by the size and scope of the series, each contributor will attempt to provide for the student and general reader the results of modern scholarship, but has been asked to assume no specialized theological or linguistic knowledge.

The volumes already planned cover the writings of the Jewish and Christian World from about 200 BC to AD 200 and are being edited as follows:

1 i *Jews in the Hellenistic World: Josephus, Aristeas, the Sibylline Oracles, Eupolemus* – J. R. Bartlett, Trinity College, Dublin
1 ii *Jews in the Hellenistic World: Philo* – R. Williamson, University of Leeds
2 *The Qumran Community* – M. A. Knibb, King's College, London
3 *Early Rabbinic Writings* – H. Maccoby, Leo Baeck College, London
4 *Outside the Old Testament* – M. de Jonge, University of Leiden
5 *Outside the New Testament* – G. N. Stanton, King's College, London
6 *Jews and Christians: Graeco-Roman Views* – M. Whittaker, University of Nottingham

A seventh volume by one of the general editors, A. R. C. Leaney, *The Jewish and Christian World 200 BC to AD 200*, examines the wider historical and literary background to the period and includes tables of dates, relevant lists and maps. Although this companion volume will preface and augment the series, it may also be read as complete in itself and be used as a work of general reference.

P. R. A.   A. R. C. L.   J. W. P.

Editor's Foreword

This volume brings together extracts from and introductions to twelve writings dealing with prominent Old Testament figures. They tell what happened to them, what God revealed to them and through them, and try to bring home to their readers what can be learned from their examples and their explicit exhortations. Often there is also an outlook on the future intended to comfort and to encourage the readers in the difficult circumstances they have to endure.

These writings all belong to the so-called 'Pseudepigrapha' of the Old Testament – a term used (rather loosely) 'to cover writings connected with biblical books, personalities or themes, which failed to be included in any canon, even among the Apocrypha' – so A. R. C. Leaney in *The Jewish and Christian World 200 BC to AD 200*, p. 158, in this series, who also gives an extensive list of writings which may be ranged under this category.

This volume, like the others in this series, is modest in scope. The extracts from the selected writings have been chosen and introduced by authors who have dealt with them also in other contexts, often in much detail. The editor is very grateful to them for consenting to share their specialist knowledge. Obviously many details have had to be omitted and divergent opinions and supporting arguments of other specialists in the field could only very seldom be mentioned. The various contributions to this volume simply aim at introducing a fascinating collection of writings and showing ways to explore this area a little further. The authors have tried to convey their own interest in and enthusiasm for these books 'Outside the Old Testament'.

A number of people have given me help and advice in the preparation of this book. I record here with gratitude the advice given by the General Editors and by my friends George W. E. Nickelsburg and Michael E. Stone. Mrs Th. C. C. M. Heesterman-Visser gave valuable secretarial help and assisted in the preparation of the final manuscript.

Acknowledgements

Excerpts from the Testament of Abraham, the Syriac Apocalypse of Baruch and the Testament of Job are reprinted by permission of Doubleday and Company, Inc. from *The Old Testament Pseudepigrapha*, volume I, edited by James H. Charlesworth, copyright © 1983 by James H. Charlesworth.

Excerpts from Pseudo-Philo: *Liber Antiquitatum Biblicarum*, from Joseph and Aseneth and from the Ascension of Isaiah are reprinted also by permission of Doubleday and Company, Inc. from *The Old Testament Pseudepigrapha* volume II, edited by James H. Charlesworth, copyright © 1985 by James H. Charlesworth.

Excerpts from the Ethiopic Book of Enoch are reproduced from Michael A. Knibb and E. Ullendorf, *The Ethiopic Book of Enoch*, volume II, 1978, by kind permission of the Oxford University Press.

Abbreviations

Josephus

War	*The Jewish War*
Ant.	*Antiquities of the Jews*
Apion	*Against Apion* or *Contra Apion*

Philo

Cher	De Cherubim
Congr	De Congressu Eruditionis Gratia
Ebr	De Ebrietate
Fug	De Fuga et Inventione
Migr Abr	De Migratione Abrahami
Op Mund	De Opificio Mundi
Praem Poen	De Praemiis et Poenis
Sobr	De Sobrietate
Som	De Somniis
Spec Leg	De Specialibus Legibus
Virt	De Virtutibus
Vit Cont	De Vita Contemplativa
Vit Mos	De Vita Mosis

Pseudepigrapha

ApAB	Apocalypse of Abraham
TAb	Testament of Abraham
2Bar	2 (Syriac) Baruch
3Bar	3 (Greek) Baruch
4Bar	4 Baruch
ApEl	Apocalypse of Elijah
1En	1 (Ethiopic) Enoch
2En	2 (Slavonic) Enoch
3En	3 (Hebrew) Enoch
4Ezra	4 Ezra
GkApEzra	Greek Apocalypse of Ezra
AscenIs	Ascension of Isaiah
MartIs	Martyrdom of Isaiah
TJob	Testament of Job
JosAsen	Joseph and Aseneth

Jub	Jubilees
LAB	*Liber Antiquitatum Biblicarum*
ApMos	Apocalypse of Moses
AsMos	Assumption of Moses
PJ	*Paraleipomena Jeremiou*
Ps-Philo	Pseudo-Philo
SibOr	Sibylline Oracles
PssSol	Psalms of Solomon
T12P	Testaments of the Twelve Patriarchs
TReu	Testament of Reuben
TSim	Testament of Simeon
TLevi	Testament of Levi
TJud	Testament of Judah
TIss	Testament of Issachar
TZeb	Testament of Zebulun
TDan	Testament of Dan
TNaph	Testament of Naphtali
TGad	Testament of Gad
TAsh	Testament of Asher
TJos	Testament of Joseph
TBenj	Testament of Benjamin

Qumran Documents

CD	Damascus Document
1QH	Hymns, Hodayot
1QM	War Scroll
1QpHab	Commentary on Habbakuk
1QS	Community Rule, or Manual of Discipline
1QSa	Messianic Rule

Other Abbreviations

AGJU	Arbeiten zur Geschichte des antiken Judentums und des Urchristentums
ALGHJ	Arbeiten zur Literatur und Geschichte des hellenistischen Judentums
AOAT	Alter Orient und Altes Testament
A.R.N.	Abot deRabbi Nathan
b.	Babylonian Talmud
CBQ	*Catholic Biblical Quarterly*
Gr.	Greek
Hebr. t.	Hebrew text

HTR	*Harvard Theological Review*
HUCA	*Hebrew Union College Annual*
JBL	*Journal of Biblical Literature*
JJS	*Journal of Jewish Studies*
JSHRZ	Jüdische Schriften aus hellenistisch-römischer Zeit
PsVTGr	Pseudepigrapha Veteris Testamenti Graece
P.Targ.	Palestinian Targum
R.	Rabbah
SBL	Society of Biblical Literature
SC	Sources chrétiennes
SCS	Septuagint and Cognate Studies
Strack-Billerbeck	H. L. Strack and P. Billerbeck, *Kommentar zum Neuen Testament aus Talmud und Midrasch*, 6 vols., Munich, 1974–5 (repr.)
StVTPs	Studia in Veteris Testamenti Pseudepigrapha
TU	Texte und Untersuchungen
y.	Yerushalmi (Palestinian Talmud)

General Introduction

M. DE JONGE

The so-called Pseudepigrapha

In the companion volume to this series, *The Jewish and Christian World 200 BC to AD 200*, A. R. C. Leaney has given a short history of the origin of Law, Prophets and Writings as an authoritative Hebrew canon of Scripture. He has also pointed to the existence of the Apocrypha of the Greek and Latin Bible and of Pseudepigrapha, a term used to denote a number of writings, other than the canonical books and the apocrypha, that profess to give genuine information about important biblical figures and to convey, through them, teaching relevant to later generations.

The word 'pseudepigraphon', in the strict sense of 'a writing with false superscription or title' (Liddell–Scott–Jones, *Greek-English Lexicon*), can only be applied to a certain number of these writings. The Testament (Assumption) of Moses, for example, gives the last words of Moses (in a narrative setting) and the Testaments of the Twelve Patriarchs give the parting words of the sons of Jacob; the apocalypses 1 Enoch and 2 Baruch record visions seen by Enoch and Baruch, again in a narrative setting. But other narratives are in the first place narratives about biblical figures (so, for example, Joseph and Aseneth, the Martyrdom of Isaiah, the *Paraleipomena Jeremiou* and the Testament of Job) in which the words of the central figures function within the story about them. There, too, it is of course supposed that what they did and said is of the utmost importance for the readers in their own situation.

The twelve writings introduced here form a representative selection of the much larger group of writings briefly introduced in Leaney's volume. 4 Ezra (2 Esdras) is not included here because this book, belonging to the Apocrypha of the English Bible, has already received its commentary by M. A. Knibb in R. J. Coggins and M. A. Knibb, *The First and Second Books of Esdras*, in the CBC series, Cambridge, 1979. It is important in connection with 2Bar and *PJ*.

Pseudepigraphy

It is necessary to say something here about pseudepigraphy, a very varied and complex phenomenon by no means confined to the so-called Pseudepigrapha of the Old Testament. The following considerations may be relevant:

(a) In a difficult period in the life of the people or of a group within Israel, pseudepigraphy served to transmit guidance from authoritative figures in the past. It is assumed that what is true and relevant in the present time, must have been true and relevant from of old. The heroes of the past must have experienced and taught much more than what is handed down in those writings which have gradually become authoritative. The essence of pseudepigraphy is not the false attribution of writings to people who have nothing to do with them, but the keen awareness of some sort of ongoing revelation and of the task of continuous reinterpretation of the truth and wisdom transmitted in God's history with his people.

(b) Some figures in the past had and have specific functions. Moses received the revelation of the 'written Torah' (as well as of the 'oral Torah', according to the scribes) on Mount Sinai. It does not come as a surprise, then, that Jubilees, a rewritten version of Genesis and part of Exodus, tries to bring a number of points about beliefs and practices home to his readers in the form of a revelation transmitted to Moses by an angel. Moses and the angel are the authorities behind this view of Israel's earliest history and this particular interpretation of its *halakah* (binding regulations). Another example: if a number of psalms, sung or read in certain Jewish circles, give voice to certain significant common experiences, they are collected and ascribed to Solomon, one of the composers of psalms and hymns in Scripture. Or, if the Jews are disoriented because of the destruction of Jerusalem in AD 70, some circles attempt to reconcile this disaster with the belief in God's guidance of Israel and to sustain hope in a new beginning, and for that purpose they invoke the authority of Jeremiah and his secretary Baruch, unwavering servants of God at the time of the destruction of the city before the Babylonian exile.

(c) Pseudepigraphy as a means of appeal to the authorities of the past is used for different purposes. As the introductions to the individual writings in this volume show, it is very difficult to define certain genres in this literature. Four of them, for instance, bear the title 'testament' but almost the only common element seems to be the connection with the death of an important person. It is equally difficult to describe the characteristics of apocalyptic writings – such as 1 Enoch and 2 Baruch, introduced here – because 'apocalyptic' passages or elements are also found in other documents.

Yet it may be useful to say something about the purpose of pseudepigraphy in a writing rightly regarded as a collection of testaments: the Testaments of the Twelve Patriarchs. The sons of Jacob transmit certain exhortations to their sons with the command to hand them down to future generations. Biographical examples and predictions concerning the future serve to underline the value and the strength of the ethical commands. The literary device of a 'testament' connects the readers of the present with the authorities of the past: Israel has to give heed to the wise words of its Fathers.

Pseudepigraphy in apocalyptic writings is often connected with the motif of secret tradition. Before departing from this life Ezra, under divine inspiration, commits ninety-four books to writing in forty days, with the help of five assistants. Twenty-four of these books are to be made public at once, 'but the last seventy books are to be kept back, and given to none but the wise among your people' (2 Esdras 14:37–48). Apocalyptic writings are not for everyone; they have to be handed down in certain circles (cp. 1En 104:12, 13), and are often ordered to be kept 'sealed' until the end of days (cp. Dan. 8:26; 12:9). The visions recorded in them deal with events that lie in the future for the authority who is speaking; for the readers they give guidance as to the true interpretation of what happened in the past, they assure them that what was predicted has become reality and that the events which have not yet come about will also certainly happen as predicted. In this way apocalypses transmit secret knowledge which is studied carefully in special circles occupying themselves with discerning the signs of the times and interpreting God's instructions for life and faith to his faithful ones in a dark age.

Questions of date and provenance

In the case of these writings questions of date and provenance can often be answered only with great difficulty. Although they originated in a special situation and with a claim to speak to the condition of special groups of believers in that situation, their authors could only hint at the specific circumstances they had in mind because they took their stand in the past. Next, the history of Israel in the period between 200 BC and AD 200 may be (and often has been) described as a time of continuous crisis, testing the faithfulness and perseverance of the Jewish people, particularly of the law-abiding pious circles in the nation. What was originally written for a particular period was equally relevant on later occasions. Writings were read and reread, perhaps also (partly) rewritten to fit the new situation. They were handed down not only because they were connected with a biblical person but also because they continued to be relevant.

Unfortunately we know very little about the circumstances of transmission in Jewish circles. Only lately fragments of 1 Enoch and Jubilees in Aramaic and Hebrew have come to light among the Qumran Scrolls so that we can gain at least some idea of the earliest form of these writings (see M. A. Knibb, *The Qumran Community*, in this series, forthcoming). On the whole, however, the pseudepigrapha have come down to us via Christian channels; the primary witnesses are late, and often we have to work with translations of translations. This means that the reconstruction of the oldest accessible text is very difficult and that we have to reckon with a long history of transmission often in remote parts of the Church, such as Ethiopia or Armenia where some writings still held a place of honour when they were forgotten, or only regarded as devotional literature, in other regions of Christianity.

It is essential to keep the history of transmission of each individual writing in mind while one tries to establish its most original form and content. Sometimes there are only few clearly Christian elements which can be set on one side easily, in other cases there must have been a more thorough Christian redaction. In all instances a considerable time has elapsed and much may have happened between the original composition and the copying by Christian scribes of the oldest witnesses at our disposal.

So far the so-called pseudepigrapha of the Old Testament have mainly been studied as documents reflecting the beliefs and convictions of various Jewish groups in the centuries around the beginning of Christianity, as a welcome addition to and correction of what was transmitted through other (particularly later rabbinic) channels. They remain important for that purpose, certainly in connection with the documents found at Qumran. Much less attention has been devoted to the answer to the question why they were taken over by the early Christians and what part they played in the Church, in the first centuries and also much later. The Christians recognized the authority of the Patriarchs, the Prophets and other great and wise men; they were thought to have spoken about Christ and about the life and faith of his followers, and their words in what had become the Old Testament of the Church were, at least to a great extent, regarded as inspired. How the individual pseudepigrapha fitted into this general picture is very often not clear. But the fact that they were handed down and eventually reached us in sometimes very roundabout ways testifies to the abiding value they were thought to have, at least in some parts of Christianity.

Suggestions for further reading

A recent introduction to the literature under discussion is G. W. E. Nickelsburg, *Jewish Literature Between the Bible and the Mishnah. A Historical and Literary Introduction*, Philadelphia, 1981. It deals with Daniel, (nearly) all the Apocrypha, many Pseudepigrapha and a selection of the Dead Sea Scrolls and treats them against the background of Jewish history. This is without any doubt a very useful tool for any reader who wants to study the Pseudepigrapha in greater depth.

A very full collection of Pseudepigrapha in translation is found in James H. Charlesworth (ed.), *The Old Testament Pseudepigrapha*, vols. I–II, Garden City, N.Y., 1983–5. In Germany the 'Jüdische Schriften aus hellenistisch-römischer Zeit' (JSHRZ), Gütersloh, 1973ff, are appearing in separate fascicles which will eventually make up five volumes. Editors are W. G. Kümmel, C. Habicht, O. Kaiser, O. Plöger and J. Schreiner. For serious study these two modern editions are indispensable. For quick reference the reader will do well to consult H. F. D. Sparks, *The Apocryphal Old Testament*, Oxford, 1984. This edition gives new translations of twenty five writings, with introductions and short notes. It appeared too late to be consulted by the contributors to the present volume.

Well-known (and often reprinted) are two older standard collections, the one edited by R. H. Charles, *The Apocrypha and Pseudepigrapha of the Old Testament*, vols. I–II, Oxford, 1913 and the other by E. Kautzsch, *Die Apokryphen und Pseudepigraphen des Alten Testaments*, vols. I–II, Tübingen, 1900.

Literature on the various individual writings can be found in Nickelsburg's book, in *The Old Testament Pseudepigrapha*, *The Apocryphal Old Testament* and in JSHRZ.

Further useful tools are A.-M. Denis, *Introduction aux Pseudépigraphes grecs d'Ancien Testament* (StVTPs I), Leiden, 1970; J. H. Charlesworth, *The Pseudepigrapha and Modern Research with Supplement* (SBL Septuagint and Cognate Studies 7S), Chico, 1981, and G. Delling and M. Maser, *Bibliographie zur jüdisch-hellenistischen und intertestamentarischen Literatur: 1900–1970* (TU 106[2]), Berlin, 1975.

Another useful book is M. E. Stone (ed.), *Jewish Writings of the Second Temple Period* (Compendia Rerum Iudaicarum ad Novum Testamentum, vol. II, 2), Assen-Philadelphia, 1984. It deals with the Apocrypha, Pseudepigrapha, Qumran sectarian writings, Philo and Josephus.

In their *Faith and Piety in Early Judaism*, Philadelphia, 1983, George W. E. Nickelsburg and Michael E. Stone give a number of select passages on different topics with a view to presenting many aspects of the life and thought of early Judaism. They aim at the same audience, covering a wider range of sources than those treated in this volume. Their book may well be read in connection with

Pseudo-Philo, *Liber Antiquitatum Biblicarum*
DANIEL J. HARRINGTON

Title

This book was not written under the name of Philo, nor was *Liber Antiquitatum Biblicarum* (*LAB*) its original title. The manuscripts of *LAB* were included among the Latin translations of the writings of Philo of Alexandria. But the author made no pretence of being Philo, and so the work is not technically a pseudepigraphon. Furthermore, nothing in the theology and the treatment of the Old Testament links it to Philo of Alexandria. The ascription to Philo probably rests on its similarity in form and content to the Antiquities of Josephus. That is, since one book of Antiquities was written by Josephus, this other book of Antiquities must have been written by Philo.

The Latin title *Liber Antiquitatum Biblicarum* (Book of Biblical Antiquities) first appeared in the 1552 edition published at Lyons by S. Gryphe. The word Antiquities appears on the label of one of the manuscripts and was taken over as part of the book's title (*Liber Antiquitatum*) in 1527 by its first editor, Johannes Sichardus.

The text

LAB exists in eighteen complete and three fragmentary manuscripts. The manuscripts are of German or Austrian origin, and date from the eleventh to the fifteenth century. All the Latin evidence is presented in my edition in *Pseudo-Philon, Les Antiquités Bibliques*, vol. 1. Parts of *LAB* appear in Hebrew form in the Chronicles of Jerahmeel, but those texts appear to be translations from Latin to mediaeval Hebrew. I have edited and translated the Hebrew texts in *The Hebrew Fragments of Pseudo-Philo* (for details see Bibliography).

The most important Latin manuscripts are Fulda-Kassel Theol. 4°, 3 (eleventh century) and Phillipps 461 (twelfth century). But the relations among the Latin manuscripts are such that the second major group can preserve readings that reflect the earliest stage of the Latin tradition. Furthermore, there is ample evidence (see my 'The Original Language of Pseudo-Philo's *Liber Antiquitatum Biblicarum*', *HTR* (1970),

503–14) that the Latin text was translated from Greek and that the Greek version was based on a Hebrew original. This complex history of transmission must be taken into account in translating and interpreting *LAB*.

Literary genre and aim

The author of *LAB* rewrote and expanded parts of the biblical story from Adam to David. In literary form, the work is closest to the Antiquities of Josephus and the Qumran Genesis Apocryphon. The literary form of those books has been described variously as midrash, targum, and rewritten Bible. But each of those terms raises as many problems as it resolves. At any rate, the author of *LAB* sought to include within the framework of the biblical story from Adam to David the exegetical traditions and theological ideas that were current in his time. Perhaps he wished to provide a kind of handbook for synagogue preachers. Or he may simply have wished to 'bring up to date' the biblical narratives. Attempts to narrow his audience down to a specific group (Samaritans, Hellenists, Essenes, Gnostics, Idumaeans, Galileans) have not been very convincing.

Content

The books of the Old Testament from Genesis to 1 Samuel provide the structural framework for *LAB*: Genesis (*LAB* 1–8), Exodus (*LAB* 9:1–13:2), Leviticus (*LAB* 13:3–10), Numbers (*LAB* 14–18), Deuteronomy (*LAB* 19), Joshua (*LAB* 20–4), Judges (*LAB* 25–48), and 1 Samuel (*LAB* 49–65). The story breaks off rather abruptly just before the death of Saul (65:5). The author may have intended to end on a note of repentance with Saul saying: 'Be not mindful of my hatred or my iniquity.' But it is also possible that the ending of the work was lost. How much was lost (one page, or half the book) cannot be known.

The author of *LAB* displays a very strong interest in Israel as God's people and in the covenant. His other theological interests include the evil of mixed marriages, the place of women, biblical geography, angels and demons, the after-life, God's eschatological visitation, and the relation between sin and punishment.

The seven passages selected for translation and commentary in this volume illustrate how Ps-Philo used the text of the Old Testament as a vehicle for including exegetical and other traditional material: the apocalypse of Noah (Gen. 8:21–2), the birth of Moses (Exod. 2:1–10), the death of Moses (Deut. 34:1–6), the sacrifice of Isaac (Gen. 22:1–18), the testament of Deborah (Judg. 5:7), the announcement of Samson's birth (Judg. 13:2–20), and the song of David the exorcist (1 Sam. 16:14–23). Each of these passages interweaves biblical texts and other materials, and each has relevance for New Testament study. They also illustrate the variety of literary forms used in *LAB*.

Date and place

The parallels between *LAB*, 4 Ezra (2 Esdras), and 2 Baruch are not sufficient to prove a date of composition after AD 70. A date prior to AD 70 (and perhaps around the time of Jesus) is suggested by the kind of Old Testament text used in the book, the free attitude towards the text, the interest in the sacrifices and other things pertaining to cult, and the silence about the destruction of the temple. These same points, as well as the likelihood that *LAB* was composed in Hebrew, indicate a Palestinian origin.

Bibliography

D. J. Harrington and J. Cazeaux, *Pseudo-Philon, Les Antiquités Bibliques*, vol. 1: 'Introduction et texte critiques. Traduction' (SC 229), Paris, 1976.

D. J. Harrington, *The Hebrew Fragments of Pseudo-Philo* (SBL Texts and Translations 3, Pseudepigrapha Series 3), Missoula, 1974.

C. Perrot and P. M. Bogaert, *Pseudo-Philon, Les Antiquités Bibliques*, vol. 11: 'Introduction littéraire, commentaire et index' (SC 230), Paris, 1976.

M. R. James, *The Biblical Antiquities of Philo*, New York, 1971. This edition of a book first published in 1917 contains a 169-page prolegomenon by L. H. Feldman.

C. Dietzfelbinger, *Pseudo-Philo: Antiquitates Biblicae (Liber Antiquitatum Biblicarum)* (JSHRZ 11/2), pp 91–271.

D. J. Harrington, in J. H. Charlesworth (ed.), *The Old Testament Pseudepigrapha*, vol. 11, forthcoming.

THE APOCALYPSE OF NOAH (*LAB* 3:9–10)

God's promise to Noah not to destroy the earth again by a flood provides the occasion for a revelation or apocalypse in which a scenario of eschatological events is given. The passage illustrates some of Ps-Philo's characteristic methods of composition. He quotes from Gen. 8:21–2, gives explanations and refinements of the biblical material, and adds to it an eschatological compendium based on Jewish traditions. The scenario of events consists of the interruption of the world as we know it, the resurrection of the dead, the general judgement, and the renewal of creation to be enjoyed by the just. It differs from the eschatological scenarios in the Synoptic Gospels (Mark 13:1–37, and parallels) chiefly in its total silence about the Son of Man.

9 And God said: 'I will never again curse the earth on man's account, for the tendency of man's heart is foolish from his youth; and so I will never destroy all living creatures at one time as I have done. But when those inhabiting the earth sin, I will judge them by famine or by the sword or by fire or by death; and there will be earthquakes, and they will be scattered to uninhabited places. But no more will I destroy the earth by the water of the flood. And in all the days of the earth, seedtime and harvest, cold and heat, spring and autumn will not cease day and night, until I remember those who inhabit the earth, until the appointed times are fulfilled.

10 But when the years appointed for the world have been fulfilled, then the light will cease and the darkness will fade away. And I will bring the dead to life and raise up those who are sleeping from the earth. And hell will pay back its debt, and the place of perdition will return its deposit so that I may render to each according to his works and according to the fruits of his own devices, until I judge between soul and flesh. And the world will cease, and death will be abolished, and hell will shut its mouth. And the earth will not be without progeny or sterile for those inhabiting it; and no one who has been pardoned by me will be tainted. And there will be another earth and another heaven, an everlasting dwelling place.'

9. *And God said...as I have done*: according to the quotation from Gen. 8:21, God recognized the waywardness of humanity but promised never to destroy the earth again as he did in Noah's time. *the tendency of man's heart*: the literal translation of the Hebrew text of Gen. 8:21 refers to the impulse that guides human activities along good or evil ways. *is foolish*: the Latin manuscripts read 'has left off' (*desiit*), but the conjecture 'is foolish' (*desipit*) better reflects the meaning. *in all the days*: in Gen. 8:22, God promised Noah that the natural cycle of the earth would continue. The end of that cycle depends entirely on God's decision to initiate the sequence of eschatological events. *until the appointed times are fulfilled*: compare 'until the times of the Gentiles are fulfilled' in Luke 21:24.

10. *But when the years...have been fulfilled*: the cycle ends when the period determined by God has been completed. *the light will cease*: the phrase echoes Gen. 8:21 and indicates that a new period will begin. *I will bring the dead to life*: the resurrection of the dead is a major event in the last days. *sleeping*: the idea of the dead sleeping in the earth appears in *LAB* 9:6; 19:12; 35:3; 51:5. See also 4 Ezra 7:32 and 2Bar 11:4; 21:24. *deposit*: the Latin *paratecem* reflects the Greek word *parathēkē*. The reading *partem* found in some Latin manuscripts substitutes a more familiar but less accurate word for the loan word *paratecem*. The idea of Sheol returning its deposit appears in *LAB* 33:3; 1En 51:1; 4 Ezra 4:41–3; 7:32; and 2Bar 21:23. *until I judge*: the general resurrection is the prelude to the final judgement. Until the eschatological visitation, the souls of the just are at peace (*LAB* 23:13; 28:10; 51:5) and the wicked undergo punishment for their sins (16:3; 23:6; 31:7; 36:4; 38:4; 44:10; 51:5; 63:4). *between soul and flesh*: perhaps the higher and lower aspects of the person are meant. *And the world will cease*: the idea of two worlds (this world and the world to come) is an apocalyptic commonplace. In the world to come, there will be no death and no punishment. The wicked will already be annihilated. *death will be abolished*: according to 1 Cor. 15:26, the last enemy is death. *another earth and another heaven*: the idea of a new earth and a new heaven appears in Isa. 65:17; 66:22. In Jewish and Christian apocalyptic writings (see 1En 45:4–5; 91:16; Jub 1:29; 2 Pet. 3:13; Rev. 21:1), it describes what things will be like after the resurrection and general judgement. The renewed creation will be abundant (*not without progeny or sterile*), secure (*no one...will be tainted*), and eternal (*an everlasting dwelling place*).

THE BIRTH OF MOSES (*LAB* 9:9–16)

Ps-Philo's account of the birth of Moses is clearly dependent on Exod. 2:1–10 for its narrative framework and for many of its phrases. But he adds to the biblical narrative some important traditions: the role of the spirit of God, the dreams of Miriam and of Pharaoh's daughter, the appearance of the angel, the announcement of Moses' mission in leading the escape from Egypt, the actual slaughter of the male children, the idea that Moses was born circumcised, and Melchiel as Moses' Hebrew name. Many of the motifs taken from Exod. 2:1–10 or added by Ps-Philo are present in Matthew's account of Jesus' birth and infancy, but there is no good reason to suppose that Matthew had *LAB* before him as he composed the first two chapters in his Gospel.

9 And Amram of the tribe of Levi went out and took a wife from his own tribe. When he had taken her, others followed him and took their own wives. And this man had one son and one

10 daughter; their names were Aaron and Miriam. And the spirit of God came upon Miriam one night, and she saw a dream and told it to her parents in the morning saying: 'I have seen this night, and behold a man in a linen garment stood and said to me: "Go and say to your parents: 'Behold he who will be born from you will be cast forth into the water; likewise through him the water will be dried up. And I will work signs through him and save my people, and he will exercise leadership always.'"' And when Miriam told of her dream, her parents did not believe her.

11 The strategy of the king of Egypt, however, prevailed against the sons of Israel, and they were humiliated and worn down in making

12 bricks. Now Jochebed conceived from Amram and hid him in her womb for three months. For she could not conceal him any longer, because the king of Egypt appointed local chiefs who, when the Hebrew women gave birth, would immediately throw their male children into the river. And she took her child and made for him an ark from the bark of a pine tree and placed the ark at the bank of the river.

13 Now that child was born in the covenant of God and the

14 covenant of the flesh. And when they had cast him forth, all the elders gathered and quarrelled with Amram saying: 'Are not these our words that we spoke: "It is better for us to die without having sons than that the fruit of our womb be cast into the waters?"' And Amram did not listen to those who were saying these words.

15 Now Pharaoh's daughter came down to bathe in the river, as she had seen in dreams, and her maids saw the ark. And she sent one, and she fetched and opened it. And when she saw the boy and while she was looking upon the covenant (that is, the covenant

16 of the flesh), she said: 'It is one of the Hebrew children.' And she took him and nursed him. And he became her son, and she called him by the name Moses. But his mother called him Melchiel. And

the child was nursed and became glorious above all other men, and through him God freed the sons of Israel as he had said.

9. *Amram*: the names of Moses' family are taken from Exod. 6:20. Amram's example in marrying despite the Egyptian decree against it gave the other Hebrews the courage to do likewise.

10. *the spirit of God*: the action of the Holy Spirit enables Miriam to act as a prophetess. *dream*: Exod. 2:1–10 makes no mention of Miriam's dream. For dreams in relation to the birth of Jesus, see Matt. 1:20–3; 2:12; 2:13–14; 2:19–20. *a man in a linen garment*: for angels in linen garments, see Ezek. 9:11; Mark 16:5; and Luke 24:4. *through him the water will be dried up*: Moses' future mission in leading Israel out of Egypt is connected with his being cast forth into the water just after his birth.

12. *and hid him*: the suddenness of the transition from the conception of Moses to his mother's efforts at hiding him suggests that the report of Moses' birth (see Exod. 2:2) has been accidentally omitted. *throw their male children into the river*: the actual murder of these children is inferred from Exod. 1:16–22. Compare the slaughter of the innocent children in Matt. 2:16–18.

13. *born in the covenant*: Moses was born circumcised. The term 'covenant' was used to refer to the rite that came to symbolize it (cp. Gen. 17:11). The reason why Ps-Philo could say that Moses was born circumcised is supplied in 9:15.

15. *dreams*: as was the case with Miriam in *LAB* 9:10, so here Pharaoh's daughter is directed by dreams. *one of the Hebrew children*: this quotation from Exod. 2:6 explains how Ps-Philo knew that Moses had been born circumcised. If he were not, how could Pharaoh's daughter have recognized so easily that he was one of the Hebrew children?

16. *Melchiel*: the Egyptian name 'Moses' had been an embarrassment from Exod. 2:10 onwards. Ps-Philo supplies him with a good Hebrew name Melchiel ('God is my king'?).

THE DEATH OF MOSES (*LAB* 19:8–16)

The biblical account of Moses' death is greatly expanded by Ps-Philo. The vision of the promised land in Deut. 34:1–3 is transformed into a vision of the heavens and the events of the last days, and the words of God to Moses in Deut. 34:4 are developed into a dialogue in which Moses prays twice (verses 8–9, 14) and God answers twice (verses

10–13, 15). The exegetical problem of why no one knows the place of Moses' tomb in Deut. 34:5–6 is explained by emphasizing that God himself buried him (verse 16). This passage in *LAB* is especially significant because it contains several peculiar traditions: the special heavenly source of water for the Holy Land, the staff of Moses as the sign of the covenant, Moses' death as a glorification, and the cessation of the heavenly chorus on the day of Moses' death.

8 And Moses ascended Mount Abarim as God had commanded him, and he prayed saying: 'Behold I have completed the time of my life; I have completed 120 years. And now I ask: May your mercy with your people and your pity with your heritage, Lord, be established; and may your longsuffering in your place be upon

9 the chosen race because you have loved them before all others. And you know that I was a shepherd. And when I fed the flock in the wilderness, I brought them to your mountain Horeb and then I first saw your angel on fire from the bush. But you called me from the bush, and I was afraid and turned my face. And you sent me to them and you freed them from Egypt, but their enemies you drowned in the water. And you gave them the law and the statutes which they might live in and enter on as sons of men. For who is the man who has not sinned against you? And unless your patience abides, how would your heritage be established, if you were not merciful to them? Or who will yet be born without sin? Now you will correct them for a time, but not in anger.'

10 Then the Lord showed him the land and all that is in it and said: 'This is the land that I will give to my people.' And he showed him the place from which the clouds draw up water to water the whole earth, and the place from which the river takes its water, and the land of Egypt, and the place in the firmament from which only the Holy Land drinks. And he showed him the place from which the manna rained upon the people, even unto the paths of paradise. And he showed him the measurements of the sanctuary and the number of sacrifices and the signs by which they are to interpret the heaven. And he said: 'These are what are prohibited for the

11 human race because they have sinned against me. And now your staff with which these signs were performed will be a witness

between me and my people. And when they sin, I will be angry with them but I will recall your staff and spare them in accord with my mercy. And your staff will be before me as a reminder all the days, and it will be like the bow with which I established my covenant with Noah when he went forth from the ark saying: "I will place my bow in the cloud, and it will be for a sign between me and men that never again will the flood water cover all the earth."

12 And now I will take you from here and glorify you with your fathers, and I will give you rest in your slumber and bury you in peace. And all the angels will mourn over you, and the heavenly hosts will be saddened. But neither angel nor man will know your tomb in which you are to be buried until I visit the world. And I will raise up you and your fathers from the land of Egypt in which you sleep and you will come together and dwell in the immortal dwelling place that is not subject to time.

13 But this heaven will be before me like a fleeting cloud and passing like yesterday. And when the time draws near to visit the world, I will command the years and order the times and they will be shortened, and the stars will hasten and the light of the sun will hurry to fall and the light of the moon will not remain; for I will hurry to raise up you who are sleeping in order that all who can live may dwell in the place of sanctification I showed you.'

14 And Moses said: 'If I can make another request of you, Lord; according to your great mercy be not angry with me, but show me what amount of time has passed and how much remains.'

15 And he said to him: 'There is honey, the topmost peak, the fullness of a moment, and the last drop of a cup; and time has fulfilled all things. For four and a half have passed, and two and a half remain.'

16 And when Moses heard this, he was filled with understanding and his appearance became glorious; and he died in glory according to the word of the Lord, and he buried him as he had promised him. And the angels mourned at his death, and the lightnings and the torches and the arrows all went together before

him. And in that day the hymn of the heavenly hosts was not sung because of the passing of Moses, nor was there such a day from the one on which the Lord made man upon the earth, nor shall there be such for ever, that the hymn of the angels should stop on account of men; because he loved him very much. And he buried him with his own hands on a high place and in the light of all the world.

8. *Mount Abarim*: Mount Nebo (see Deut. 32:49; Num. 27:12) is one of the mountains in the Abarim chain. *he prayed*: Ps-Philo's version of Moses' prayer (verses 8–9) contains a plea for mercy on his people, a reminder of God's care in the time of the exodus (see Exod. 13:1–6), and a final plea for patience and mercy. *in your place*: that is, heaven. The reading found in some manuscripts 'into/toward your place' would refer to the land of Israel.

9. *as sons of men*: in the light of the following quotation from 1 Kings 8:46 ('For who is the man who has not sinned against you?'), this expression seems to describe human beings in their weakness and their tendency toward sin.

10. *from which only the Holy Land drinks*: in Moses' vision of the land and of the heavens, he is shown the source of water set aside for the Holy Land. For the description of Israel as the Holy Land, see Zech. 2:12; 2 Macc. 1:7; 4 Ezra 13:48; and 2Bar 63:10. *the sanctuary*: for the idea of the pattern of the tabernacle, see Exod. 25:9. *the signs*: the signs of the zodiac are most probably meant. *me*: that is, God. The Latin manuscripts read 'themselves', but this probably reflects a mistake in transition from Hebrew to Greek. God is clearly the speaker.

11. *your staff*: the idea of Moses' staff as a sign of the covenant like the rainbow (see Gen. 9:13, 15) is not found elsewhere in Jewish writings.

12. *glorify you*: the death of Moses is described as a glorification. Compare the presentation of Jesus' death as a glorification in John's Gospel (e.g. 3:14; 7:39; 12:23, 32f). *neither angel nor man will know your tomb*: the idea that no one knows the exact location of Moses' tomb is based on Deut. 34:6. According to verse 16, God himself buried Moses and only he knows where. *the land of Egypt*: if this phrase is not simply a gloss inserted into the text, the idea must be that Moses and his ancestors were buried outside the land of Israel and so must be raised up from there.

13. *heaven*: this is most likely a reference to the new heaven and the new earth that will follow God's visitation. But *celum* ('heaven') may

be a mistake for *seculum* ('age'). *shortened*: for God's shortening the days
of suffering, see Mark 13:20 (Matt. 24:22).

15. *honey*: perhaps the last drop of honey is meant. On the basis of
4 Ezra 4:48–50; 6:9–10, it is possible to emend this and the following
phrase to read 'an instant, the topmost part of a hand'. At any rate,
the point is that not much time remains before God's eschatological
visitation. *two and a half remain*: it is not clear what system of calculation is being used. But since more than half of the time had passed
before Moses' death, by the time of Ps-Philo the end must be considered very near. According to Dan. 12:7 three and a half times ('a
time, two times and half a time') remained before the end; perhaps
Ps-Philo was suggesting that now the end is even nearer than it was in
the time when Daniel was composed.

16. *glorious*: for Moses' death as a glorification, see verse 12. *he buried
him*: the exegetical problem raised by Deut. 34:6 ('no man knows the
place of his burial to this day', RSV) is solved by insisting that God
buried Moses and only he knows the exact place. *the hymn of the
heavenly hosts was not sung*: other Jewish traditions say that the angels
ceased their singing on the days of the flood, the crossing of the Reed
Sea, and the destruction of the Jerusalem temple. In this case only, they
cease for a man.

THE SACRIFICE OF ISAAC (*LAB* 32:1–4)

The story of God's command to Abraham to sacrifice his son Isaac in
Gen. 22:1–18 has fascinated biblical exegetes and theologians for
thousands of years. In the first century, the Genesis account was
apparently being read in association with the Suffering Servant passage
in Isa. 52:13–53:12 and perhaps in the context of the passover or
New Year festivals. Isaac is presented as a martyr who willingly offered
himself as a sacrifice to God. For recent discussions of the many
parallels and the theological and historical problems connected with
this motif, see the articles by R. J. Daly, 'The Soteriological Significance
of the Sacrifice of Isaac', *CBQ* 39 (1977), 45–75; and P. R. Davies and
B. D. Chilton, 'The Aqedah: A Revised Tradition History', *CBQ* 40
(1978), 514–46. Although there may be allusions to the Isaac-pattern in
Rom. 8:32; Jas. 2:21–3; and Heb. 11:17–20, it is odd that the New
Testament writers did not exploit it more often and more extensively
in explaining the death of Jesus.

1 Then Deborah and Barak the son of Abino and all the people
   together sang a hymn to the Lord on that day saying: 'Behold the

Lord has shown us his glory from on high, as he did in the height of the heavenly places, when he sent forth his voice to confuse the languages of men. And he chose our nation and took Abraham our father out of the fire and chose him over all his brothers and kept him from the fire and freed him from the bricks destined for the building of the tower. And he gave him a son at the end of his old age and took him out of a sterile womb. And all the angels were jealous of him, and the worshipping hosts envied him.

2   And since they were jealous of him, God said to him: "Kill the fruit of your body for me, and offer for me as a sacrifice what has been given to you by me." And Abraham did not argue, but set out immediately. And as he was setting out, he said to his son: "Behold now, my son, I am offering you as a holocaust and am delivering you into the hands that gave you to me."

3   But the son said to his father: "Hear me, father. If a lamb of the flock is accepted as sacrifices to the Lord with an odour of sweetness and if for the wicked deeds of men animals are appointed to be killed, but man is designed to inherit the world, how then do you now say to me: 'Come and inherit life without limit and time without measure?' Yet have I not been born into the world to be offered as a sacrifice to him who made me? Now my blessedness will be above that of all men because there will be nothing like this; and about me future generations will be instructed and through me the peoples will understand that the Lord has made the soul of a man worthy to be a sacrifice."

4   And when he had offered the son upon the altar and had bound his feet so as to kill him, the Most Powerful hastened and sent forth his voice from on high saying: "You shall not slay your son, nor shall you destroy the fruit of your body. For now I have appeared so as to reveal you to those who do not know you and have shut the mouths of those who are always speaking evil against you. Now your memory will be before me always, and your name and his will remain from one generation to another."'

1. *all the people*: the story of the sacrifice of Isaac (Gen. 22:1–18) is set in the context of the hymn of Deborah and Barak (Judg. 5:1). The

presence of the people is reminiscent of the scene for the Song of Moses in Exodus 15. Even though what follows is called a hymn, it is not possible to detect a hymnic structure (if there ever was one). *shown us his glory*: the phrase echoes Deut. 5:24; see also John 1:14. *in the height of the heavenly places*: Ps-Philo 'corrects' the statement in Gen. 11:5 that God came down to see the city and the tower of Babel. *took Abraham our father out of the fire*: according to Gen. 11:28, 31, Abraham and his family dwelt in Ur of the Chaldeans. On the basis of the verbal coincidence between the city's name and the Hebrew word for fire (ʾûr) and the proximity of the references to Ur and the tower of Babel in Genesis 11, Ps-Philo (or his source) presented in *LAB* 6 the story of Abraham's refusal to join in building the tower of Babel and his subsequent rescue from the fiery furnace. For other Jewish sources regarding Abraham in the fiery furnace after the pattern set in Daniel 3, see G. Vermes, *Scripture and Tradition in Judaism* (SPB 4; Leiden: Brill, 1961), pp. 85–90. *the worshipping hosts envied him*: for the angels' envy of Abraham, see Jub 17:16. According to Wisd. of Sol. 2:23–4, God's creation of man in his image (see Gen. 1:26) aroused the envy of the devil.

2. *what has been given to you by me*: both God and Abraham interpret the sacrifice of Isaac as the return of a gift to its giver. *I am offering*: in contrast to Gen. 22:1–18, Abraham here shows no uncertainty and makes no effort to conceal his plan from Isaac.

3. *man is designed to inherit the world*: the point of Isaac's objection is that animals, not human beings, are the proper material for sacrifices. *Yet have I not been born...to be offered as a sacrifice to him who made me*: conscious of his role as a sacrificial victim, Isaac willingly accepts it. That Isaac readily presented himself as a sacrifice is also stated in *LAB* 18:5 and 40:2. *there will be nothing like his*: although this phrase could conceivably allude to Christian attempts to interpret Jesus' death in light of the Isaac-pattern, it more probably refers to the prohibition of child sacrifice.

4. *to reveal you to those who do not know you*: other manuscripts read 'to reveal myself (God) to those who do not know me'. *those who are always speaking evil against you*: this phrase refers back to the jealous angels described in verse 1.

THE TESTAMENT OF DEBORAH (*LAB* 33:1–6)

The story of Deborah's efforts at saving Israel from its enemies is told in Judges 4–5, but nothing is said there about her death. Ps-Philo constructs the story of her death by putting in her mouth a testament or farewell speech in *LAB* 33:1–6. The passage is significant as part of Ps-Philo's general tendency of giving special prominence to the women of the biblical story. It also is remarkable for its teaching on life after death and before the last judgement: After death persons can neither repent (33:2) nor do further evil (33:3), and the righteous departed cannot intercede for the living (33:5). A lament in poetic form (33:6) concludes the passage.

1 And when the days of her death drew near, she sent and gathered all the people and said to them: 'Listen now, my people. Behold I am warning you as a woman of God and am enlightening you as one from the female race. And obey me like your mother, and heed

2 my words as people who will also die. Behold I am going today on the way of all flesh, on which you also will come. Only direct your heart to the Lord your God during the time of your life, because after your death you cannot repent of those things in which you

3 live. For then death is sealed up and brought to an end, and the measure and the time and the years have returned their deposit. For even if you seek to do evil in hell after your death, you cannot because the desire for sinning will cease and the evil impulse will lose its power, because even hell will not restore what has been received and deposited to it unless it be demanded by him who has made the deposit to it. Now therefore, my sons, obey my voice; while you have the time of life and the light of the law, make straight your ways.'

4 And while Deborah was saying these words, all the people raised up their voice together and wept and said: 'Behold now, mother, you will die, and to whom do you commend your sons whom you are leaving? Pray therefore for us, and after your departure your soul will be mindful of us for ever.'

5 And Deborah answered and said to the people: 'While a man is still alive he can pray for himself and for his sons, but after his end he cannot pray or be mindful of anyone. Therefore do not hope in your fathers. For they will not profit you at all unless you be found like them. But then you will be like the stars of the heaven, which now have been revealed among you.'

6   And Deborah died and slept with her fathers and was buried in the city of her fathers. And the people mourned for her seventy days, and while they were mourning for her, they said these words as a lamentation:

'Behold there has perished a mother from Israel,
and the holy one who exercised leadership in the house of Jacob.
She firmed up the fence about her generation,
and her generation will grieve over her.'

And after her death the land had rest for seven years.

1. *a woman of God*: this variation on the expression 'man of God' (see 1 Sam. 9:6–7) suggests that Deborah was a prophet (see Judg. 4:4) like Samuel.

2. *Behold I am going today on the way of all flesh*: Deborah speaks in terms taken from Josh. 23:14.

3. *the evil impulse will lose its power*: the idea that the inclination toward sin loses its power after death, not simply in the messianic era, is unique to *LAB*. *by him who has made the deposit*: in God's eschatological visitation, Sheol will return the souls that had been deposited to it between the time of death and the last judgement.

5. *after his end he cannot pray or be mindful of anyone*: that the just cannot intercede after the last judgement is well known from 4 Ezra 7:102–12; 2 Bar 85:12; 2 En 53:1. But Ps-Philo refers to the period before the last judgement. A similar point is made in the parable of the rich man and Lazarus in Luke 16:19–31. *the stars of the heaven*: the life of the blessed is described in terms of astral immortality in Dan. 12:2–3; 1En 104:2; 4 Ezra 7:97, 125; 2Bar 51:10.

6. *mother from Israel*: the phrase is based on Judg. 5:7 ('until you arose, Deborah, arose as a mother in Israel', RSV). *seven years*: according to Judg. 5:31, the land was at rest for forty years.

THE ANNOUNCEMENT OF SAMSON'S BIRTH (*LAB* 42:1–10)

In the story of the announcement of Samson's birth, Ps-Philo closely follows the text of Judg. 13:2–20 but makes some important additions: the name of Samson's mother Eluma, his genealogy, the argument between Samson's parents, Eluma's prayer, the announcement of the child's name before his birth, the wife's vow of silence, and her husband's uncertainty regarding the angel's message. These additional features (as well as the elements of the biblical account) have parallels in the announcements of the births of John the Baptist and Jesus in Luke 1:5–38. But rather than assume that Luke used *LAB* or vice versa, it is best to see Luke 1:5–38 and *LAB* 42:1–10 as independent developments of Judg. 13:2–20.

1 Now there was a man from the tribe of Dan, whose name was Manoah, son of Edoc, son of Odon, son of Eriden, son of Fadesur, son of Dema, son of Susi, son of Dan. And he had a wife whose name was Eluma the daughter of Remac, and she was sterile and did not bear children to him. And every day Manoah her husband was saying to her: 'Behold the Lord has shut up your womb so that you may not bear children, and now let me go that I may take another wife lest I die without fruit.' And she said: 'Not me has the Lord shut up that I may not bear children, but you that I may not bear fruit.' And he said to her: 'Would that this could

2 be tested and proved!' And they were quarrelling daily, and both were very sad because they were without fruit. One night the wife went up to the upper chamber and prayed saying: 'Behold you, Lord God of all flesh, reveal to me whether it has not been granted to my husband or to me to produce children, or to whom it may be forbidden or to whom it may be allowed to bear fruit in order that whoever is forbidden may weep over his sins because he remains without fruit. Or if both of us have been deprived, then reveal to us also so that we might bear our sins and be silent before you.'

3 And the Lord heard her voice and sent his angel to her in the morning, and he said to her: 'You are the sterile one who does not bring forth, and you are the womb that is forbidden so as not to bear fruit. But now the Lord has heard your voice and paid attention to your tears and opened your womb. And behold you will conceive and bear a son, and you will call his name Samson. For this one will be dedicated to your Lord. But see that he does not taste from any fruit of the vine and eat any unclean thing because (as he himself has said) he will free Israel from the hand of the Philistines.' And when the angel of the Lord had spoken these words, he departed from her.

4 And she came into the house to her husband and said to him:

'I am placing my hand upon my mouth, and I will be silent before you all the days because I have boasted in vain and have not believed your words. For the angel of the Lord came to me today and revealed to me, saying: "Eluma, you are sterile, but you

5   will conceive and bear a son."' And Manoah did not believe his wife, and being perplexed and sad he himself also went to the upper chamber and prayed and said: 'Behold I am not worthy to hear the signs and wonders that God has done among us or to see

6   the face of his messenger.' And while he was speaking these words, the angel of the Lord came again to his wife. But she was in the field, and Manoah was in his house. And the angel said to her: 'Run and announce to your husband that God has accounted him worthy to hear my voice.'

7   And the wife ran and called to her husband, and he hurried to come to the angel in the field. The angel said to him: 'Go into your wife and do all these things.' But he said: 'I am going, but see to it, sir, that your word be accomplished regarding your servant.'And he said: 'It will be accomplished.'

8   And Manoah said to him: 'If I can, let me persuade you to enter my house and eat bread with me; and know that, when you go, I will give you gifts that you may take along with you to offer as a sacrifice to the Lord your God.' And the angel said to him: 'I will not enter your house with you, nor eat your bread nor take your gifts. For if you offer sacrifice from what is not yours, I cannot

9   show favour to you.' And Manoah built an altar upon the rock and offered sacrifices and holocausts. And when he had cut up the meats and placed them on the altar, the angel reached out and touched them with the tip of his staff. And fire came forth from the rock, and it devoured the holocausts and sacrifices. And the angel of the Lord went up from there with the flame of fire.

10 But Manoah and his wife saw these events and fell on their faces and said: 'Surely we will die because we have seen the Lord face to face.' And Manoah said: 'It is not enough that I have seen him but I even asked his name, not knowing that he was the minister of God.' Now the angel who came was named Fadahel.

1. *son of Edoc, son of Odon*: the genealogy of Samson is not found in Judg. 13:2, and this one was probably constructed by Ps-Philo. Compare the sections in the New Testament genealogies that have no Old Testament basis (see Matt. 1:13–16; Luke 3:23–7). *Eluma*: this name for Samson's mother is not given elsewhere in Jewish literature. *she was sterile*: Eluma's sterility (see Judg. 13:2) is paralleled in the cases of Sarah, Rebecca, Rachel, Hannah and Elizabeth (see Luke 1:7). *now let me go*: the argument between Manoah and Eluma is not part of the biblical story. That Manoah should *ask* for a divorce was unusual in a Jewish setting, but see Mark 10:12 ('and if she divorces her husband'). *Would that this could be tested and proved!*: a literal translation of the Latin text is 'the law makes evident our experiment'. The Hebrew original was probably misread in the transition to Greek.

2. *upper chamber*: for other references to the upper storey or roof as the place of prayer, see Dan. 6:10 and Acts 1:13–14; 9:39; 20:8. Prayer is also an important theme in the Lucan infancy narrative. *prayed*: Eluma asks to know whether she or her husband is responsible for their failure to have children. According to verse 3, it was her fault.

3. *angel*: the angel announces that Eluma's prayer has been heard and promises her a son. Compare this development of the Samson story with the announcements on the births of John the Baptist and Jesus in Luke 1:5–38. *see that he does not taste*: according to Judg. 13:4–5, 13, it is Samson's mother rather than Samson who must abstain. But compare this with the angel's command about John the Baptist in Luke 1:15 ('and he shall drink no wine nor strong drink'). *as he himself has said*: the 'he' is God. For the announcement of the hero's name and mission before his birth, see Luke 1:13–17 and 1:31–3.

4. *I will be silent*: Eluma's vow of silence is presented as a consequence of her unbelief. Compare the silence imposed on Zechariah in Luke 1:20, 22.

5. *prayed*: Manoah's uncertainty and confusion parallel Joseph's bewilderment in Matt. 1:19. In both cases, the resolution comes through the appearance of an angel.

7. *in the field*: some manuscripts add 'in spirit/anger' or 'in Ammo'. *see to it, sir, that your word be accomplished*: Manoah does not believe completely what the angel had told Eluma and him. Compare Judg. 13:13–14 and Josephus, *Ant.* v. 8.3 (281), where Manoah's doubt is stressed.

8. *If I can*: Manoah's diffidence suggests that he recognizes the superhuman nature of the angel. *sacrifice from what is not yours*: if

Manoah gave the gifts to the angel to be offered as sacrifices to God, those sacrifices would then not be the property of Manoah. The sacrifices would be the angel's, not Manoah's.

9. *the angel reached out*: the description of what the angel did is taken from the Gideon story in Judg. 6:21.

10. *Fadahel*: according to Judg. 13:18, the angel's name was 'Wonderful' (*Peli'y*). Perhaps *pl'y'l* in the Hebrew original, which in Greek would be Phalael, was misread as Phada(h)el (the *l* and *d* are very similar in Greek uncial script). The name Fadael does occur, however, in Jewish mystical texts. Though Manoah knew something about the angel's nature, he did not know his name.

THE SONG OF DAVID THE EXORCIST (*LAB* 60:1–3)

In retelling the story of David's skill as a musician to soothe the troubled spirit of Saul (see 1 Sam. 16:14–23), Ps-Philo gives a sample of David's songs. The song is addressed to the evil spirit troubling Saul and reminds the spirit of its place in the plan of creation described in Genesis 1. It also warns that one of David's descendants (most likely Solomon, but perhaps the future messiah) will rule over the evil spirit. The song abounds in parallelisms and uses many phrases from the Old Testament. The esoteric content of the song does not necessarily demand that it be attributed to Gnostic or Essene circles.

1   And in that time the spirit of the Lord was taken away from Saul, and an evil spirit was choking him. And Saul sent and brought David, and he played a song on his lyre by night. And this was the song that he played for Saul in order that the evil spirit might depart from him.

2   Darkness and silence were before the world was made,
     And silence spoke a word and the darkness became light.
     Then your name was pronounced, in the drawing together of what had been spread out,
     The upper part of which was called heaven and the lower part was called earth.
     And the upper part was commanded to bring down rain according to its season,
     And the lower part was commanded to produce food for all things that had been made.

And after these was the tribe of your spirits made.

3   And now do not be troublesome as one created on the second day.

But if not, remember Tartarus where you walk.

Or is it not enough for you to hear that, through what resounds
before you, I sing to many?

Or do you not remember that you were created from a resounding
echo in the chaos?

But let the new womb from which I was born rebuke you,

From which after a time one born from my loins will rule over you.

And as long as David sang, the spirit spared Saul.

1. *(the) spirit of the Lord*: the introductory paragraph consists of
phrases taken from 1 Sam. 16:14, 19, 23. *by night*: no specific time is
given in the biblical account. In *LAB* 9:15; 28:4; 32:16; 53:3–4;
56:3, revelations occur by night. *that the evil spirit might depart*: David
acts as an exorcist. Other references to Jewish exorcists occur in the
Qumran texts, Genesis Apocryphon xx.16–24 and Prayer of Nabo-
nidus 1.4, and, of course, the Gospels.

2. *Darkness and silence*: the idea of the primordial darkness and
silence is based on Gen. 1:1–2 and is also found in 4 Ezra 6:39; 7:30;
and 2Bar 3:7. *silence spoke a word*: the same theme appears in Ignatius'
letters to the Magnesians (8:2) and the Ephesians (19:1) as well as the
Gospel of Truth 37:10–12. *your name*: the name of the demon addressed
in the song, not the name of God. *the tribe of your spirits*: this phrase
probably includes all the spirits, whether good or bad.

3. *as one created on the second day*: according to Jub 2:2, the spirits
were created on the first day. But according to 2En 29:1 they were
created on the second day. The latter tradition is used here to remind
the evil spirit of its inferior status. *remember Tartarus*: if an inferior place
in the order of creation does not humble the evil spirit, then the fact
that he dwells in hell should do so. *I sing to many*: but according to
verse 1, David sings to Saul alone by night. At any rate, the sound of
David's song should remind the evil spirit that it too was created by the
sound of God's word. *the new womb*: the phrase may refer to the Davidic
dynasty or perhaps to Eve. *one born from my loins will rule over you*: for
references to Solomon as an exorcist, see Wisd. of Sol. 7:17–22 and
Josephus, *Ant.* VIII.2.5 (45–9).

The Ethiopic Book of Enoch
MICHAEL A. KNIBB

Enoch literature

The number of writings associated with the name of Enoch is an indication of the fascination which this figure held for later generations, a fascination aroused no doubt by the enigmatic statement of Gen. 5:24, 'Having walked with God, Enoch was seen no more, because God had taken him away' (cp. Ecclus. 44:16; 49:14; Heb. 11:5). Three writings in particular are important, known respectively as the Ethiopic, the Slavonic, and the Hebrew book of Enoch, or, for convenience, as 1, 2 and 3 Enoch. The first of these is so called because it is only in the Ethiopic language that a complete version has come down to us. The second, a work composed in Greek but extant only in two Slavonic versions, describes Enoch's ascent through the heavens to the presence of God and the instructions he gave during a temporary return to earth; at the end of the book Enoch is taken back to heaven, this time permanently. The Slavonic book shows some points of contact with 1 Enoch and perhaps dates from the first century AD. The third writing, a somewhat later work composed in Hebrew, is important for the development of Jewish mysticism.

The Ethiopic Enoch

In the form known to us from the Ethiopic version 1 Enoch consists of five main sections: (1) The book of Watchers (chapters 1–36). (2) The Parables of Enoch (chapters 37–71). The contents of these two sections are summarized below, pp. 29 f, 43 f. (3) The book of Astronomy (chapters 72–82). This contains amongst other things a description of the movements of the sun and the moon as the author understood them; the material is important for the calendar which it attests because this same calendar, attested also in the book of Jubilees, was the one used by the Qumran community. (4) The book of Dreams (chapters 83–90). This section gives an account of two dream-visions seen by Enoch, of which the first (chapters 83–4) is concerned with the flood. The second (chapters 85–90, sometimes known as the Animal Apocalypse because human beings are represented in it by animals) is far longer and much more important. In allegorical form, it records biblical history from Adam to the outbreak of the Maccabean revolt; the final part of the apocalypse is a prophecy of the defeat of the forces opposing the Jews and of the last judgement which the author believed would follow immediately. The literary form of this work is related to that of Dan. 2; 7; 8; 2 Esdras 11–12; 13. (5) The Epistle of Enoch (chapters 91–107; the name is used for this section in the Greek version of the book). These chapters are presented as an exhortation by Enoch to his sons and have something of the form of a testament; in them the author addresses his contemporaries, encouraging the righteous to stand firm and denouncing and threatening the sinners. The last part of this section (chapters 106–7) is apparently from the book of Noah (see below, p. 30) and recounts the miraculous birth of Noah. Chapter 108 is a later appendix to the book.

The pentateuchal (five-part) structure outlined above refers to the book in its present (Ethiopic) form; the Qumran discoveries have made it clear that these traditions originally had a different shape. Fragments of eleven manuscripts of Enoch in Aramaic were discovered amongst the Qumran scrolls, and these fragments confirmed the view that 1 Enoch was composed in Aramaic. The manuscripts fall into two distinct groups. On the one hand, fragments from seven manuscripts correspond to parts of the first, fourth and fifth sections of the Ethiopic book (chapters 1–36; 83–90; 91–107). The indications are that these parts of 1 Enoch, together with a work known as the book of Giants, circulated at Qumran as separate writings and were also copied out in combination – with the book of Giants apparently as the second of the four elements – to form a four-part corpus of Enochic writings, a tetrateuch. On the other hand, the fragments from the other four manuscripts belong to a book of Astronomy which at Qumran circulated separately from the other Enochic writings; the third section of the Ethiopic book (chapters 72–82) is based on the Qumran book of Astronomy, but is much shorter and differs quite substantially. No fragments were discovered corresponding to the second section of the Ethiopic book (chapters 37–71), the Parables.

The Aramaic writings associated with Enoch were translated into Greek, and parts of this Greek version, of which the most important cover 1:1–32:6 and 97:6–107:3, are extant. The Ethiopic version was made from the Greek, although it seems likely that in some cases the Ethiopic translators also made direct use of an Aramaic text of Enoch. It is, however, difficult to trace in detail the stages by which the

Enochic writings known to us from the Qumran fragments acquired the pentateuchal form which they have in the Ethiopic version, i.e. with the Parables in place of the book of Giants, and with the astronomical material inserted in the middle of the book. Fragments of translations of I Enoch into other ancient languages are also known. For full details concerning the text of Enoch see M. A. Knibb, *The Ethiopic Book of Enoch*, vol. II.

Provenance

Although fragments of four of the five writings incorporated in the present Ethiopic book of Enoch were found at Qumran, these are not Qumran writings in the narrow sense, but rather works taken over by the community. In fact the background to the emergence of much of this material is to be found in the circumstances of the third and early second centuries BC when the Jews in Palestine were increasingly affected in a variety of ways by the Greeks. The material may be regarded as a reaction to the events of the period and to the threat that, in the eyes of pious Jews, was posed to the Jewish faith by the encroachment of Hellenism. The oldest element is the book of Astronomy, dating from the third century BC; the interest in astronomy reflects a concern over the calendar, and underlying the material (as well as material in Jubilees and the Qumran scrolls) is a dispute about the proper calendar to be followed. The book of Watchers, discussed in more detail below, is from the end of the third or the beginning of the second century BC. The Epistle of Enoch is of later date, most probably from the early decades of the second century BC and reflecting the situation in which the threat posed by Hellenism was coming to a crisis-point, but possibly from the latter part of the second century BC. Finally, the book of Dreams stems from the period between the outbreak of the Maccabean revolt and the death of Judas Maccabeus in 160 BC; it is concerned to encourage those fighting for their faith to stand firm in the certainty of victory and may be compared with the material in Dan. 7–12. (The Parables are a much later work and reflect different circumstances; see below, p. 44.)

The extracts presented here are from the book of Watchers and from the Parables because these form in many respects the most important parts of the book.

Bibliography

R. H. Charles, *The Book of Enoch*, 2nd edn., Oxford, 1912.

R. H. Charles, 'Book of Enoch', in *The Apocrypha and Pseudepigrapha of the Old Testament in English*, vol. II, pp. 163–281.

The Ethiopic Book of Enoch 29

M. A. Knibb, in consultation with E. Ullendorff, *The Ethiopic Book of Enoch: A New Edition in the Light of the Aramaic Dead Sea Fragments*, Oxford, 1978, vol. II: 'Introduction, Translation and Commentary'.

M. A. Knibb, 'The Book of Enoch', in H. F. D. Sparks (ed.), *The Apocryphal Old Testament*, Oxford, 1984, pp. 169–319.

E. Isaac gives an English translation in J. H. Charlesworth (ed.), *The Old Testament Pseudepigrapha*, vol. I, pp. 5–89.

S. Uhlig, 'Das äthiopische Henochbuch', in JSHRZ v/6, pp. 461–780.

THE BOOK OF WATCHERS

The book of Watchers is, with the exception of the book of Astronomy, the oldest part of 1 Enoch and the basis upon which the other sections have been built; there are allusions to it and echoes of it in the Parables, the book of Dreams and the Epistle. It is not all of one piece, but acquired its present form by a process of accretion. After an introductory section (chapters 1–5) the nucleus is formed by the story of the fall from heaven of the Watchers, i.e. angels (chapters 6–16; cp. Dan. 4:13, 17, 23). To this has been appended an account of Enoch's journey to the edge of the world where he sees the places of punishment of the fallen angels and the disobedient stars, as well as the range of seven mountains in the north-west, on the middle one of which is situated the throne of God (chapters 17–19). Chapter 20, a list of the seven archangels and their functions, forms the introduction to the account of a second journey (chapters 21–36). In the first part of this journey Enoch visits places already described in chapters 17–19, and thus chapters 21–5 may be regarded as another version of the earlier journey in which the material has been reordered and expanded. Thereafter Enoch goes to Jerusalem (chapters 26–7), and then far away to the east to the Garden of Righteousness (chapters 28–32). In the last part of the journey Enoch circles the earth and observes certain astronomical and meteorological phenomena (chapters 33–6); this material is related to the material in the book of Astronomy. For the accounts of these two journeys the author made use of a wide range of biblical and extra-biblical traditions. In particular he drew together in chapters 21–32 a number of different biblical traditions relating to the mountain of God (cp. Ps. 48:2; Isa. 14:12–15; Ezek. 28:11–19; Exod. 24:10) and to the garden of Eden with its tree of knowledge and tree of life (Gen. 2–3). The underlying theme, announced already in the introduction (chapters 1–5), is that of judgement. The places which Enoch is above all concerned to describe are the mountain on which God will sit when he visits the earth as judge, the place where the dead wait until the day of judgement, and the places where the wicked (both angels and men) and the righteous will either be punished or enjoy a life of bliss. With this in mind we may turn to the story of the Watchers.

The story of the fall of the Watchers, which draws its inspiration from Gen. 6:1–4, falls into two distinct parts (chapters 6–11; 12–16), and in the first of these Enoch is not mentioned. It seems likely that chapters 6–11 were taken over by the author of 1 Enoch, and that they come originally from a work known to have existed in antiquity, but now lost, the so-called book of Noah; other parts of 1 Enoch (e.g. chapters 106–7) also seem to have been taken from this work.

It should be noted that the translation which follows is based on the Ethiopic version, and for the most part on one particular manuscript, not on any attempted reconstruction of the original text of the book. A selection of significant variant readings from the Ethiopic version and from the Greek version (Greek[a]) is given in the footnotes, but only occasional reference has been made to a second Greek version (Greek[s]) preserved in the work of the historian Syncellus and covering 6:1–10:14 and 15:8–16:1. The fragmentary Aramaic text is also only mentioned occasionally.

THE FALL OF THE WATCHERS

6:1 And it came to pass, when the sons of men had increased, that in
2 those days there were born to them fair and beautiful daughters. And the angels, the sons of heaven, saw them and desired them. And they said to one another: 'Come, let us choose for ourselves wives from the children of men, and let us beget for ourselves children.'
3 And Semyaza, who was their leader, said to them: 'I fear that you may not wish this deed to be done, and (that) I alone will pay for
4 this great sin.' And they all answered him and said: 'Let us all swear an oath, and bind one another with curses not to alter this plan, but
5 to carry out this plan effectively.'[a] Then they all swore together and
6 all bound one another with curses to it. And they were in all two hundred, and they came down on Ardis which is[b] the summit of Mount Hermon. And they called the mountain Hermon, because
7 on it they swore and bound one another with curses. And these (are) the names of their leaders: Semyaza, who was their leader, Urakiba, Ramiel, Kokabiel, Tamiel, Ramiel, Daniel, Ezeqiel, Baraqiel,

Asael, Armaros, Batriel, Ananel, Zaqiel, Samsiel, Sartael, ...,

8 Turiel, Yomiel, Araziel. These are the leaders of the two hundred angels, and of all the others with them.[c]

7:1 And they took wives for themselves, and everyone chose for himself one each. And they began to go in to them and were promiscuous[d] with them. And they taught them charms and spells,

2 and showed to them the cutting of roots and trees.[e] And they became pregnant and bore large giants, and their height (was) three

3 thousand cubits. These devoured all the toil of men, until men were

4 unable to sustain them. And the giants turned against them in order

5 to devour men. And they began to sin against birds, and against animals, and against reptiles and against fish, and they devoured one

6 another's flesh and drank the blood from it.[f] Then the earth complained about the lawless ones.

8:1 And Azazel taught men to make swords, and daggers, and shields and breastplates. And he showed them the things after these, and the art of making them: bracelets, and ornaments,[g] and the art of making up the eyes and of beautifying the eyelids, and the most precious and choice stones, and all (kinds of) coloured dyes.

2 And the world was changed.[h] And there was great impiety and much fornication, and they went astray, and all their ways became

3 corrupt. Amezarak[i] taught all those who cast spells and cut roots,[j] Armaros the release of spells, and Baraqiel astrologers,[k] and Kokabiel portents, and Tamiel[l] taught astrology, and Asradel[m] taught the

4 path of the moon. And at the destruction of men they cried out, and their voices reached heaven.

---

a *but...effectively*: Greek[a] 'until we have accomplished it and have done this deed.'

b *on Ardis which is*: corrupt; read 'in the days of Jared on', cp. Greek[s] and Aram.

c Some Eth. mss. 'These are their leaders of tens, and of all the others with them'; Greek[a] 'These are their leaders ⟨over⟩ tens'.

d *and were promiscuous*: Greek[a] 'and to defile themselves'.

e Greek[a] (partly supported by some Eth. mss.) 'charms and spells and the cutting of roots, and showed to them plants'.

f *from it*: Greek[a] and one Eth. ms. omit.

g *the things...ornaments*: Greek[a] 'metals, and the art of working them, and bracelets, and ornaments'. Eth. 'the things after these' probably derives from a corrupt translation of the word for 'metals'.

h *And the world was changed*: so Eth., but probably corrupt; Greek omits.

i   *Amezarak*: so Eth. (or a similar form), but corrupt for 'Semzaya' (so Greek[a]).
j   *all...roots*: Greek[a] 'spells and the cutting of roots'.
k   Greek[a] 'astrology'.
l   *Tamiel*: so Eth.; Greek[a] 'Sathiel'; both corrupt for 'Ziqiel'.
m   *Asradel*: so Eth. (or a similar form), but corrupt for 'Sahriel'; Greek[a] 'Seriel'.

The story of the fall of the Watchers, as already indicated, draws on and expands the story of the sons of the gods in Gen. 6:1–4, although it is likely that extra-biblical traditions, stemming from Greek or ancient Near Eastern mythology, have had a strong influence on the form which the story has acquired in Enoch. In Genesis the myth serves to explain the origin of the Nephilim, men of gigantic stature (cp. Num. 13:33). The Nephilim are not regarded as the source of evil, but the story of the marriage of the sons of the gods and the daughters of men occurs immediately before the flood narrative and implicitly is a further sign of the corruption of the earth, the corruption which caused God to bring the flood. In Enoch the myth has explicitly become an account of the origins of evil and corruption (cp. 7:3–6). However, it is apparent that the basic story, according to which the Watchers descended to earth because of their lust for the daughters of men (6:1–7:6; 8:4), has been expanded by the insertion of a somewhat different mythological tradition; according to this the Watchers descended in order to teach mankind, and it is the knowledge which they bring that is the source of evil (7:1b; 8:1–3). With these two different myths are associated two different angelic leaders: Semyaza (in the original Aramaic, Šemiḥazah) with the first, and Azazel (in the Aramaic, 'Asa'el) with the second. The story of the Watchers is mentioned in other writings of the period, particularly Jubilees, and here too the distinction between the two different myths can be observed: cp. CD ii.18–19; Jub 4:22; 5:1–11; 7:21–5 with Jub 4:15; 8:3–4.

The story of the Watchers provides an explanation of the origin of evil and in this respect may be compared with other such explanations, the story of Adam (cp. Gen. 2–3; Rom. 5:12–14) and the idea of the evil inclination (see the comment on 2 Esdras 3:20 in the Cambridge Bible Commentary on 2 Esdras, pp. 117–18). It was not used in isolation from what was happening in contemporary society, but rather in response to those events. The author wrote in a situation in which the community he represented was experiencing hardship and loss of life (cp. 7:3–5; 8:4; 9:1, 9), and the background to the use of the myth in the book of Watchers – however it may have been used in earlier contexts – is probably to be found in the difficult circumstances which faced the Jews as a consequence of the wars between the Seleucids and the Ptolemies at the end of the third century BC (cp. Josephus, *Ant.* XII.3.3 (129–44)). There is in any case clear evidence that this part of the book of Watchers, and probably the book of Watchers as a whole, had acquired more or less its present form by about 175 BC. In this period the Jews were increasingly exposed to hellenistic cultural influences, and the attitude of pious Jews towards the outward manifestations of Hellenism probably underlies the references to the teaching brought by the Watchers: of the arts of war (8:1), of the cosmetic arts, seen to be responsible for the corruption of society (8:1–2), of magic and astrology (8:3, cp. 7:1*b*). The explanation for all the evils which were overtaking society was seen by the author to lie in events which happened in the primeval period; the activities of the Watchers and their giant sons, and the evil knowledge brought by the Watchers. In the sequel (see chapters 10–11) the author announces judgement on those who were responsible for evil and holds out the prospect of a life of bliss for the righteous; as we have seen, the theme of judgement and of reward for the righteous underlies both the introduction (chapters 1–5) and the account of Enoch's journeys (chapters 17–36).

6:3. *Semyaza*: in the original Aramaic 'Šemiḥazah', probably meaning 'my name has seen' (where 'my name' refers to God).

6:7. The forms of the names given in the two Greek versions and in the Ethiopic differ in varying degrees from one another and from the forms in the original Aramaic; for details see the translations of Enoch listed in the Bibliography. The list of names as given here follows that of the Ethiopic version in which the seventeenth of the twenty names has dropped out of the text.

7:5. The giants turn from mankind to animals, and then against one another. *and drank the blood*: eating flesh with the blood still in it is prohibited in Gen. 9:4, cp. Jub 7:28–9; Acts 15:20; the fact that the giants drank the blood made their crime all the worse.

8:1. *Azazel*: in the Aramaic the name was ''Asa'el' ('God has made', cp. the Old Testament name 'Asahel' (e.g. 2 Sam. 2:18)). The Ethiopic version of the tenth name in 6:7 is 'Asael' (the Greek differs), but here, as elsewhere, the Ethiopic has 'Azazel', the Greek versions 'Azael'.

8:3. Greek[s], partly supported by the Aramaic, has a longer text in this verse than Eth. Greek[a].

8:4. The cry of mankind for justice stands parallel to that of the earth in 7:6.

THE PRAYER OF THE ARCHANGELS

9:1 And then Michael, Gabriel, Suriel and Uriel[a] looked down from heaven and saw the mass of blood that was being shed on the

2 earth and all the iniquity that was being done on the earth. And they said to one another: 'Let the devastated earth cry out with

3 the sound of their cries unto the gate of heaven.[b] And now, to you O holy ones of heaven, the souls of men complain, saying: "Bring

4 our suit before the Most High."' And they said to their Lord, the King: 'Lord of Lords, God of Gods, King of Kings![c] Your glorious throne (endures) for all the generations of the world, and your name (is) holy and praised for all the generations of the

5 world, and blessed and praised! You have made everything, and power over everything is yours. And everything is uncovered and open before you, and you see everything, and there is nothing

6 which can be hidden from you. See then what Azazel has done, how he has taught all iniquity on the earth and revealed the eternal

7 secrets which were made in heaven. And Semyaza has made known spells, (he) to whom[d] you gave authority to rule over those

8 who are with him. And they went in to the daughters of men together,[e] and lay with those women, and became unclean, and

9 revealed to them these[f] sins. And the women bore giants,[g] and thereby the whole earth has been filled with blood and iniquity.

10 And now behold the souls which[h] have died cry out and complain unto the gate of heaven, and their lament has ascended, and they[i] cannot go out in the face of the iniquity which is being committed

11 on the earth. And you know everything before it happens, and you know this and what concerns each of them.[j] But you say nothing to us. What ought we to do with them about this?'

a *Michael...Uriel*: so some Eth. mss.; Greek 'Michael, Uriel, Raphael and Gabriel'; Aram. apparently 'Michael, Sariel, Raphael and Gabriel'.

b Greek[a] 'The sound of those who cry out on the earth (reaches) unto the gates of heaven'.

c Greek[a], 'of the ages'.

d *and revealed...to whom*: so some Eth. mss., but text uncertain; other Eth. mss. 'and they have revealed the eternal secrets which were made in heaven. (And) Semyaza has brought knowledge to men, (he) to whom'; Greek[a] 'and has revealed the eternal secrets, the things in heaven which men practise ⟨and⟩ know. And (what) Semyaza (has done), to whom.'

e Two Eth. mss. 'of men on the earth'; Greek 'of the men of the earth'.
f Some Eth. mss. Greek 'all'.
g Greek^a 'titans'.
h Some Eth. mss. Greek^a 'of those who'.
i Some Eth. mss. Greek 'it'.
j *and what...them*: Greek 'but you leave them alone'.

3. The archangels speak to the other angels. *holy ones*: i.e. angels; for this usage cp. Dan. 4:13, 17, 23; 8:13.

11. This verse, which forms the climax of the prayer, epitomizes the problem faced by the author and makes it clear that in the end it was one of theodicy: how can the all-powerful and all-knowing God permit evil?

THE DIVINE REPLY

10:1   And then the Most High, the Great and Holy One, spoke and
2   sent Arsyalalyur^a to the son of Lamech, and said to him: 'Say to
      him in my name "Hide yourself", and reveal to him the end which
      is coming, for the whole earth will be destroyed, and a deluge is
      about to come on all the earth, and what is in it will be destroyed.
3   And now teach him that he may escape, and (that) his offspring
4   may survive for the whole earth.'^b And further the Lord said to
      Raphael: 'Bind Azazel by his hands and his feet, and throw him
      into the darkness. And split open the desert which is in Dudael, and
5   throw him there. And throw on him jagged and sharp stones, and
      cover him with darkness; and let him stay there for ever, and
6   cover his face, that he may not see light, and that on the great day
7   of judgement he may be hurled into the fire. And restore the earth
      which the angels have ruined, and announce the restoration of the
      earth, for I shall restore the earth,^c so that not all the sons of men
      shall be destroyed through the mystery of everything which the
8   Watchers made known^d and taught to their sons. And the whole
      earth has been ruined by the teaching of the works of Azazel, and
9   against him write down all sin.' And the Lord said to Gabriel:
      'Proceed against the bastards and the reprobates and against the
      sons of the fornicators, and destroy the sons of the fornicators and
      the sons of the Watchers from amongst men. And send them out,
      and send them against one another, and let them destroy them-
10   selves in battle, for they will not have length of days. And they

will all petition you, but their fathers will gain nothing in respect of them, for they hope for eternal life, and that each of them will

11 live life for five hundred years.' And the Lord said to Michael: 'Go, inform[e] Semyaza and the others with him who have associated with the women to corrupt themselves with them in all their

12 uncleanness. When all their sons kill each other, and when they see the destruction of their beloved ones, bind them for seventy generations under the hills[f] of the earth until the day of their judgement and of their consummation, until the judgement which

13 is for all eternity is accomplished. And in those days they will lead them to the abyss of fire; in torment and in prison they will be

14 shut up for all eternity. And then he[g] will be burnt and from then on destroyed with them; together they will be bound until the

15 end of all generations. And destroy all the souls of lust[h] and the

16 sons of the Watchers, for they have wronged men. Destroy all wrong from the face of the earth, and every evil work will cease. And let the plant of righteousness and truth appear, and the deed will become a blessing; righteousness and truth will they plant[i] in

17 joy for ever. And now all the righteous will escape, and will live until they beget thousands; and all the days of their youth and

18 their sabbaths[j] they will fulfil in peace. And in those days the whole earth will be tilled in righteousness, and all of it will be planted

19 with trees, and it will be filled with blessing. And all pleasant trees they will plant on it, and they will plant on it vines, and the vine which is planted on it will produce fruit[k] in abundance; and every seed which is sown on it, each measure will produce a thousand,

20 and each measure of olives will produce ten baths of oil. And you, cleanse the earth from all wrong, and from all iniquity, and from all sin, and from all impiety, and from all the uncleanness which is

21 brought about on the earth; remove them from the earth. And all the sons of men shall be righteous, and all the nations shall serve

22 and bless me and all shall worship me. And the earth will be cleansed from all corruption, and from all sin, and from all wrath, and from all torment; and I will not again send a flood[l] upon it for all generations for ever.

11:1   And in those days I will open the storehouses of blessing which
        (are) in heaven that I may send them down upon the earth, upon
2   the work and upon the toil of the sons of men. Peace and truth will
        be united for all the days of eternity and for all the generations of
        eternity.'

a *Arsyalalyur*: so Eth. (or a similar form), but corrupt; Greekᵃ 'Istrael', perhaps originally
  'Israel'; Greekˢ 'Uriel'. Underlying Aramaic probably 'Sariel'.
b Some Eth. mss. 'for all generations'; Greek 'for all the generations of eternity'.
c Some Eth. mss. 'that the earth may be restored'; Greek 'that they may heal the plague'.
d *made known*: correction; Eth. and Greek texts corrupt.
e Greekˢ 'bind'.
f Greek 'in the valleys'.
g *And then he*: so some Eth. mss., referring to Semyaza; other Eth. mss. Greekᵃ differ;
  Greekˢ 'And whoever is condemned and destroyed from now on will be bound with
  them until the end of their generation.'
h Greekᵃ 'the spirits of the reprobate'.
i Or 'will be planted'.
j *and their sabbaths*: so Eth. Greekᵃ, but a mistranslation of 'and their old age', as Aram.
  confirms.
k Some Eth. mss. Greekᵃ 'wine'.
l *a flood*: some Eth. mss. Greekᵃ omit.

In response to their prayer the four archangels are sent by God respectively to Noah (10:1–3), to Azazel (10:4–8), to the giants (10:9–10),
and to Semyaza and his associates (10:11–11:2). The instructions given
by God are intended to have the effect that Noah is saved from the
coming flood, Azazel, Semyaza and the Watchers are imprisoned until
the final judgement, the giants kill each other in battle, and the earth is
restored.

10:1–3. The reference to Noah and the flood is appropriate in the
context, even though there has been no mention of Noah before,
because in Genesis the story of the sons of the gods is the immediate
prelude to the flood narrative. But the reference to Noah has a deeper
significance here, as elsewhere in 1 Enoch; the flood serves as the type
of the final judgement, and Noah as the type of the righteous individual
who will find salvation at that judgement.

4–8. The imprisonment of Azazel until the day of judgement.
Dudael: not the name of a real place, but the explanation of the name is
uncertain. Greekᵃ has 'Dadouel', Greekˢ 'the desert Doudael'.
Watchers: for this name for angels see Dan. 4:13, 17, 23; it is used to
refer both to fallen angels (so here) and to faithful angels (cp. 12:2, 3;
20:1, 'the holy angels who keep watch'). The idea underlying the term
is apparently that the angels 'keep watch' on God's behalf, and comparison has been drawn with the 'watchmen' of Isa. 62:6, as well as

with the eyes of God's throne-chariot (Ezek. 1:18) and the 'eyes of the LORD ranging over the whole earth' (Zech. 4:5(10)).

9–10. The self-destruction of the giants. *eternal life*: the following words (cp. also verse 17) indicate that for the author 'eternal life' meant a very long life, a life approaching the length of that lived by the patriarchs before the flood (cp. Gen. 5).

10:11–11:2. The imprisonment of Semyaza and his associates until the day of judgement.

12. *seventy generations*: perhaps influenced by the tradition of the seventy years of exile, Jer. 25:11–12; 29:10; Dan. 9:2, 24.

15. The instructions given to Gabriel (verse 9–10) are repeated in a generalized form.

10:16–11:2. The instructions about the restoration of the earth in the time of the Watchers become a description of the earth as it will be after the final judgement, an earth cleansed from all corruption and marvellously fruitful (cp. Amos 9:13–15), upon which men live long lives and have many children.

16. *the plant of righteousness and truth*: for the symbolic use of plant imagery cp. 93:10; CD 1.7.

11:1. Cp. Deut. 28:12.

2. Cp. Ps. 85:10.

ENOCH'S DEALINGS WITH THE WATCHERS

The story of the Watchers is continued in chapters 12–16, but here with the involvement of Enoch. He is introduced somewhat abruptly in 12:1, and there is a break between chapters 11 and 12. Enoch is commissioned to deliver the message of judgement to the Watchers (chapter 12) and this he does (13:1–3). The Watchers, fearful and ashamed, ask Enoch to write a petition on their behalf and to present it before God (13:4–5). Enoch writes a petition, reads it out, and in consequence experiences a dream-vision in which, as we subsequently learn, the message of judgement on the Watchers is reaffirmed (13:6–8). He returns to the Watchers to tell them of his vision (13:9–10). Chapters 14–16 are an account of the vision; Enoch, after some introductory words (14:1–7), describes his ascent to the throne-room of God (14:8–24) and the message which he received from God for the Watchers (15:1–16:4). Only 14:8–16:4 is given here.

It would appear that chapters 12–16 stem from the author of the book of Watchers himself; they serve as an elaboration of the material in chapters 6–11, which, as we have seen, was probably taken over from the book of Noah. Much of what is said in the earlier chapters is repeated, but one significant new point is made: the continuing existence of evil in the world is attributed to the activities of the spirits which are held to have come from the giants (cp. 15:8–12).

ENOCH'S ASCENT TO THE THRONE-ROOM OF GOD

14:8 And the vision appeared to me as follows: Behold clouds called me in the vision, and mist called me, and the path of the stars and flashes of lightning hastened me and drove me, and in the vision winds caused me to fly and hastened me and lifted me up into

9 heaven. And I proceeded until I came near to a wall which was built of hail-stones, and a tongue[a] of fire surrounded it, and it began to

10 make me afraid. And I went into the tongue[a] of fire and came near to a large house which was built of hail-stones, and the wall of that house (was) like a mosaic (made) of hail-stones, and its floor (was)

11 snow. Its roof (was) like the path of the stars and flashes of lightning, and among them (were) fiery Cherubim, and their

12 heaven (was like) water. And (there was) a fire burning around its

13 wall, and its door was ablaze with fire. And I went into that house, and (it was) hot as fire and cold as snow, and there was neither pleasure nor life[b] in it. Fear covered me and trembling took hold

14 of me. And as I was shaking and trembling, I fell on my face. And I

15 saw in the vision, and behold, another house, which was larger than the former, and all its doors (were) open before me, and (it was)

16 built[c] of a tongue[d] of fire. And in everything it so excelled in glory and splendour and size that I am unable to describe to you its glory

17 and size. And its floor (was) fire, and above (were) lightning and

18 the path of the stars, and its roof also (was) a burning fire. And I looked and I saw in it a high throne, and its appearance (was) like ice[e] and its surrounds[f] like the shining sun and the sound of

19 Cherubim. And from underneath the high throne there flowed out rivers of burning fire so that it was impossible to look at it.

20 And he who is great in glory[g] sat on it, and his raiment was

21 brighter than the sun, and whiter than any snow. And no angel could enter and look at the face of him who is honoured and

22 praised, and no (creature of) flesh could look at him. A sea of fire burnt around him, and a great fire stood before him, and none of those around him came near to him. Ten thousand times ten

23 thousand (stood) before him, but he needed no holy counsel. And the Holy Ones[h] who were near to him did not leave by night or

24 day, and did not depart from him. And until then I had a covering on my face,[i] as I trembled. And the Lord called me with his own mouth and said to me: 'Come hither, Enoch, to my holy word.'

25 And he lifted me up[j] and brought me near to the door. And I looked,[k] with my face down.

a One Eth. ms. Greek[a] 'tongues'.
b Some Eth. mss. 'no pleasure of life'; Greek[a] 'no food of life'.
c Greek[a] (partly supported by one Eth. ms.) 'another door open before me, and a house larger than the former, and all of it (was) built'.
d Some Eth. mss. Greek[a] 'tongues'.
e Or 'crystal'.
f Or 'its wheels'.
g Some Eth. mss. Greek[a] 'the Great Glory'.
h Text uncertain, perhaps read with one Eth. ms. 'but he needed no counsel. And the most Holy Ones'; Greek[a] differs.
i Greek[a] 'I had been prostrate on my face'.
j *to my...me up*: Greek[a] 'and hear my word. And one of the Holy Ones came to me, and raised me, and stood me up.'
k Greek[a] 'And I bowed'.

The account of Enoch's ascent in a visionary state to the throne-room of God is the earliest example of such an ascent-vision which was to become an important element in other pseudepigraphical writings (cp. e.g. 2 Enoch, the Ascension of Isaiah) and in later Jewish mystical writings. The author of Enoch to some extent drew his inspiration from Ezekiel's vision of the throne-chariot of God, and in Enoch as in Ezekiel (cp. 1:1–3:3) the vision is followed by a commission to deliver a message of judgement. The description of the ascent to the throne-room in Enoch serves to authenticate the message which Enoch there received from God. The heavenly region is presented as if it were a palace or temple-complex; Enoch first enters a courtyard (verse 9), then an outer building (verses 10–14*a*), and finally an inner building, larger than the first one (verse 15), but conceived of as a holy of holies (verses 14*b*–25).

8. A comparable description of an ascent is given in 39:3: 'And at that time clouds and a storm-wind carried me off from the face of earth, and set me down at the end of heaven.'

9. The courtyard. *and it began to make me afraid*: fear is a frequent motif in accounts of visions in the apocalyptic writings, cp. e.g. Dan. 7:15; 8:17-18; 10:8-10. In this vision fear is mentioned at the end of the descriptions of each of the three parts of the heavenly temple which Enoch enters, cp. verses 13*b*-14*a*, 24.

10-14*a*. The outer house.

14*b*-25. The inner house.

18-19. The throne of God. For the description cp. Dan. 7:9-10; Isa. 6:1-5; Ezek. 1:26-8*a*.

20. *He who is great in glory*: or 'the Great Glory' (see the footnote). Underlying this title is the use of the term 'glory', particularly in Ezekiel and the Priestly writing, as a technical term to refer to God's presence, cp. Ezek. 1:28*a*; Exod. 40:34-8. *and his raiment was...whiter than any snow*: cp. Dan. 7:9.

22. *Ten thousand times ten thousand*: cp. Dan. 7:10.

25. *And he lifted me up*: as is clear from the Greek (see the footnote), it is an angel who does this; this too is a characteristic feature of visions in apocalyptic writings, cp. Dan. 8:18; 10:10.

GOD'S MESSAGE TO THE WATCHERS

15:1   And he answered me and said to me with his voice: 'Hear!ª Do not be afraid, Enoch, (you) righteous man and scribe of righteous-
2   ness. Come hither and hear my voice. And go, say to the Watchers of heaven who sent you to petition on their behalf: "You ought to petition on behalf of men, not men on behalf of
3   you. Why have you left the high, holy and eternal heaven, and lain with the women and become unclean with the daughters of men, and taken wives for yourselves, and done as the sons of the
4   earth and begotten giant sons. And you (were) spiritual, holy, living an eternal life, (but) you became unclean upon the women,ᵇ and begat (children) through the blood of flesh, and lusted after the blood of men,ᶜ and produced flesh and blood as they do who
5   die and are destroyed. And for this reason I gave them wives, (namely) that they might sow seed in them and (that) children might be born by them, that thus deeds might be done on the
6   earth.ᵈ But you formerly were spiritual, living an eternal, immortal
7   life for all the generations of the world. For this reason I did not

arrange wives for you because the dwelling of the spiritual ones[e]

8 (is) in heaven. And now the giants who were born from body and
flesh[f] will be called evil spirits upon the earth, and on the earth

9 will be their dwelling. And evil spirits came out from their flesh[g]
because from above[h] they were created; from the holy Watchers
was their origin and first foundation. Evil spirits they will be on

10 the earth, and spirits of the evil ones they will be called.[i] And the
dwelling of the spirits of heaven is in heaven, but the dwelling of
the spirits of earth, who were born on the earth, (is) on earth.

11 And the spirits of the giants...which do wrong[j] and are corrupt,[k]
and attack and fight and break on the earth, and cause sorrow; and

12 they eat no food and do not thirst,[l] and cause offence.[m] And these
spirits will rise against the sons of men and against[n] the women
because they came out (from them). In the days[o] of slaughter and

16:1 destruction and the death of the giants, wherever the spirits have
gone out from (their) bodies, their flesh shall be destroyed[p] before
the judgement; thus they will be destroyed[q] until the day of the
great consummation is accomplished upon the great age, upon the

2 Watchers and the impious ones." And now to the Watchers who
sent you to petition on their behalf, who were formerly in

3 heaven – and now (say): "You were in heaven, but (its) secrets[r]
had not yet been revealed to you and a worthless mystery you
knew. This you made known to the women in the hardness of
your heart, and through this mystery the women and the men

4 cause evil to increase on the earth." Say to them therefore: "You
will not have peace."'

a *with his voice*: Hear: some Eth. mss. Greek[a] 'and his voice I heard'.
b *upon the women*: so Eth., but corrupt for Greek[a] 'through the blood of the women'.
c *and lusted after the blood of men*: possibly an addition or corrupt – the idea of murderous intent is out of place here.
d Greek[a] (partly supported by some Eth. mss.) 'that nothing might be lacking to them on the earth'.
e Some Eth. mss. Greek[a] add 'of heaven'.
f One Eth. ms. Greek 'from the spirits and flesh'.
g Or 'from their bodies'.
h Greek[a] 'from men'.
i *and spirits...called*: Greek[a] omits together with verse 10.
j Text obscure, perhaps originally 'The spirits of the giants, the Nephilim, do wrong.'
k Two Eth. mss. Greek 'and cause corruption' or 'and cause destruction'.

l Greek 'and they do not eat, but fast and thirst'.
m Correction based on one Eth. ms. Greek.
n Greek 'and of'.
o Two Eth. mss. Greek 'From the days'.
p Eth. corrupt; read 'from the souls of their flesh, they will destroy', cp. Greek.
q Eth. corrupt; read with Greek 'they will destroy'.
r Greek[a] 'every secret'.

15:8–12. The continuing existence of evil in the world is attributed to the activities of spirits which came out of the bodies of the giants.

15:9b–10. This is lacking in Greek[s] (see the textual note) and may well be a secondary addition in Greek[a] Eth.; the text merely repeats what has already been said in verses 7b–8.

15:11. The text in the Ethiopic and Greek versions is corrupt and uncertain, but the main point is clear; the verse provides a list of the evils caused by the spirits of the giants.

15:12–16:1. The Ethiopic text is in part corrupt (see the textual notes). The meaning is clearer in the Greek; the evil spirits are allowed to carry on their activities and remain unpunished until the day of judgement; cp. Jub 10:1–11.

16:3. The knowledge which the Watchers brought to earth (8:1–3) is now said to have been incomplete and worthless; it is for this reason that it was the cause of sin.

THE PARABLES OF ENOCH

Chapters 37–71 of 1 Enoch have been given the title 'the Parables' because each of the three sections into which the material is divided (chapters 38–44; 45–57; 58–69) is called in the text a 'parable' (or 'similitude', as the word is sometimes translated). The Parables describe Enoch's journey through heaven, and much of the interest and importance of this material derives from the fact that a great deal of what he sees and is told on his journey relates to an individual called by various names, of which the most important are 'the Chosen One' and 'the Son of Man', who acts on God's behalf as judge at the final judgement (cp. John 5:27). Not all the material in these chapters is concerned with this individual, and traditions about Noah, perhaps from the lost book of Noah (see above, p. 30), form another significant element. Chapter 37 provides an introduction, and there are two separate conclusions, chapters 70 and 71; in the second of these, possibly a little later than the rest of the material, Enoch himself is identified as the one about whom we have been told throughout the Parables, i.e. as the Son of Man.

The concern with the Son of Man has led to the Parables being considered in relation to the traditions in the gospels about the Son of Man. Some scholars have thought that the Parables are Christian, but this is very unlikely because the Parables lack any reference to the life, death and resurrection of Jesus; here the difference from the Testaments of the Twelve Patriarchs, a work Jewish in origin but clearly Christian in its present form, is particularly significant. In fact the Parables are a Jewish work and are rooted firmly in traditions stemming from the Old Testament; they build upon what is said about the 'one like a man' of Dan. 7, but also draw upon traditions relating to the Davidic Messiah (cp. Isa. 11) and to God's servant (cp. Isa. 49). It is a matter of debate whether the Parables, as a Jewish work, might have exercised some limited influence on the gospel traditions; but their real importance – apart from their interest in their own right – lies in the fact that they show us how Jews contemporary with the early Christians used and interpreted the material in Dan. 7 about the 'one like a man'.

It is very difficult to attach a precise date to the Parables. As we have seen, no fragments corresponding to this section of 1 Enoch were discovered at Qumran, and this writing is not a Qumran work. However, it was not written in isolation from the other traditions associated with Enoch, but represents in some respects a continuation of them. There are reasons to think that the Parables were composed during the period in which Rome controlled affairs in Palestine (see the comment on 46:7); more precisely it seems likely that they date from the first century AD – in the writer's opinion from towards the end of that century. It should be noted that for this section of Enoch we have available only an Ethiopic text.

The extract given here (chapters 45–51) has been chosen both because of its intrinsic interest and because it forms a distinct element in the Parables, marked off from what precedes and what follows.

THE INTRODUCTION TO THE SECOND PARABLE

45:1 And this (is) the second parable about those who deny the name
2 of the dwelling of the holy ones and of the Lord of Spirits. They will not ascend into heaven, nor will they come upon earth: such will be the lot of the sinners who deny the name of the Lord of Spirits,
3 who will thus be kept for the day of affliction and distress. On that day the Chosen One[a] will sit on the throne of glory, and will choose their works, and their resting-places will be without number; and

their spirits within them will grow strong when they see my
Chosen One[b] and those who appeal to my holy and glorious name.

4 And on that day I will cause my Chosen One to dwell among them,
and I will transform heaven and make it an eternal blessing and

5 light. And I will transform the dry ground and make it a blessing,
and I will cause my chosen ones to dwell upon it; but those who

6 commit sin and evil will not tread upon it. For I have seen, and
have satisfied with peace, my righteous ones, and have placed them
before me; but for the sinners my judgement[c] draws near before me,
that I may destroy them from the face of the earth.

a Some Eth. mss. 'my Chosen One'.
b Some Eth. mss. 'my chosen ones'.
c *but for the sinners my judgement*: so some Eth. mss.; others omit 'my' or read 'but the
judgement of the sinners'.

Chapter 45 forms the introduction to the second parable and indicates
the major themes of the material which it contains: the judgement of
the wicked, the role of the Chosen One, and the blessed fate of the
righteous after the judgement.

1. *parable*: the word 'parable' is used in the Old Testament to refer
both to the short proverbial sayings that form much of the content of
Proverbs and Ecclesiasticus, and to prophetic utterances, particularly of
a figurative kind (cp. Num. 23:7, 18 (NEB 'oracle'); Ezek. 17:2;
20:49; Micah 2:4 (NEB 'poem'). It is in the latter sense that the word
is used here, cp. 1:3. *deny the name of the dwelling of the holy ones and of
the Lord of Spirits*: denying the name of the Lord of Spirits – which
means denying his existence – is a charge frequently brought against
the wicked in the Parables, cp. e.g. 46:7; 48:10; here it is linked with
the charge that they deny the reality of the heavenly world. *Lord of
Spirits*: this title for God, used very frequently in the Parables, is perhaps
based on the title that occurs in Num. 16:22; 27:16, 'God of the spirits
of all mankind'. However, in 39:12, 'Holy, holy, holy, Lord of
Spirits; he fills the earth with spirits', a link is made with Isa. 6:3 and
thus with the common Old Testament title for God, 'LORD of hosts'.
Cp. 2 Macc. 3:24, 'The Ruler of spirits and of all powers', and 1QH x.8
'Lord of all spirits'.

2. *nor will they come upon earth*: sinners will be excluded from the
earth which will be transformed after the judgement, cp. verse 5.
the day of affliction and distress: i.e. the day of judgement.

3. *the Chosen One*: this title for the individual who acts as God's

agent in the judgement of the wicked is inherent in the fact that he has been chosen by God (46:3; 48:6; 49:4; cp. Isa. 42:1). The individual is also called 'Son of Man' (46:2, and frequently), 'the Righteous One' (38:2), 'the Righteous and Chosen One' (53:6), and 'Messiah' (48:10; 52:4). *choose*: so all Eth. mss., but probably a mistranslation of an Aramaic word which can mean both 'to choose' and 'to test'; the latter would make more sense here – the Chosen One 'tests' the works of those whom he judges. *their works...their resting-places...their spirits*: we might have expected the text to refer to the judgement of the sinners (verse 2), but it makes no sense to say of sinners that 'their resting-places will be without number'. But if the text refers to the judgement of the righteous, there is no antecedent for the possessive pronouns. It is likely that there is a break between verses 1–2 and 3–6.

4–6. In the new era after the judgement the righteous will live on a transformed earth (cp. 10:16–11:2; 51:4–5) with the Chosen One in their midst (cp. 62:14). *I will transform heaven...I will transform the dry ground*: cp. Isa. 65:17; 66:22. *but for the sinners my judgement*: the Chosen One (or 'Son of Man') has only a delegated authority as judge (cp. 69:27, 'the whole judgement was given to the Son of Man'); the judgement is God's, and so here God himself is depicted as the judge, just as he plays an active part in the judgement scenes in chapters 62 and 63. See further the comment on chapter 50.

THE HEAD OF DAYS AND THE SON OF MAN

46:1   And there I saw one who had a head of days, and his head (was) white like wool; and with him (there was) another, whose face had the appearance of a man, and his face (was) full of grace, like one
2   of the holy angels. And I asked one of the holy angels who went with me, and showed me all the secrets, about that Son of Man, who he was, and whence he was, (and) why he went with the Head
3   of Days. And he answered me and said to me: 'This is the Son of Man who has righteousness, and with whom righteousness dwells; he will reveal all the treasures of that which is secret, for the Lord of Spirits has chosen him, and through uprightness his lot has
4   surpassed all before the Lord of Spirits for ever. And this Son of Man whom you have seen will rouse the kings and the powerful from their resting-places, and the strong from their thrones, and will loose the reins of the strong, and will break the teeth of the

5   sinners. And he will cast down the kings from their thrones and
    from their kingdoms, for they do not exalt him, and do not praise
    him, and do not humbly acknowledge whence (their) kingdom was
6   given to them. And he will cast down the faces of the strong, and
    shame will fill them, and darkness will be their dwelling, and worms
    will be their resting-place; and they will have no hope of rising
    from their resting-places, for they do not exalt the name of the
7   Lord of Spirits. And these are they who judge the stars of heaven,
    and raise their hands against the Most High, and trample upon the
    dry ground, and dwell upon it; and all their deeds show iniquity,
    and their power (rests) on their riches, and their faith is in the gods
    which they have made with their hands, and they deny the name of
8   the Lord of Spirits. And they will be driven from^a the houses of his
    congregation, and of the faithful who depend on the name of the
    Lord of Spirits.

        a Some Eth. mss. 'And they persecute'.

The Parables are essentially an account of a journey by Enoch through
heaven (39:3 tells how he was carried up there), and a basic element of
the material in the Parables consists of descriptions of scenes witnessed
by Enoch in heaven. These scenes relate to different aspects of the final
judgement of the wicked, and linked to the descriptions are statements
about the judgement and about the blessed fate of the righteous; in
chapters 45–51 the statement-form predominates. The material is only
loosely linked together, and the various descriptions and statements
overlap to a considerable extent, each depicting the same events from a
slightly different perspective. The material in chapter 46 has a threefold
structure: (1) Enoch describes what he sees (God accompanied by a
figure like a man, verse 1); (2) he asks about the significance of what he
has seen (verse 2); (3) the angel who accompanies him provides an
answer (verses 3–8). The statement from the angel explains who the
manlike figure is and gives an account of the judgement which he will
carry out. The description of the scene in heaven (verse 1) is based on
the Son of Man vision of Dan. 7 (see verses 9–10, 13–14) and the
chapter as a whole provides a reinterpretation of the material in Dan. 7.
    1. *one who had a head of days, and his head (was) white like wool*:
cp. Dan. 7:9. *another, whose face had the appearance of a man*: cp. Dan.

7:13, 'one like a man coming with the clouds of heaven'. The NEB translation 'one like a man' is what the underlying Aramaic expression means, although it is literally 'one like a son of man' (see the NEB footnote to Dan. 7:13).

2. *I asked...about that Son of Man*: here for the first time the author uses the expression 'Son of Man', taken from Dan. 7:13, to refer to the one he elsewhere calls 'the Chosen One'. 'Son of Man' is probably not a title since it is almost always qualified in some way, frequently by the demonstrative adjective 'that'; it is rather a description, that man-like figure, the demonstrative referring back to the account of what Enoch had seen in 45:1. The immediate answer to Enoch's question is given in verses 3–8, but in fact all the material in chapters 46–51 serves as an answer to the question.

3. *the Son of Man who has righteousness, and with whom righteousness dwells*: thus he can be called 'the Righteous One' (38:2) and 'the Righteous and Chosen One' (53:6); for righteousness as a quality possessed by the Messiah see Isa. 9:7; 11:4–5; Jer. 23:5. *he will reveal all the treasures of that which is secret*: the Son of Man as judge will uncover everything that is stored secretly away, particularly sin, cp. 49:4. *for the Lord of Spirits has chosen him*: hence he is called 'the Chosen One'.

4–8. The judgement of the Son of Man. In contrast to the passive role of the one like a man in Dan. 7, the Son of Man in Enoch plays an active part as God's agent in the judgement of the wicked.

4. *will rouse the kings and the powerful from their resting-places, and the strong from their thrones*: perhaps based on Isa. 14:9*b*. As in Isa. 14, esp. 9*b*, the kings and the powerful, although dead, are depicted as sitting on their thrones. *will break the teeth of the sinners*: cp. what is said of God in Ps. 3:7; 58:6.

6. *worms will be their resting-place*: cp. Isa. 14:11*b*. *they will have no hope of rising*: the author is no doubt thinking of the final punishment of the wicked, for it is clear from 51:1–2 that sinners and righteous rise from the dead to be judged.

7. *these are they who judge the stars of heaven, and raise their hands against the Most High*: underlying this description of the arrogant behaviour of 'the kings and the powerful' (verse 4) is the myth of the 'bright morning star' (Isa. 14:12–15 (see verses 13–14); cp. Dan. 8:10). However, it is possible that the text is not in order. *and trample upon the dry ground, and dwell upon it*: elsewhere 'the kings of the earth and the strong' (48:8; cp. verse 4 above) or 'the kings and the mighty and the exalted' (cp. e.g. 62:1, 3) are said to possess the dry ground (i.e. the

earth); such expressions suggest that the rulers who are condemned here possessed world-wide dominion. This could hardly have been said of native Jewish rulers. *their faith is in the gods which they have made with their hands*: the charge of idolatry again can hardly be applied to Jewish rulers. The indications are that foreign rulers, namely the Romans, must at least be included amongst the wicked, and this suggests that the Parables were composed during the period of Roman domination of Palestine.

THE BLOOD OF THE RIGHTEOUS CRIES FOR VENGEANCE

47:1   And in those days the prayer of the righteous and the blood of the righteous will have ascended from the earth before the Lord of

2   Spirits. In these days the holy ones who dwell in the heavens above will unite with one voice, and supplicate, and pray, and praise, and give thanks, and bless in the name of the Lord of Spirits, because of the blood of the righteous which has been poured out, and (because of) the prayer of the righteous, that it may not cease[a] before the Lord of Spirits, that justice may be done to them, and

3   (that) their patience may not have to last for ever. And in those days I saw the Head of Days sit down on the throne of his glory, and the books of the living were opened before him, and all his host, which (dwells) in the heavens above, and his council were

4   standing before him. And the hearts of the holy ones were full of joy that the number of righteousness[b] had been reached,[c] and the prayer of the righteous had been heard, and the blood of the righteous had been required before the Lord of Spirits.

a Or 'that it may not be in vain'.
b Two Eth. mss. 'of the righteous'.
c Some Eth. mss. 'had drawn near'.

This chapter takes up the theme familiar from Gen. 4:10, and present in other parts of 1 Enoch (cp. 7:6; 8:4; 22:5–7), that innocent blood that has been shed cries out to God and will be avenged by him (cp. Matt. 23:35). From a literary point of view the chapter is only loosely linked with the preceding one, although it is also concerned with the theme of the last judgement. Verses 1 and 2 are presented as a continuation of the speech of the angel in 46:3–8, but are tied to that material merely by the common introductory formula 'And in those days'.

In verses 3 and 4 there is another description of a scene in heaven relating to the judgement.

2. The angels in heaven intercede on behalf of the righteous, cp. 9:1–11. *and praise...in the name of the Lord of Spirits*: these words hardly seem appropriate in the context and may have come in by inadvertence.

3. God himself takes his seat as judge; see the comment on 45:4–6. The description of the scene is based on Dan. 7:9–10. *the books of the living were opened before him*: cp. Dan. 7:10, 'the books were opened'; see also Exod. 32:32–3; Ps. 69:28; Dan. 12:1; Mal. 3:16.

4. *the number of righteousness had been reached*: or perhaps 'of the righteous' (see the footnote). In any case there underlies this statement the idea that God had determined in advance the number of the righteous, cp. 2 Esdras 4:33–7; Rev. 6:9–11; because that number had been reached, the judgement was about to begin.

THE NAMING OF THE SON OF MAN

48:1 And in that place I saw an inexhaustible spring of righteousness, and many springs of wisdom surrounded it, and all the thirsty drank from them and were filled with wisdom, and their dwelling

2 (was) with the righteous and the holy and the chosen. And at that hour that Son of Man was named in the presence of the Lord of

3 Spirits, and his name (was named) before the Head of Days. Even before the sun and the constellations were created, before the stars of heaven were made, his name was named before the Lord of

4 Spirits. He will be a staff to the righteous and the holy,[a] that they may lean on him and not fall, and he (will be) the light of the nations, and he will be the hope of those who grieve in their

5 hearts. All those who dwell upon the dry ground will fall down and worship before him, and they will bless, and praise, and

6 celebrate with psalms the name of the Lord of Spirits. And because of this he was chosen and hidden before him before the world was

7 created, and for ever. But the wisdom of the Lord of Spirits has revealed him to the holy and the righteous, for he has kept safe the lot of the righteous, for they have hated and rejected this world of iniquity, and all its works and its ways they have hated in the name of the Lord of Spirits; for in his name they are saved, and he

8 is the one who will require their lives. And in those days the kings
   of the earth and the strong who possess the dry ground will have
   downcast faces because of the works of their hands, for on the day

9 of their distress and trouble they will not save themselves. And I
   will give them into the hands of my chosen ones; like straw in the
   fire, and like lead in water, so they will burn before the righteous,
   and sink before the holy, and no trace will be found of them.

10 And on the day of their trouble there will be rest on the earth,
   and they will fall down before him[b] and will not rise; and there
   will be no one who will take them with his hands and raise them,
   for they denied the Lord of Spirits and his Messiah. May the name
   of the Lord of Spirits be blessed!

a *and the holy*: some Eth. mss. omit.   b Some Eth. mss. 'before them'.

Verses 1–2 form a description of a scene in heaven in which Enoch
witnesses the naming of the Son of Man. Linked to this in verses 3–7 is
a statement about the attributes and functions of the Son of Man,
particularly his role as helper and saviour of the righteous. Verses 8–10
are another passage about the judgement of the wicked; they form a
continuation of the statement in verses 3–7, but are joined to it only by
the formula 'And in those days'. There are no close links between
chapter 48 and the preceding chapter, except that 47:3 describes the
enthronement of God, and 48:2 presupposes a situation in which God
sits enthroned in his heavenly court. The transition from the description of the scene (verses 1–2) to statement (verses 3–10) is unmarked,
nor is it clear who the speaker is (Enoch or the angel); in verse 9 God
himself is the speaker. The material in verses 2–6 has been clearly
influenced by what is said about God's servant in Isa. 49:1–7.

   1. The source of righteousness and wisdom, here spoken of as if they
were objective realities, is conceived to be in heaven; for the idea cp.
Pss. 85:11; 89:14; 97:2 and Job 28:23–4; Ecclus. 24:1–24; Baruch
3:29; 1 Enoch 42 (not presented here). The numerous references to
wisdom in chapters 48–9 indicate that the material has been influenced
by the wisdom tradition.

   2. *that Son of Man was named in the presence of the Lord of Spirits*:
cp. Isa. 49:1b.

   3. *Even before the sun and the constellations were created . . . his name was
named*: in verse 2 Enoch saw the Son of Man being named, but we are
now informed that he had already been named before the creation of

the world. Naming implies existence, and there is here the idea of the pre-existence of the Son of Man; the Son of Man exists already in heaven where he is kept by God until the moment comes for him to act, cp. verse 6; 62:7; 2 Esdras 12:32; 13:26. The idea of pre-existence perhaps reflects the influence of the wisdom tradition; there are similarities between what is said here about the Son of Man and what is said in Prov. 8:23–6 about the pre-existent figure of wisdom.

4. *and he (will be) the light of the nations*: cp. Isa. 49:6*b*. Also the fact that the Son of Man is to be *a staff to the righteous* corresponds to the fact that part of the task of God's servant is 'to restore the tribes of Jacob, to bring back the descendants of Israel' (Isa. 49:6*a*).

5. *will fall down and worship*: cp. Isa. 49:7*b*.

6. *he was chosen*: cp. Isa. 49:7*b*, 'because of the Holy One of Israel who has chosen you'. *and hidden*: cp. Isa. 49:2; 2 Esdras 13:52. *before the world was created*: for the idea of pre-existence see the comment on verse 3.

7. *the wisdom of the Lord of Spirits has revealed him*: perhaps, as has been suggested, through Old Testament prophecy. God's wisdom here acts almost as an independent entity, cp. Prov. 8; Ecclus. 24; 1 Enoch 42. The influence of the wisdom tradition is again apparent.

8. *the kings of the earth*: cp. Ps. 2:2.

9. The righteous participate in the judgement of the wicked. *like straw in the fire, and like lead in water*: the imagery is taken from Exod. 15:7, 10, part of the song celebrating God's defeat of Pharaoh, but cp. also Obad. 18; Mal. 4:1.

10. *for they denied the Lord of Spirits and his Messiah*: cp. Ps. 2:2; the author is drawing on material relating to the Davidic Messiah, as he also does in chapter 49. *Messiah*: see the comment on 45:3 and the Cambridge Bible Commentary on 1 and 2 Esdras, pp. 168–9.

THE WISDOM OF THE CHOSEN ONE

49:1 For wisdom has been poured out like water, and glory will not
2 fail before him for ever and ever. For he (is) powerful in all the secrets of righteousness, and iniquity will pass away like a shadow, and will have no existence; for the Chosen One stands before the Lord of Spirits, and his glory (is) for ever and ever, and his power
3 for all generations. And in him dwells the spirit of wisdom, and the spirit which gives understanding, and the spirit of knowledge and of power, and the spirit of those who sleep in righteousness.

4   And he will judge the things that are secret, and no one will be able to say an idle word before him, for he (has been) chosen before the Lord of Spirits, in accordance with his wish.

This chapter draws on what is said in Isa. 11:1–9 about the shoot from the stock of Jesse in order to describe the qualifications of the Chosen One for his task as judge (cp. verse 4). The links with the preceding and following chapters are – as we have seen for the other sections – only light; but there is a thematic link with 48:3–7 inasmuch as the latter material described the qualifications and functions of the Son of Man. From a literary point of view the statement-form continues – as it does now until the end of chapter 51.

1. *wisdom has been poured out like water*: cp. Isa. 11:9b. *before him*: the Messiah (cp. 48:10), i.e. the Chosen One/Son of Man.

2. *the Chosen One stands before the Lord of Spirits*: cp. 48:2, the naming of the Son of Man before the Lord of Spirits/Head of Days.

3. *the spirit of wisdom, and the spirit which gives understanding, and the spirit of knowledge and of power*: closely based on Isa. 11:2. *the spirit of those who sleep in righteousness*: perhaps the thought is that the Chosen One will be inspired by the same spirit as that which inspired the righteous dead; cp. 46:3 and the title 'the Righteous One' (38:2).

4. *And he will judge...an idle word before him*; this corresponds to Isa. 11:3–4a.

> He shall not judge by what he sees
> nor decide by what he hears;
> he shall judge the poor with justice.

THE SALVATION OF THOSE WHO REPENT

50:1   And in those days a change will occur for the holy and the chosen; the light of days will rest upon them, and glory and honour
2   will return to the holy. And on the day of trouble calamity will be heaped up over the sinners, but the righteous will conquer in the name of the Lord of Spirits; and he will show (this) to others that
3   they may repent and abandon the works of their hands. And they will have no honour before[a] the Lord of Spirits, but in his name they will be saved; and the Lord of Spirits will have mercy on
4   them, for his mercy (is) great. And he (is) righteous in his judgement, and before his glory iniquity will not (be able to) stand at his

judgement: he who does not repent before him will be destroyed.

5 'And from then on I will not have mercy on them', says the Lord
   of Spirits.

a Some Eth. mss. 'in the name of'.

Chapter 50 forms a further statement about the judgement and its
aftermath; it is linked to what precedes only by the introductory
formula 'And in those days'. It is noticeable that in this chapter, in
contrast to chapters 49 and 51, the Lord of Spirits himself is the judge
(cp. 47:3), and there is no mention of the Chosen One/Son of Man.
This follows from the fact that the Chosen One/Son of Man acts only
with a delegated authority, and the judgement is God's judgement (see
the comment on 45:4–6); but inasmuch as the Chosen One/Son of
Man does function as God's agent similar things can be said about the
two figures. The fact remains that there is a certain element of in-
consistency here which serves to highlight the loose style of composition. The chapter begins by referring to the fates which await the
righteous and the sinners, but then mentions another group, those who
are saved through their repentance.

   1. *the light of days*: for light as a symbol of salvation cp. Isa. 58:8, 10
(and elsewhere in Isa. 56–66).

   2. *the righteous will conquer*: cp. 48:9, the righteous participate in the
judgement.

   4. *he (is) righteous*: cp. what is said about the righteousness of the Son
of Man in 46:3. *iniquity will not (be able to) stand*: cp. the similar
expression in 49:2 ('will have no existence').

THE RESURRECTION AND FINAL JUDGEMENT

51:1 And in those days the earth will return that which has been
      entrusted to it, and Sheol will return that which has been entrusted
      to it, that which it has received, and destruction will return what it
2   owes. And he will choose the righteous and holy from among
3   them, for the day has come near that they must be saved. And in
      those days the Chosen One[a] will sit on his throne[b], and all the
      secrets of wisdom will flow out from the counsel of his mouth, for
4   the Lord of Spirits has appointed him and glorified him. And in
      those days the mountains will leap like rams, and the hills will skip
      like lambs satisfied with milk, and all will become angels in heaven.

5 Their faces will shine with joy, for in those days the Chosen One
will have risen; and the earth will rejoice, and the righteous will
dwell upon it, and the chosen will go and walk upon it.

a Some Eth. mss. 'my Chosen One'.   b Some Eth. mss. 'on my throne'.

Another statement introduced by the formula 'And in those days'
concerning the theme of judgement. Here we are informed that the
judgement will be preceded by the resurrection of the dead, cp. Dan.
12:2; 1 Enoch 22; 90:33; 91:10; 2 Esdras 7:32, 37.

1. *Sheol...and destruction*: or perhaps 'Sheol...and Abaddon', for
underlying the Ethiopic word is the place-name 'Abaddon' (Job 26:6;
28:22; Ps. 88:11; cp. Rev. 9:11). In this passage 'Sheol' and 'Abaddon'
are used synonymously as names for the place where the dead wait
until the resurrection, cp. 2 Esdras 7:32.

2. *And he*: the subject is not named until verse 3, but we are meant
to understand that it is the Chosen One who acts as judge.

3. *the Chosen One will sit on his throne*: or 'on my throne' (see the
textual note); it is in any case clear that the throne is God's throne
(cp. 47:3), and that the Chosen One sits on it by virtue of his enthronement by God (cp. 61:8, 'And the Lord of Spirits set the Chosen One
on the throne of (his) glory'). See also 45:3. *all the secrets of wisdom*:
cp. 49:3, the endowment of the Chosen One with the spirit of wisdom.
for the Lord of Spirits has appointed him: the Chosen One acts with
delegated authority as God's agent.

4-5. After the judgement the righteous live a life of bliss on a
transformed earth, cp. 45:4-6.

4. *the mountains will leap like rams, and the hills...like lambs*: cp.
Ps. 114:4, 6.

5. *the Chosen One will have risen*: i.e. in order to act; cp. the rising of
God in judgement, Ps. 76:8-10. *the righteous will dwell upon it*: cp.
Ps. 37:3, 9, 11, 29, 34.

The Testament of Abraham

E. P. SANDERS

The Testament of Abraham is a Jewish work, probably of Egyptian origin, which is generally dated to the latter part of the first century AD. It is most closely related to the Testaments of Isaac and Jacob, both of which are dependent on it. It has many themes in common with several other works, most notably 2En and 3Bar. It should not be confused with the Apocalypse of Abraham, even though the latter work also describes a heavenly tour (chapters 15–29).

The textual witnesses

TAb exists in two major recensions, and the original text is not recoverable. The longer recension (TAb A) is attested by a great number of Greek manuscripts and supported on the whole by a Rumanian version. The shorter recension (TAb B) is attested by several Greek manuscripts and supported on the whole by the Slavonic version, another Rumanian version, and by the Coptic, the Arabic and the Ethiopic versions. The fullest available list is that given in A.-M. Denis, *Introduction aux Pseudépigraphes grecs d'Ancien Testament*, pp. 32–4. The oldest extant witness is a fifth-century fragmentary Coptic text (unfortunately still unpublished).

There is considerable disagreement with regard to the earliest form of the work and the relationship between the two major recensions. It seems most likely that the longer recension better reflects the contents of the original work, although the shorter recension may in some cases preserve the earlier wording. Substantial verbatim agreement between the two recensions in Greek indicates that they have an ultimate common ancestor, even though the two recensions as they have been preserved differ from each other in two major and several minor ways. The selections in the present volume are from the longer recension.

Content

The narrative as we now have it in the long recension is as follows: When it is time for Abraham to die, God sends the archangel Michael to tell him so that he can make a will. It is also hoped that Abraham will voluntarily surrender his soul to Michael. Abraham, however, is recalcitrant and refuses to go. He requests first to be shown all the inhabited world. After consulting with God, Michael conducts Abraham on a tour. Abraham sees people engaged in sin and calls down death upon them. God tells Michael to stop the tour; for he, unlike Abraham, is compassionate and postpones the death of sinners so that they may repent. Abraham is then conducted to the place of judgement so that he may see what happens to souls after they depart from their bodies and thus be led to repent of his severity. He learns that souls are tried in three ways: by fire, record and balance; and that there are three judgements: by Abel, by the twelve tribes of Israel and finally by God. Abraham intercedes on behalf of a soul which is judged neither wicked nor righteous and then, repenting of his former harshness, on behalf of those whom he had caused to die. God saves the former and restores the latter. Abraham is taken back home, where he still declines to surrender his soul. God sends Death, who shows him his ferocity and who finally takes his soul by a deception. His soul is conducted to heaven by angels.

Central theme

The central portion of the work is the description of the judgement of souls. Each of the three images of judgement (fire, balance and records) is traditional, and the author combines them graphically, though without explaining how they actually function. That is, the image of testing by fire, if carried through logically, would imply that evil deeds are consumed. But in this case the weighing of deeds against one another, or the weighing of souls (see 12:13 and 13:10), could not take place. The author, however, was not concerned with logical consistency; he wanted, rather, to convey graphically the conviction that people are accountable for their deeds at the judgement.

God's mercy is especially emphasized even in the account of his strict justice in punishing wrong-doing. Abraham is far readier to condemn than God, who will delay death in order to allow time for repentance. One of the main themes of the judgement scene is that Abraham was wrong to call down death on sinners. God's compassion is emphasized by the contrast to Abraham's willingness to condemn hastily.

Just as the author combined different modes of judgement, he also combined different levels: by Abel immediately after death, by the twelve tribes of Israel, and by God. The relationship among these levels is again not fully explained. God's judgement is said to be final, and the point may be to allow for intercessory prayer between Abel's judgement and God's. The reference to judgement by the twelve tribes of Israel deserves special comment. The judgement of Gentiles by Israel (or of the wicked by the righteous) is known from other literature, and it has apparently been incorporated in the present work as a traditional motif. There is, however, no description of judgement by Israel, and the description of the judgement scene does not seem to leave room for it. What is particularly noteworthy about the reference to judgement by Israel, however, is that this is the only distinctively Jewish element of the work. The sins which are mentioned (adultery, theft, murder and the like) are those which are heinous in all cultures, and the virtues which are stressed (hospitality and compassion) are also universal. The judgement is of all the children of Adam, which clearly puts Jew and Gentile on equal footing, and all are judged by the same standards. Thus the Testament of Abraham bears witness to the existence of a form of Judaism which insisted on high morals and which stressed compassion, but which did not draw a sharp distinction between Jew and Gentile.

A testament?

The setting for the tour of the inhabited world and the view of the judgement of souls is provided by the story of Abraham's approaching death, the need to make a will, and his reluctance to die. It is this setting which has given to the work the title 'testament'. The work, however, is not actually a testament. No will is made and there is no death-bed scene in which the passing patriarch exhorts his survivors to live virtuous lives. The author has simply drawn on the testament genre to provide a framework for the central section of the work. In a similar way the motif of reluctance to die, which probably comes from stories about Moses, is employed to provide the occasion for the tour of the inhabited world and the view of the judgement.

Bibliography

Study of the Testament of Abraham is hampered by the lack of a modern critical text. The only edition, of both the long and the short recensions, is that by M. R. James, *The Testament of Abraham* (Texts and Studies II 2), Cambridge, 1892 (reprint Nendeln/Liechtenstein, 1967). The same text is reprinted with a new English translation in M. E. Stone, *The Testament of Abraham, the Greek Recensions* (SBL Texts and Translations 2, Pseudepigrapha Series 2), Missoula, 1972. Two of the most important studies are unpublished doctoral dissertations.

There are, however, a number of works readily available which provide information about texts, versions, and other relevant literature:

Mathias Delcor, *Le Testament d'Abraham* (StVTPs 2), Leiden, 1973.

George W. E. Nickelsburg, jr. (ed.), *Studies on the Testament of Abraham* (SCS 6), Missoula, 1976.

E. P. Sanders, 'The Testament of Abraham', in J. H. Charlesworth (ed.), *The Old Testament Pseudepigrapha*, vol. I, pp. 871–902.

E. Janssen, 'Testament Abrahams' in JSHRZ III 2, pp. 193–256.

GOD'S MESSAGE TO ABRAHAM

1:1 Abraham lived the measure of his life, 995 years. All the years of his life he lived in quietness, gentleness and righteousness, and the

2 righteous man was very hospitable: for he pitched his tent at the crossroads of the oak of Mamre and welcomed everyone – rich and poor, kings and rulers, the crippled and the helpless, friends and strangers, neighbours and passers-by – (all) on equal terms did the pious, entirely holy, righteous and hospitable Abraham welcome.

3 But even to him came the common and inexorable bitter cup of

4 death and the unforeseen end of life. Therefore the Master God called his archangel Michael and said to him: 'Commander-in-chief Michael, go down to Abraham and tell him about his death, so that

5 he may arrange for the disposition of his possessions. For I have blessed him "as the stars in the sky and the grains of sand on the sea-shore", and he lives in abundance, (having) a large livelihood and many possessions, and he is very rich. But above all others he is righteous in every goodness, (having been) hospitable and loving

6 until the end of his life. But you, archangel Michael, go to Abraham, my beloved friend, announce his death to him, and give him this

7 assurance: "At this time you are about to leave this vain world and depart from the body, and you will come to your own Master among the good."'

2:1 So the Commander-in-chief left the presence of God and went down to Abraham at the oak of Mamre, and he found the righteous Abraham in the nearby field, sitting beside yokes of plough-oxen with the sons of Masek and other servants, twelve in number.

1:2. *oak of Mamre*: see Gen. 18:1. The grammatical form shows the influence of the LXX.

1:4. *Michael*: on Michael as God's principal messenger or as the chief angel cp. ApMos 3:2; 13:2; 22:1; Rev. 12:7.

1:4. *Commander-in-chief*: cp. 3Bar 11:6; 13:3; 2En 22:6; 33:10; JosAsen 14:7; GkApEzra 4:24. The title is apparently Egyptian Jewish.

1:5. *as the stars*: Gen. 22:17 is taken to refer to Abraham's wealth rather than to the number of his descendants.

1:6. *beloved friend*: cp. Isa. 41:8; Jas. 2:23; ApAb 9, 10; Philo, Sobr 56. Also in the Islamic tradition Abraham is regarded as friend of God.

2:1. *Masek* as a proper name: LXX Gen. 15:2.

Abraham, taking Michael to be a handsome soldier, invites him home and provides him with hospitality. Michael, however, finds it difficult to tell Abraham that he must die. At the beginning of the meal, Michael goes outside (2:2–4:5).

MICHAEL'S APPEAL AND GOD'S REPLY

4:5   He ascended into heaven in the twinkling of an eye and stood
6   before God and said to him: 'Master, Lord, let your Might know that I cannot announce the mention of death to that righteous man, because I have not seen upon earth a man like him – merciful, hospitable, righteous, truthful, God-fearing, refraining from every evil deed. And so now know, Lord, that I cannot announce the
7   mention of death.' Then the Lord said: 'Michael, Commander-in-chief, go down to my friend Abraham, and whatever he should say to you, this do; and whatever he should eat you also eat with him.
8   And I shall send my holy spirit upon his son Isaac, and I shall thrust the mention of his death into Isaac's heart, so that he will see his father's death in a dream. Then Isaac will relate the vision, you will interpret it, and he himself will come to know his end.'

Michael enquires about how to comport himself during the meal, since incorporeal beings do not eat. God explains that a spirit will consume everything on the table (4:9–10). God continues:

4:11   'Only interpret well the things of the vision, so that Abraham will come to know the sickle of death and the unforeseen end of life, and so that he might make arrangements for the disposition of all his belongings; for I have blessed him more than "the grains of sand of the sea" and "as the stars in the sky".'

After the meal, Isaac has a dream which Michael interprets as predicting Abraham's death (5:1–7:9).

ABRAHAM'S CONTINUED RELUCTANCE

7:10 Abraham said to the Commander-in-chief: 'O most surprising wonder of wonders! And is it you, then, who are about to take
11 my soul from me?' The Commander-in-chief said to him: 'I am Michael, the Commander-in-chief who stands before God, and I was sent to you that I might announce to you the mention of death. And then I shall return to him just as we were commanded.'
12 And Abraham said: 'Now I do know that you are an angel of the Lord, and you were sent to take my soul. Nevertheless, I will not by any means follow you, but you do whatever he commands.'
8:1 When the Commander-in-chief heard this statement he immediately became invisible. And he went up into heaven and stood before God and told (him) everything which he saw at
2 Abraham's house. And the Commander-in-chief also said this to the Master: 'Your friend Abraham also said this: "I will not by any means follow you, but you do whatever he commands."
3 Almighty Master, what do your Glory and (your) immortal
4 Kingship command now?' God said to the Commander-in-chief
5 Michael: 'Go to my friend Abraham one more time and say this to him: "Thus says the Lord your God, who led you into the promised land, who blessed you more than 'the grains of sand of
6 the sea' and 'the stars in the sky', who opened the womb of the barren Sarah and graciously granted to you Isaac, the fruit of the
7 womb in old age. Truly I say to you that 'blessing I will bless you and multiplying I will multiply your seed', and I will give to you whatever you ask of me; for I am the Lord your God and besides
8 me there is no other. Tell me why you are resisting me and why there is grief in you? And why have you resisted my archangel

9 Michael? Do you not know that all those who (spring) from Adam and Eve die? And not one of the prophets escaped death, and not one of those who reign has been immortal. Not one of the fore-fathers has escaped the mystery of death. All have died, all have departed into Hades, all have been gathered by the sickle of Death.

10 But to you I did not send Death. I did not allow a fatal disease to befall you. I did not permit the sickle of Death to come upon you. I did not allow the nets of Hades to entwine you. I did not ever

11 want any evil to come upon you. But for (your) good comfort I sent my Commander-in-chief Michael to you, in order that you might come to know of your departure from the world and that you might make arrangements for the disposition of your house and everything that belongs to you, and so that you might bless Isaac your beloved son. And now know that I have done these

12 things not wanting to grieve you. And so why did you say to my Commander-in-chief: 'I will not by any means follow you'? Why did you say these things? Do you not know that if I give permission to Death, and he should come to you, then I should see whether you would come or not come?"'

8:6. *opened the womb*: cp. Gen. 18:11–14.

8:7. *blessing I will bless you*: the quotation is from Gen. 22:17. The Greek retains the Hebraism. The Hebrew idiom means 'I will surely bless'. *there is no other*: cp. Exod. 20:3; Deut. 4:35, 39; 5:7; 2En 36:1.

Michael carries out his commission, but Abraham is still recalcitrant. This time he asks 'to see all the inhabited world' before his death. Michael conveys the request to God, who agrees (9:1–8).

ABRAHAM'S TOUR OF THE INHABITED WORLD

10:1 And the archangel Michael went down and took Abraham on a chariot of cherubim and lifted him up into the air of heaven and led him onto the cloud, as well as sixty angels. And on the carriage

2 Abraham soared over the entire inhabited world. And Abraham beheld the world as it was that day: some were ploughing, others leading wagons; in one place they were pasturing (flocks), else-where abiding (with their flocks) in the fields, while dancing and

sporting and playing the zither; in another place they were
wrestling and pleading at law; elsewhere they were weeping, then
also bearing the dead to the tomb. And he also saw newlyweds
3 being escorted in procession. In a word, he saw everything which
4 was happening in the world, both good and evil.. Then continuing on, Abraham saw men bearing swords, who held in their
hands sharpened swords, and Abraham asked the Commander-in-
5 chief: 'Who are these?' And the Commander-in-chief said: 'These
are robbers, who want to commit murder and rob and burn and
6 destroy.' Abraham said: 'Lord, Lord, heed my voice and command
7 that wild beasts come out of the thicket and devour them.' And as
he was speaking wild beasts came out of the thicket and devoured
8 them. And he saw in another place a man with a woman, engaging
9 in sexual immorality with each other, and he said: 'Lord, Lord,
command that the earth open and swallow them up.' And
immediately the earth split in two and swallowed them up.
10 And he saw in another place men breaking into a house and
11 carrying off the possessions of others, and he said: 'Lord, Lord,
command that fire come down from heaven and consume them.'
And as he was speaking fire came down from heaven and con-
12 sumed them. And immediately a voice came down from heaven
to the Commander-in-chief, speaking thus: 'O Michael, Commander-in-chief, command the chariot to stop and turn Abraham
13 away, lest he should see the entire inhabited world. For if he were
to see all those who pass their lives in sin, he would destroy
everything that exists. For behold, Abraham has not sinned and
14 he has no mercy on sinners. But I made the world, and I do not
want to destroy any one of them; but I delay the death of the
15 sinner until he should convert and live. Now conduct Abraham
to the first gate of heaven, so that there he may see the judgements
and the recompenses and repent over the souls of the sinners
which he destroyed.'

10:2. *abiding*: cp. Luke 2:8. *wrestling*: for evidence that Jews in the
diaspora watched and perhaps participated in sports and theatre, see
Philo, Ebr 177.

THE PLACE OF JUDGEMENT

11:1 Michael turned the chariot and brought Abraham towards the
2   east, to the first gate of heaven. And Abraham saw two ways. The
    first way was 'narrow' and 'strait' and the other 'wide' and
3   'spacious'. (And he saw there two gates. One gate was wide),
    corresponding to the wide way, and one gate was narrow, corres-
4   ponding to the narrow way. And outside the two gates of that
    place they saw a man seated on a golden throne. And the ap-
5   pearance of that man was terrifying, like the Master's. And they
    saw many souls being driven by angels and being led through the
    wide gate, and they saw a few other souls and they were being
6   brought by angels through the narrow gate. And when the
    wondrous one who was seated on the throne of gold saw few
    entering through the narrow gate, but many entering through the
    wide gate, immediately that wondrous man tore the hair of his
    head and the beard of his cheeks, and he threw himself on the
7   ground from his throne crying and wailing. And when he saw
    many souls entering through the narrow gate, then he arose from
    the earth and sat on his throne, very cheerfully rejoicing and
8   exulting. Then Abraham asked the Commander-in-chief: 'My
    lord Commander-in-chief, who is this most wondrous man who is
    adorned in such glory, and sometimes he cries and wails while at
9   other times he rejoices and exults?' The incorporeal one said: 'This
    is the first-formed Adam who is in such glory, and he looks at the
10 world, since everyone has come from him. And when he sees
    many souls "entering through" the narrow gate, then he arises
    and sits on his throne rejoicing and exulting cheerfully, because
    this narrow gate is (the gate) of the righteous, "which leads to
    life", and those who enter through it come into paradise. And on
    account of this the first-formed Adam rejoices, since he sees the
11 souls being saved. And when he sees "many" souls "entering
    through" the wide gate, then he pulls the hair of his head and casts
    himself on the ground crying and wailing bitterly; for the wide
    gate is (the gate) of the sinners, "which leads to destruction" and

to eternal punishment. And on account of this the first-formed Adam falls from his throne, crying and wailing over the destruction of the sinners; for many are the ones who are destroyed, while few are the ones who are saved. For among seven thousand there is scarcely to be found one saved soul, righteous and undefiled.'

12:1 While he was yet saying these things to me, behold (there were) two angels, with fiery aspect and merciless intention and relentless look, and they drove myriads of souls, mercilessly beating them 2 with fiery lashes. And the angel seized one soul. And they drove 3 all the souls into the wide gate towards destruction. Then we too 4 followed the angels and we came inside that wide gate. And between the two gates there stood a terrifying throne with the 5 appearance of terrifying crystal, flashing like fire. And upon it sat 6 a wondrous man, bright as the sun, like unto a son of God. Before 7 him stood a table like crystal, all of gold and byssus. On the table lay a book whose thickness was six cubits, while its breadth was 8 ten cubits. On its right and on its left stood two angels holding 9 papyrus and ink and pen. In front of the table sat a light-bearing 10 angel, holding a balance in his hand. (On) (his) left there sat a fiery angel, altogether merciless and relentless, holding a trumpet in his hand, which contained within it an all-consuming fire (for) testing 11 the sinners. And the wondrous man who sat on the throne was the 12 one who judged and sentenced the souls. The two angels on the right and on the left recorded. The one on the right recorded 13 righteous deeds, while the one on the left (recorded) sins. And the one who was in front of the table, who was holding the balance, 14 weighed the souls. And the fiery angel, who held the fire, tested 15 the souls. And Abraham asked the Commander-in-chief Michael: 'What are these things which we see?' And the Commander-in-chief said: 'These things which you see, pious Abraham, are 16 judgement and recompense.' And behold, the angel who held the 17 soul in his hand brought it before the judge. And the judge told one of the angels who served him: 'Open for me this book and 18 find for me the sins of this soul.' And when he opened the book he

found its sins and righteous deeds to be equally balanced, and he
neither turned it over to the torturers nor (placed it among) those
who were being saved, but he set it in the middle.

13:1   And Abraham said: 'My lord Commander-in-chief, who is this
all-wondrous judge? And who are the angels who are recording?
And who is the sunlike angel who holds the balance? And who is
2   the fiery angel who holds the fire?' The Commander-in-chief
said: 'Do you see, all-pious Abraham, the frightful man who is
seated on the throne? This is the son of Adam, the first-formed,
3   who is called Abel, whom Cain the wicked killed. And he sits
here to judge the entire creation, examining both righteous and
sinners. For God said: "I do not judge you, but every man is
4   judged by man." On account of this he gave him judgement, to
judge the world until his great and glorious parousia. And then,
righteous Abraham, there will be perfect judgement and recom-
5   pense, eternal and unalterable, which no one can question. For
every person has sprung from the first-formed, and on account of
6   this they are first judged here by his son. And at the second
parousia they will be judged by the twelve tribes of Israel, both
7   every breath and every creature. And, thirdly, they shall be judged
by the Master God of all; and then thereafter the fulfilment of that
judgement will be near, and fearful will be the sentence and there
8   is none who can release. And thus the judgement and recompense
of the world is made through three tribunals. And therefore a
matter is not ultimately established by one or two witnesses, but
"every matter shall be established by three witnesses".

9   'The two angels, the one on the right and the one on the left,
these are those who record sins and righteous deeds. The one on
the right records righteous deeds, while the one on the left
10   (records) sins. And the sunlike angel, who holds the balance in his
hand, this is the archangel Dokiel, the righteous balance-bearer,
and he weighs the righteous deeds and the sins with the righteous-
11   ness of God. And the fiery and merciless angel, who holds the fire in
his hand, this is the archangel Puruel, who has authority over fire,
12   and he tests the work of men through fire. And if the fire burns

up the work of anyone, immediately the angel of judgement takes him and carries him away to the place of sinners, a most bitter

13 place of punishment. But "if the fire tests" "the work of anyone" and does not touch it, this person is justified and the angel of righteousness takes him and carries him up to be saved in the lot

14 of the righteous. And thus, most righteous Abraham, all things in all people are tested by fire and balance.'

The soul which was placed in the middle had good and bad deeds evenly balanced. Abraham and Michael join in intercessory prayer, and the soul is saved. Further, Abraham requests God to restore to life the sinners on whom he had called down death (14:1–13). God replies:

14:14 'Abraham, Abraham, I have heeded your voice and your supplication and I forgive you (your) sin; and those whom you think that I destroyed, I have called back, and I have led them into

15 life by my great goodness. For I did punish them in judgement for a time. But those whom I destroy while they are living on the earth, I do not requite in death.'

11:2. *two ways*: the theme of two ways is common in Jewish and Christian literature. The adjectives in inverted commas in 11:2, however, are the same as those in Matt. 7:13f, and here TAb is probably dependent on Matthew.

11:3. *And he saw there*: the text is corrupt. I follow James's reconstruction.

11:4. *they saw*: either the person or the number of the verb changes here. The greek *idon* could also be 'I saw'.

11:5. *many...few*: cp. Matt. 22:14; 4Ezra 7:48; 8:3.

11:9. *first-formed*: cp. Wisd. of Sol. 7:1; 10:1; ApMos, introduction (ed. Tischendorf, p. 1).

11:10–11. *entering through, which leads to*: the phrases in inverted commas are probably dependent on Matt. 7:13.

12:1. *to me*: here the change to the first person is clear.

12:7. *byssus*: fine linen.

12:12. *recorded*: on judgement by deeds recorded in a book or books, cp. 1En 81:1f; Sifre Deut. 307; Ab. 2:1; b.Ned. 22a; b.Roš ha-Šanah. 16b, 32b; 2En 52:15, and elsewhere.

12:13. *weighed the souls*: the theme of weighing *deeds* is much more common (see e.g. 1En 41:1; 4Ezra 3:34; 2En 52:15). The image of weighing *souls* is generally regarded as Egyptian. See Delcor, *Testament d'Abraham*, p. 67.

12:14. *tested the souls*: on testing by fire cp. Ps. 66:10–12; Zech. 13:9; Jer. 6:29; Wisd. of Sol. 3:6.

13:4. *parousia*: 'appearance'. The final judgement is often connected with Christ's parousia in Christian literature: 1 Thess. 4:15; 1 John 2:28. On God's parousia see Jas. 5:7; 2 Pet. 3:12. In Mal. 3:2 the judgement is related to God's coming, although the word parousia does not occur.

13:6. *the twelve tribes*: this incorporates and modifies the traditional motif of the judgement of Gentiles by Israel. See Dan. 7:22 LXX; Jub 32:19; IQpHab 5:4; and elsewhere. Cp. Matt. 19:28.

13:8. *every matter*: a quotation from Deut. 19:15.

13:10. *he weighs the righteous deeds*: here deeds are weighed, not souls (contrast 12:13).

13:13. *if the fire tests*: the wording is probably influenced by 1 Cor. 3:13.

14:15. *do not requite*: it is a standard Jewish view that those who are punished by premature death are not further punished. See E. P. Sanders, *Paul and Palestinian Judaism*, Philadelphia/London, 1977, pp. 168–74.

ABRAHAM'S RETURN AND EVENTUAL DEATH

Michael conducts Abraham back home, but he is still unwilling to die. Michael again has recourse to God (15:1–11):

15:12 'Lord Almighty, behold I have heeded your friend Abraham with regard to everything that he mentioned to you and I have fulfilled his request: I showed him your power and the entire earth under heaven as well as the sea; I showed him judgement and recompense by means of a cloud and chariots. And again he has
13 said, "I will not follow you."' And the Most High said to the angel: 'Does my friend Abraham say still again, "I will not follow
14 you?"' The archangel said: 'Lord Almighty, thus he speaks, and I refrain from touching him because from the beginning he has been your friend and he did everything which is pleasing before
15 you. And there is no man like unto him on earth, not even Job, the wondrous man. And for this reason I refrain from touching him. Command, then, Immortal King, what is to be done.'

16:1   Then the Most High said: 'Call Death here to me, who is
       called the (one of) abominable countenance and merciless look.'

Death is called for and sent to Abraham, being commissioned to bring
Abraham's soul to heaven, but by gentle means, since Abraham is God's
friend. After a long exchange about the horrible ways in which most
people meet death, during which Death reveals his ferocious appearance, Abraham asks him to resume the comely appearance in which
Death first met him. Abraham is still reluctant to accept his fate, and he
asks more questions about the various kinds of death (16:2–20:2).
Finally Death says:

20:3   'Now behold, I have told you everything that you have asked.
       Now I tell you, most righteous Abraham, set aside every wish
       and leave off questioning once and for all, and come, follow me as
4   the God and Judge of all commanded me.' Abraham said to
       Death: 'Leave me yet a little while, that I may rest on my couch,
5   for I feel very faint of heart. For from the time when I beheld you
       with my eyes, my strength has failed; all the limbs of my flesh
       seem to me to be like a lead weight, and my breath is very
       laboured. Depart for a little; for I said, I cannot bear to see your
6   form.' Isaac his son came and fell upon his breast weeping. Then
       also his wife Sarah came and embraced his feet wailing bitterly.
7   Also all his male and female servants came and encircled his couch
8   wailing greatly. And Abraham entered the depression of death. And
       Death said to Abraham: 'Come, kiss my right hand, and may
9   cheerfulness and life and strength come to you.' For Death
       deceived Abraham. And he kissed his hand and immediately his
10   soul cleaved to the hand of Death. And immediately Michael the
       archangel stood beside him with multitudes of angels, and they
       bore his precious soul in their hands in divinely woven linen.
11   And they tended the body of the righteous Abraham with divine
       ointments and perfumes until the third day after his death. And
       they buried him in the Promised Land at the oak of Mamre,
12   while the angels escorted his precious soul and ascended into
       heaven singing the Thrice-Holy hymn to God, the Master of all,
       and they set it (down) for the worship of the God and Father.

13 And after great praise in song and glorification had been offered to
the Lord, and when Abraham had worshipped, the undefiled voice

14 of the God and Father came speaking thus: 'Take, then, my friend
Abraham into paradise, where there are the tents of my righteous
ones and (where) the mansions of my holy ones, Isaac and Jacob,
are in his bosom, where there is no toil, no grief, no moaning, but

15 peace and exultation and endless life.' (Let us too, my beloved
brothers, imitate the hospitality of the patriarch Abraham and let
us attain to his virtuous behaviour, so that we may be worthy of
eternal life, glorifying the Father and the Son and the Holy
Spirit: to whom be the glory and the power forever. Amen.)

20:10. *they bore his...soul*: cp. TJob 47:11; 52:2, 5; ApMos 33:2.

20:11. *they buried him*: the soul is taken and the body buried:
TJob 52:10f; ApMos 32–42, and elsewhere.

20:12. *Thrice-Holy*: cp. Isa. 6:3.

20:14. *in his bosom*: illogically the patriarchs are considered to be
already in heaven.

20:15. A Christian exhortation and doxology. Although the work
was preserved by Christian scribes, there are few Christian elements.
Besides the conclusion, see also 11:2, 10f, and 13:13 above.

The Testaments of the Twelve Patriarchs
HARM W. HOLLANDER

Structure and genre

The *Testaments of the Twelve Patriarchs* (T12P), a pseudepigraphon originally written in Greek, consists of twelve parts or 'testaments'. Each Testament contains the last words of one of the twelve sons of Jacob addressed to his sons (and other relatives) at the end of his life. It has a stereotyped structure. The 'farewell speech' which forms the bulk of a Testament is always preceded by an introductory passage indicating that what is to follow is the Patriarch's farewell discourse and giving some details about the circumstances under which the speech was delivered. All Testaments end with a small passage giving some information about the Patriarch's death and burial. The framework and above all the stereotyped introductory and concluding passages have been grafted upon Old Testament examples, particularly upon Gen. 49 (Jacob's 'farewell speech' to his sons).

The 'farewell speech' itself usually consists of three parts. First, the Patriarch tells his sons about his life in the past and describes his own moral behaviour (the biographical part). Above all, his former relation towards Joseph forms a constituent element in the description of his ethical attitude in the past. Some of the Patriarchs, like Simeon, Dan and Gad, plead guilty and point to their sins, which consist of vices like hatred, jealousy, envy, anger and lying. Zebulun, however, stresses his goodness to Joseph. The biographical part serves as a kind of introduction to the second part, the parenetic (that is, hortatory) section. Now the patriarch turns to his sons to exhort them not to fall into the same sins or, if he has been a virtuous man, to exhort them to imitate him. This part usually contains all kinds of details about particular virtues or vices. This section runs into the third part of the speech, where the Patriarch foretells what will happen to his sons in the future and usually adds some words about the future salvation of the people of Israel (and the Gentiles), which will be brought about by God 'at the end of times' (the passage dealing with the future or the eschatological part). For a fine example of this tripartite structure, see TIss (translated and commented on below).

71

The T12P do not provide the only examples of 'farewell discourses'. There are plenty of examples in the Old Testament, in other Jewish writings as well as in the New Testament, e.g. Gen. 49; Deut. 33; Josh. 23; I Kings 2:1–10; John 13–17; Acts 20:17–38 (and in early Christian literature). Nevertheless, the 'farewell discourse' as a *genre* with its particular features is a rather late literary product. It was a favourite genre in the intertestamental period and one of the first examples is found in the book of Tobit (chapters 4 and 14). In all instances of 'last words' – 'testament' may be a misleading term, since 'farewell discourses' are not juridical at all and can quite easily do without the actual term *diathēkē*, 'testament' – the emphasis lies undeniably upon the parenesis. The T12P are no exception to the rule. At his death-bed the Patriarch makes a final and dramatic call on his sons who are standing around his bed, to be obedient to God and to do his commandments. Besides he seems to be inspired in those moments just before his death and has acquired knowledge of future events.

Joseph as an ideal of virtue

One of the basic elements of the pareneses of the T12P is the exemplary role of Joseph. He is a good example for his sons in his own farewell speech, and he is introduced as an illuminating example in some of the other Testaments. Above all he is a representative of the author's ideal of man. For the author, a 'good man' is somebody who loves God and his neighbour. Love to God is put into practice by keeping God's – obviously moral – commandments. Love to one's neighbour requires a noble social behaviour. It implies above all mercy and compassion, forgiveness, sympathy, sexual purity, steadfastness and endurance, and it is characterized by 'singleness' or 'simplicity', that means by absolute integrity. TBenj, the twelfth and last Testament, contains some kind of résumé summing up in one continuous discourse all the scattered statements concerning the author's ethical ideal of man (see TBenj 4–6 translated and commented on below).

Traditions and sources

In the parenetic sections of the Testaments the author clearly shows his great dependence on the Old Testament, or rather on the Septuagint. In particular the Psalms and Jewish wisdom literature (above all Proverbs, Job, Ecclesiastes, and the book of Jesus Sirach) have influenced the author deeply. On the other hand, the hellenistic background is obvious, far more than in the wisdom books found in the Septuagint. The parenesis of the T12P cannot be considered as typical Jewish or typical Christian. Moreover, Christianity adopted (nearly) all the standard topics of Jewish parenesis.

Certainly, the author made use of all kinds of oral and written sources. It is even possible that he belonged to a school or circle of wisdom where biblical passages and every kind of source and tradition were discussed. If this is considered a likely explanation for the composition of the parenetic sections, it seems certain for the biographical and eschatological passages. For here we have at our disposal some (old and fragmentary) manuscripts found partly in the Cairo Genizah, partly at Qumran and partly elsewhere, showing that the author of the T12P was acquainted with stories and traditions very similar to those found in these documents. This is particularly obvious from the biographical sections in the T12P where the author gives much more information about the Patriarchs' lives than can be drawn from Genesis alone.

As for the eschatological sections, the situation seems to be more complex. There is not only a great variety in the sections in the T12P that deal with the future, but Jewish and Christian elements seem to be mixed up here. Nevertheless, two or three regularly recurring 'patterns' can be distinguished. First, there are the so-called 'Sin–Exile–Return' passages, giving a description of Israel's future sins, their punishment by God (exile) and finally God's compassion and Israel's return to the promised land. These passages obviously have their background in the 'deuteronomistic kerygma'. Secondly, there are 'Levi–Judah' passages, where the Patriarch exhorts his sons to honour Levi and Judah, since the priesthood has been given to Levi and the kingship to Judah, and Israel's salvation will spring from these two tribes. Connected with the latter motif, some passages are found dealing with the future Messiah (and the future resurrection), and here the Christian elements are most numerous and prominent, such as when the Patriarchs refer to the coming of Jesus Christ who will save Israel together with the Gentiles. For an example, see TJud 24 translated and commented on below.

Jewish or Christian?

This brings us to the rather difficult question of whether the T12P are originally Jewish (with some Christian additions or interpolations) or Christian. In spite of the many ingenious attempts to argue for different stages of redaction or extensive interpolations in an originally Jewish document, it seems wiser to regard the text as a literary product and as a coherent unity. That means, to regard the text either as a Christian composition in which a number of Jewish sources and traditions have been incorporated, or as a Jewish document which was thoroughly christianized so that it has become impossible to remove 'Christian' elements without affecting the whole of the T12P. In any case, the text of the T12P as it lies before us now seems to be an attempt of a Christian in the second century to show Jews and Christians that the Jews were wrong in having rejected Jesus Christ as God's Messiah and that their own famous forefathers had foretold their disobedience and had warned them, when they gave their final exhortations to their sons and instructed them to pass their teachings on to their children (and so on). Nevertheless, the Christian author (or redactor) of the T12P also points to the future salvation, not only of the (righteous) Gentiles (the Christians), but also of the people of Israel, as foretold by the Patriarchs.

Witnesses to the text

Remarkably, there are only a few clear references to the T12P in early Christian literature (in Origen and Jerome), which implies that the role of the T12P within the early Church was not very important. The 'history' of the T12P until the ninth or tenth century remains rather obscure. At least from that time onwards the T12P was a popular writing as is attested by the fifteen manuscripts, some of them containing a continuous Greek text and others only excerpts, dating from the tenth to the eighteenth century, and by the many versions (Armenian, Slavonic, Serbian, Latin and New Greek) all made from the Greek text. (For details see the Leiden edition of 1978.)

Bibliography

GREEK TEXT:

The Testaments of the Twelve Patriarchs. A Critical Edition of the Greek Text, ed. M. de Jonge, in co-operation with H. W. Hollander, H. J. de Jonge, Th. Korteweg (PsVTGr 1 2), Leiden, 1978.

MODERN TRANSLATIONS:

J. Becker, 'Die Testamente den zwölf Patriarchen' (JSHRZ III/1), pp. 15–163.
R. H. Charles, *The Testaments of the Twelve Patriarchs, Translated from the Editor's Greek Text and Edited, with Introduction, Notes, and Indices*, London, 1908.

SECONDARY LITERATURE:

J. Becker, *Untersuchungen zur Entstehungsgeschichte der Testamente der zwölf Patriarchen* (AGJU 8), Leiden, 1970.

R. Eppel, *Le Piétisme juif dans les Testaments des Douze Patriarches*, Paris, 1930.

H. W. Hollander, *Joseph as an Ethical Model in the Testaments of the Twelve Patriarchs* (StVTPs 6), Leiden, 1981.

H. W. Hollander, M. de Jonge, *The Testaments of the Twelve Patriarchs. A Commentary* (St VTPs 8), Leiden, 1985.

M. de Jonge, *The Testaments of the Twelve Patriarchs. A Study of their Text, Composition and Origin*, 2nd edn., Assen, 1975.

M. de Jonge, ed., *Studies on the Testaments of the Twelve Patriarchs. Text and Interpretation*, Leiden, 1975.

THE TESTAMENT OF ISSACHAR ON SIMPLICITY

Each Testament centres round a particular theme, usually a virtue or a vice that has played some part in the Patriarch's own life. If possible, it is linked up with some data about the Patriarch found in the Genesis stories or in Jewish tradition. In the case of Issachar the author of the T12P deals with the Patriarch's life and work as a farmer, a theme suggested by the Greek translation of Gen. 49:14–15: '...having seen the resting-place that it was good, and the land that it was fertile, he subjected his shoulders to labour and became a farmer'. Next, being aware of the positive appreciation of the farmer's life and virtues in Greek and hellenistic thought, he introduces the virtue of 'simplicity' as characteristic of Issachar, since agriculture, hard work and 'simplicity' in food, clothing, dwelling and other aspects of life, were considered as belonging together. In T12P 'simplicity' or 'singleness' means the integrity of the pious man who has chosen God wholeheartedly and who is obedient to him alone, which includes the fulfilment of the two great commandments and fidelity to the law. For the virtue of 'simplicity' elsewhere, cp., e.g., 1 Macc. 2:37, 60; Job 1:1 (LXX, variant); 1:8 (LXX, variant); Matt. 6:22; Luke, 11:34; Col. 3:22; Eph. 6:5.

Issachar's birth and namegiving: TIss 1–2

This section retells (and changes) the story of the mandrakes, the apples that bring fertility, found in Gen. 30:14–18 LXX (see also 30:19–24).

1:1 A Copy of the words of Issachar.
After having called his sons he said to them:
Listen, children, to Issachar your father,
give ear to (his) words, you beloved of the Lord.

2 I was born as the fifth son to Jacob, in exchange for the mandrakes.
3 For Reuben brought the mandrakes from the field, and Rachel,
4 meeting him before, took them. But Reuben wept and at his
5 voice my mother Leah came out. – Now these (mandrakes) were
sweet-smelling apples which the land of Aram produced on a high
6 place below a ravine of water. – Rachel said: 'I shall not give them
to you, for they will be to me instead of children.'

7 – Now there were two apples. – And Leah said: 'Let it suffice you
that you have taken the husband of my virginity; would you take
8 these also?' But she said: 'Behold, Jacob shall be yours this night
9 for the mandrakes of your son.' But Leah said to her: 'Do not
boast or vaunt yourself; for Jacob is mine and I am the wife of his
10 youth.' But Rachel said: 'How so? For he was betrothed to me
11 first and for my sake he served our father for fourteen years. What
can I do for you? For the craft and the cunning of men have
12 multiplied and craft prospers on earth. If not, you would not be
seeing the face of Jacob; for you are not his wife, but by craft you
13 were led in in my place. And my father deceived me, and
removing me that night, he did not let me see it (or: him); for if
14 I had been there this had not happened.' And Rachel said: 'Take
one mandrake, and for this one I shall hire him to you for one
15 night.' And Jacob knew Leah, and she conceived and bore me;
and on account of the hire I was called Issachar.

2:1 Then an angel of the Lord appeared to Jacob, saying: 'Two
children will Rachel bear, because she has despised intercourse with
2 a man and has chosen continency.' And if my mother Leah had
not paid the two apples for the sake of intercourse, she would have
borne eight sons. Therefore she bore six, and Rachel bore the two,
3 because on account of the mandrakes the Lord visited her. For he
saw that for the sake of children she wished to have intercourse
4 with Jacob and not for lust of pleasure. For on the next day she

gave Jacob up again, in order that she might receive also the other mandrake. Therefore, on account of the mandrakes, the Lord
5 listened to Rachel. For though she desired them she did not eat them, but she dedicated them in the house of the Lord, offering them to the priest of the Most High who was there at that time.

1:1. Usual superscription and introduction.

1:2. Theme of chapter 1.

1:3–4. Explanatory story, cp. Gen. 30:14. Rachel intervenes and takes the mandrakes (cp. verses 7, 14; and 2:4).

1:5. Note about the mandrakes. *the land of Aram*: the Hebrew Bible speaks of Paddan-Aram and Laban the Aramean, the Septuagint of Mesopotamia and Laban the Syrian. In the T12P, see TJud 10:1, 'Tamar...from Mesopotamia, daughter of Aram'.

1:6. Extra, compared to Gen. 30:14–18.

1:7a. Mention of two mandrakes necessary as introduction to 2:4; cp. 1:14; 2:2.

1:7b–14. This passage gives an extended version of Gen. 30:15, with details taken from Gen. 29:15–30.

1:7. *the husband of my virginity*: cp. Joel 1:8 LXX; Ecclus. 15:2.

1:9. *wife of his youth*: cp. Prov. 5:18; Mal. 2:14f (and Ecclus. 15:2).

1:10. *How so?* introduces an objection. *he served our father*: cp. Gen. 29:15, 18, 20, 25, 30, etc. The *fourteen years* are mentioned in Gen. 31:41; there they are connected with two daughters, but the view that Jacob served this period for Rachel is in tune with the story in Genesis.

1:11. *For the craft and the cunning of men have multiplied*: cp. verses 12f; see Gen. 6:5. *seeing the face of Jacob*: 'to see the face of' is a standard expression in the Old Testament, see Gen. 32:21(20); 33:10; 43:3, 5, etc., and cp. also Acts 20:25, 38, etc.

1:14. *one mandrake*: see on verse 7a. *hire him*: cp. Gen. 30:16.

1:15. Cp. Gen. 30:17. For 'to know' in this sense, see Gen. 4:1, 17, 25, etc. For verse 15b, cp. Gen. 30:18.

Chapter 2 continues the story of chapter 1; it refers freely to the events mentioned in Gen. 30:19–24 and emphasizes Rachel's continency and piety.

2:1. *an angel of the Lord appeared to*: cp. Exod. 3:2; Judg. 6:12; 13:3; Tobit 12:22; Luke 1:11; Acts 7:30.

2:2. Leah sells two apples for two nights with Jacob and 'loses' two children. Instead of eight sons for Leah and none for Rachel, the division will now be six for Leah and two for Rachel. *visited her*: the

same expression is used in Gen. 21:1 in the case of Sarah and in
1 Sam. 2:21 in the case of Hannah.

2:3. The idea that the only purpose of marriage is the procreation
of children is often found in hellenistic, Jewish hellenistic and early
Christian literature.

2:4. This verse explains verses 1 and 3. *listened to*: cp. Gen. 30:22.

2:5. Because of extreme piety Rachel dedicated the mandrakes in a
temple, offering them to the priest. Wishing to emphasize the unbroken
continuity in the succession of priests, the author introduces 'the priest
of the Most High', adapting the terminology from Gen. 14:18
(Melchizedek, 'the priest of God, the Most High').

Issachar's life and work as a farmer and his 'simplicity': TIss 3

3:1 When, therefore, I grew up, my children,
     I walked in uprightness of heart,
     and I became a farmer for my fathers and my brothers,
     and I brought in fruits from the fields according to their season.

2   And my father blessed me, seeing that I walk in simplicity.

3   And I was not a busy-body in my affairs,
     nor wicked and malicious against my neighbour;

4   I did not slander anyone
     nor did I censure the life of a man
        walking (as I did) in singleness of eyes.

5   Therefore, at the age of thirty I took myself a wife,
     for my labour wore away my strength,
     and I did not think of pleasure with a woman,
     but because of my toil sleep overcame me.

6   And always my father rejoiced in my simplicity;
     for if I laboured on anything,
     I offered all the choice fruit and all the first fruit,
     first through the priest to the Lord,
     then to my father, and then I myself (took from it).

7   And the Lord doubled the goods in my hands.
     And also Jacob knew that God aided my simplicity.

8   For upon everyone who was poor and everyone who was
           oppressed
        I bestowed the good things of the earth in singleness of heart.

3:1-2. *General picture.* Issachar who works as a farmer also for his family, is blessed by his father because of his virtuous life. *uprightness*: this term finds its origin in the Old Testament; it simplies true service of God by keeping his commandments, and like 'simplicity' it denotes integrity and complete obedience. *and I became a farmer*: Gen. 49:14-15 LXX, 'Issachar...became a farmer'.

3:3-4. These verses describe the faults which man should avoid. *not a busy-body*: simplicity excludes meddlesome curiosity.

3:5. Issachar's attitude towards women, introduced by the clause 'in singleness of eyes' (verse 4); cp. 7:2; and TBenj 6:2-3. 'Singleness of eyes' leads to chastity.

3:6-8. The hard-working farmer offers to God and helps his father and the needy. Cp. Ecclus. 7:27-36.

3:7. *And the Lord doubled*: this theme is particularly found in traditions concerning Job; cp. Job 42:10 LXX; TJob 4:7; 44:5; 53:8. Job was rewarded because he was steadfast in his troubles and did not give up his trust in God, but also his generosity towards the poor is mentioned.

3:8. *poor...oppressed*: helping the poor is a well-known theme in the Old Testament, Jewish and Christian literature; this help is often carried out in the provision of food; see TJos 3:5; TJob 10:6; 12:1; 13:4; Philo, Spec Leg II.105; Virt 90; 97. *the good things of the earth*: cp. Ezra 9:12; Isa. 1:19; 1 Esdras 8:82; TJob 17:3; Philo, Det Pot Ins 156.

The parenetic section of the Testament: TIss 4:1-5:3

4:1   And now, listen to me, children,
            and walk in singleness of heart,
                for I have seen (that) all the pleasure of the Lord (rests) upon it.

2   The single(-minded) man does not covet gold,
            he does not overreach his neighbour,
            he does not desire a variety of food,
            he does not want varied apparel,

3   he does not plan to live a long time,
        but he only waits for the will of God,

4   and the spirits of deceit have no power against him.
            For he does not look to welcome the beauty of a woman,
            lest he would pollute his mind with perversion;

5   no envy will invade his thoughts,

no malice will make his soul pine away
nor does he think of money-getting with insatiable desire.

6   For he walks in uprightness of life
and looks at all things in simplicity,
not welcoming with the eyes bad things that come from the
deceit of the world,
lest he would see anything in the commandments of the
Lord in a perverted way.

5:1 Keep, therefore, the law of God, my children,
and acquire simplicity,
and walk in guilelessness,
not meddling with the commandments of the Lord and
the affairs of your neighbour.

2   But love the Lord and your neighbour,
show mercy to the poor and the weak.

3   Bow down your back to farming,
and be at work in the works of the earth in all sorts of farm work,
offering gifts to the Lord with thanksgiving.

4:1. Direct parenesis; central theme: 'singleness' (of heart); cp. 3:8; 5:1.

4:2–6. Description of the 'single-minded' man.

4:2. The combination of ideas expressed in the four negative phrases constitutes a hellenistic *topos*. 'Simple' life advocates simple food, plain clothing, modest houses and the absence of greediness.

4:3. *he does not plan to live a long time*: the motif that the righteous man should not ask God for a long life is derived from the story of Solomon who asked for wisdom instead of wealth or a long life or the lives of his enemies (1 Kings 3: 10f; 2 Chron. 1:11). *he only waits for the will of God*: cp. TGAD 7:1ff; Jas. 4:15. Man cannot take his future in his own hands.

4:4–5. Waiting only for the will of God means that 'the spirits of deceit' will have no hold on a person. Consequently, vices connected with these spirits are foreign to the 'single-minded' man's nature. *he does not look to welcome the beauty of a woman*: warnings against 'the beauty of women' are often found in the T12P. *make his soul pine away*: cp. Ecclus. 18:18; 31:1; Plutarch, *De sera numinis vindicta* 27 (Mor. 566 A), '...that the intelligent part of the soul is dissolved away...by pleasure'.

4:6. *in uprightness of life...in simplicity*: cp. 3:1. The expression *the deceit of the world* (cp. Justin, *Dialogue* 113:6) characterizes the real nature of all the evils mentioned in this chapter.

5:1-3. Direct parenesis.

5:1. *walk in guilelessness*: cp. Ps. 26:1, 11; 84:11; and Hermas, *Visio* 2, 3, 2.

5:2. *love the Lord and your neighbour*: sums up the essential in keeping the law of God (cp. verse 1a). The love for one's neighbour is specified as: *show mercy to the poor and the weak*; with this phrase the author returns to 3:8.

5:3. Likewise, in this verse, the author takes up themes of chapter 3. *Bow down your back to farming*: cp. Gen. 49:15 LXX. *offering gifts to the Lord*: cp. 3:6.

The blessings bestowed on Issachar and his tribe, on Levi and Judah (a 'Levi-Judah' passage), and on Gad: TIss 5:4-8

5:4   Because with the first fruits of the earth the Lord blessed you
        even as he blessed all the saints from Abel until now.

5   For no other portion is given to you than that of the fatness of the
        earth whose fruits are raised by toil.

6   Because our father Jacob blessed me with blessings of the earth
        and first fruits.

7   And Levi and Judah were glorified among the sons of Jacob,
        for (to them) the Lord gave an inheritance among them,
            and to the one he gave the priesthood
            and to the other the kingdom.

8   Do you, therefore, obey them
            and walk in the simplicity of your father.
        For also to Gad it has been given to destroy the bands
            that come against Israel.

5:4-6. The tribe of Issachar has been charged by God with agriculture. This is motivated by a reference to Jacob's blessing of Issachar (cp. 3:2) found in Gen. 49:15 LXX.

5:7-8. Now the Patriarch emphasizes the particular privileges and tasks allotted to Levi and Judah and asks his sons to obey them. *priesthood...kingdom*: see TJud 21:2; 17:3; TLevi 5:2; 8:2; see also Ecclus. 45:6-7 and 45:23-6.

5:8c. A clear reference to Gen. 49:19 LXX. Why Gad's task is mentioned here is not quite clear.

The part of the Testament dealing with the future (introduced by the 'Levi–Judah' passage in 5:7–8), giving a 'Sin–Exile–Return' passage: TIss 6:1–4

6:1   I know, my children, that in the last times

your sons will forsake simplicity and will cleave to insatiable desire,
and leaving guilelessness they will draw near to wickedness,
and forsaking the commandments of the Lord
                                they will cleave to Beliar,

2   and leaving (their) farm work
                                they will follow after their wicked
            thoughts
        and they will be dispersed among the nations and will serve their
            enemies.

3   And do you, therefore, say this to your children
        in order that, if they sin, they may quickly return to the Lord.

4   For he is merciful and will deliver them, to bring them back into
            their land.

6:1–2a. Description of the future sins of Issachar's children. They will give up their farm work, and consequently, simplicity, guilelessness, in short, the law of God. *in the last times*: in the future, cp. Gen. 49:1. *Beliar*: the prince of the spirits of deceit, God's adversary who will be destroyed by Jesus at the end of times. Beliar, or Belial, is also found elsewhere as the name of the devil: see, e.g., 1QS 1.18, 24; II.5; CD IV.13, 15; V.18; Jub 15:33; AscenIs 4:2; 2 Cor. 6:15.

6:2b. Exile; cp. TJud 23:3; TNaph 4:2; and also Deut. 28:48; Jer. 15:14.

6:3. Repentance (cp. TJud 23:5; TZeb 9:7; TDan 5:6; TNaph 4:3; and also 1 Sam. 7:3; Isa. 31:5f, etc.). *do you...say this to your children*: this is one of the sentences in which the purpose of the Testaments is explicitly mentioned; future generations are warned.

6:4. Return.

The concluding section of the Testament: TIss 7:7–9

After some other verses about the Patriarch's exemplary life ending with a reference to the two great commandments practised by Issachar (TIss 7:1–6), we read finally:

7:7   Do you also these things, my children,
and every spirit of Beliar will flee from you
and no deed of wicked men will rule over you
and every wild beast you will subdue,
having with you the God of heaven,
walking together with men in singleness of heart.

8   And he commanded them that they should carry him up to
Hebron, and bury him there in the cave with his fathers. And

9   he stretched out his feet and died, the fifth (son of Jacob), at a
good old age, (still) having every limb sound; and being strong
he slept the eternal sleep.

7:7. General exhortation. *every spirit of Beliar . . . you will subdue*: on
the virtuous man the spirits of evil, wicked men and wild beasts have
no hold (cp. TDan 5:1; TNaph 8:4; TBenj 3:3-5; 5:1-2). *having
with you the God of heaven*: cp. TDan 5:2. God's presence in the life
of the good man is expressed in various ways in TBenj 6:1, 3, 4.
Now, this idea takes an eschatological turn: *walking together with men
in singleness of heart*, referring to the coming of God in Jesus Christ.
This phrase, and thereby the whole verse, is, therefore, most probably
understood as referring to the eschatological future realized in Jesus
Christ. Cp. TJud 24:1 where a similar phrase occurs in connection
with the coming of Christ on earth (translated and commented on
below).
7:8-9. Usual concluding passage. *that they should carry him up to
Hebron, and bury him there with his fathers*: cp. Gen. 23:19; 25:9f;
35:27ff; 49:29ff; 50:13. *and he stretched out his feet*: cp. TLevi 19:4;
TGad 8:4; TJos 20:4; and Gen. 49:33; Jub 23:1. *at a good old age*:
cp. TBenj 12:2; and Gen. 15:15; 25:8; 1 Chron. 29:28. *(still) having
every limb sound; and being strong*: cp. Deut. 34:7.

THE ETHICS OF THE T12P

A fine example of the ethics of the T12P is found in the Testament of
Benjamin, particularly in TBenj 3-6. In this Testament the author
gives one continuous discourse concerning his ethical ideal of man.
This résumé centres round the 'good man' (the man with a 'good
mind'), the personification of this ideal. And since Joseph corresponds
to this ethical ideal, it is he who is introduced as an illuminating

example, whereas the role of Benjamin himself is restricted to a minimum.

First we find exhortations to fear and love God, to keep his commandments and to love one's neighbour, together with an explanation of the beneficial effects of such an attitude and a clear reference to the career of Joseph (TBenj 3). Then Benjamin gives a first description of the ideal of the 'good man' in chapter 4:

4:1 See, children, the end of the good man.
Be followers, therefore, of his compassion with a good mind,
   that you also may wear crowns of glory.

2 The good man has not a dark eye.
For he shows mercy to all men,
   even though they are sinners;

3   even though they devise with to do him harm,
by doing good he overcomes the evil,
   because he is shielded by the good.
But he loves the righteous as his own soul.

4 If anyone is glorified, he is not envious;
if anyone is rich, he is not jealous;
if anyone is valiant, he eulogizes him;
the virtuous man he trusts and praises;
on the poor man he has mercy;
with the weak man he feels sympathy;
unto God he sings praises.

5 As for him who has the fear of God, he protects him as with a shield;
him who loves God he helps;
him who rejects the Most High he admonishes and turns back;
and him who has the grace of a good spirit he loves as his own soul.

4:1. Direct parenesis. *the end of the good man*: the 'exaltation' of Joseph, his kingship given by God as a reward for his pious attitude during the time of his distress and humiliation as a slave and as a prisoner. Benjamin's sons are exhorted to be Joseph's imitators. *compassion*: one of Joseph's main virtues in the T12P.

4:2-5. Description of the good man's attitude towards others.

4:2a. *has not a dark eye*: the good man's mind is not 'blinded' or 'darkened' by evil spirits or vices; cp. 3:2; TDan 2:4; TGad 5:7; TJud 13:6; 14:1.

4:2b-3. *he shows mercy to all men . . . he loves the righteous as his own soul*: this twofold attitude of the good man shows qualities that belong to God, for traditionally it is God who 'has mercy on all men' (cp. Wisd. 11:23; and also 15:1; Ecclus. 18:13; Rom. 11:32) and who 'loves the righteous' (cp. Ps. 146:8; and also Prov. 15:9). *by doing good he overcomes the evil*: cp. 5:2, 4f; TJos 18:2; and esp. Rom. 12:21, 'but use good to defeat evil'.

4:4. In this verse, the good man's attitude towards some specific groups of people (and towards God) is mentioned by way of a climax: towards honourable and rich men, towards virtuous men, towards the poor and weak, and finally towards God. *if anyone is glorified, he is not envious; if anyone is rich, he is not jealous*: cp. TGad 7:1ff. The background of the motif of envy and jealousy because of another's wealth and glory is to be found in Greek and Jewish Hellenism (see, e.g., Plutarch, *De recta ratione audiendi* 5 (Mor. 39 E), 'Now the man who is stung by the wealth, or repute, or beauty possessed by another, is merely envious; for he is depressed by the good fortune of others'; Philo, Praem Poen 168; Vit Mos I.246f). *valiant . . . virtuous*: these terms express two of the four main virtues in Greek philosophy, and form a well-known combination in hellenistic and Jewish hellenistic literature. *the poor man . . . the weak man*: cp. TIss 5:2; and also Prov. 22:22; 31:9; Polycarp, *Philippians* 6:1. The attitude of mercy towards the poor is a traditional topic in wisdom literature and Jewish hellenistic writings. *he feels sympathy*: cp. TZeb 6:5; 7:3f.

4:5. Like verses 2-3, this verse deals with the good man's attitude towards sinners on the one hand and righteous men on the other. *he protects him as with a shield . . . he helps*: once more, just as in verses 2-3, the good man is characterized by qualities that belong to God: 'protecting (as with a shield)' and 'helping' the righteous ones are usually actions of God (cp. Deut. 33:29; Ps. 20:1; Prov. 30:5; Isa. 31:5; Rom. 8:28). *he loves as his own soul*: cp. verse 3.

The wholesome effects of such behaviour upon others, in particular
upon wicked men: TBenj 5

5:1　If you have a good mind, children,
　　　　both wicked men will be at peace with you
　　　　and the profligate will reverence you and turn unto good
　　　　and the covetous will not only cease from their passion,
　　　　　　but even give the objects of their covetousness to those
　　　　　　who are afflicted.

2　　If you do well,
　　　　both the unclean spirits will flee from you
　　　　and even the beasts will fear you.

3　　For where there is light of good works in the mind,
　　　　darkness flees away from him.

4　　For if anyone does violence to a holy man, he repents;
　　　　for the holy man is merciful to his reviler and holds his
　　　　peace.

5　　And if anyone betrays a righteous soul, and the righteous man is
　　　　humbled for a little – praying (all the time) –,
　　　　not long after he appears more glorious,
　　　　　　even as was Joseph my brother.

5:1–2. Wicked men will change for the better, and behave more positively when meeting a good man. Likewise, the 'unclean spirits' and wild beasts will flee away and dread him; see TBenj 3:3–5. *will be at peace with you*: cp. Ecclus. 6:5f; Prov. 15:28a LXX.

5:3. The 'change of behaviour' mentioned in verses 1–2 is formulated in more general terms in this verse. *darkness*, as represented by wicked men, unclean spirits, wild beasts, etc. together with all their dreadful activities cannot rule over the good man; cp. Philo, Som I.117.

5:4–5. The good man's attitude towards sinners and wicked men is described in another two conditional sentences. This time his attitude towards those who do wrong *to him* is dealt with. *praying*: for salvation from his troubles or for the one who has betrayed him. *more glorious, even as was Joseph*: a reference to Joseph's kingship in Egypt.

Another description of the good man's behaviour: TBenj 6

6:1   The disposition of the good man is not in the power of the deceit
      of the spirit of Beliar;
         for the angel of peace guides his soul.

2   He does not gaze passionately upon corruptible things,
      nor does he gather together riches for desire of pleasure;

3   he does not delight in pleasure,
      he does not grieve his neighbour,
      he does not sate himself with luxuries,
      he does not err in the uplifting of the eyes;
         for the Lord is his portion.

4   The good disposition does not admit of glory or dishonour from
      men,
      and it does not know any guile or lie, fighting or reviling;
         for the Lord dwells in him and lights up his soul.
      And he rejoices towards all men always.

5   The good mind has not two tongues,
         of blessing and of cursing, of contumely and of honour,
         of sorrow and of joy, of quietness and of confusion,
         of hypocrisy and of truth, of poverty and of wealth;
         but it has one disposition, uncorrupt and pure, concerning
         all men.

6   It has no double sight, nor double hearing;
         for in everything which he does, or speaks, or sees,
            he knows that the Lord looks on his soul.

7   And he cleanses his mind
         that it is not condemned by God and men.
      And every work of Beliar also is twofold and has no singleness.

    6:1. Introduction to the whole chapter. The good man's disposition
is not in the power of Beliar, the prince of the evil spirits; the last verse
refers to the twofold works of Beliar, so making explicit what it means
to be in his power. The good man, however, is guided by the angel of
peace. And what that means, is explained in verses 2–7. *the angel of
peace*: this angel performs many functions in the T12P: he guides the

soul of the righteous man, he welcomes him at his death and comforts him with eternal life (TAsh 6:6), and he strengthens the people of Israel that it may not fall into wickedness (TDan 6:5).

6:2–4. In these verses, some of the actions or rather abstinences of the good man are mentioned.

6:2. The good man's attitude towards wealth. *corruptible things*: this term is traditionally applied above all to riches, gold and silver; see, e.g., Philo, Cher 48; Congr 112; 1 Pet. 1:18.

6:3. Other abstinences of the good man, which belong rather to the social sphere. *he does not delight in pleasure…he does not err in the up-lifting of the eyes*: these phrases belong together, both giving a picture of the good man's attitude in sexual affairs; cp. TJud 13:6; 14:2; TIss 3:4f; 7:2ff; and Ecclus. 23:4; 26:9. The eyes above all are connected with the desire of impurity, cp. PssSol 4:4f; Matt. 5:28, etc. *he does not grieve his neighbour, he does not sate himself with luxuries*: these phrases, too, are related. 'Not grieving' one's neighbour implies helping oppressed, poor and hungry men by providing them with the things they need. *for the Lord is his portion*: cp. Ps. 73:26; 119:57.

6:4. *does not admit of glory or dishonour from men*: the good man is depicted as a kind of hellenistic philosopher who does not care what people think of him; cp. 2 Cor. 6:8; Dio Chrysostom VIII.15f; LXVII.3; Epictetus 1.24.6; Philo, Som 1.124f, etc. Instead *he rejoices towards all men always*: cp. 2 Cor. 6:10, 'in our sorrows, we have always cause for joy'; Epictetus III.5.8f, 'I fell sick, when it was your (God's) will; so did other men, but I willingly. I became poor, it being your will, but with joy.' Plutarch, *De tuenda sanitate praecepta* 25 (Mor. 136 CD); Diognetus 5.11ff, etc. *for the Lord dwells in him*: cp. TZeb. 8:2; TDan 5:1; TJos 10:2f; and also Philo, Sobr 62, and esp. Hermas, *Mandate* 3:1; 10:1, 6; Barnabas 16:8ff. *and lights up his soul*: cp. 4:2; TGad 5:7.

6:5–7. This section gives a description of some qualities of the good man, having as its central theme the opposition double–single. The good man is the one who is 'single' or 'simple', not an hypocrite (cp. TIss).

6:5. The good man belongs to the right side, he is 'one-sided': he blesses and does not curse, honours and does not revile, rejoices and has no sorrow, is quiet and not in confusion, tells the truth and is not hypocritical, is poor and not wealthy. *of sorrow and of joy, of quietness and of confusion*: these phrases refer to the good man's inner condition, which is not disturbed by all kinds of bad desires and passions.

6:6. The good man knows he cannot hide himself from God. Again,

he is depicted as different from the hypocrite, who is not aware of the
fact that God not only looks on his deeds but even knows his in-
tentions.

   6:7a. *he cleanses his mind*: he makes his mind 'pure', that is, free from
pains, from bad desires and passions.

   6:7b. The good man's activities are not twofold, as are all of
Beliar's works, but they are characterized by 'singleness', which sums
up all the good features and activities of the good man.

THE COMING OF THE MESSIAH: TJUD 24

After a section that describes the future sins of Judah's tribe, its punishment and its repentance together with the return to the promised land
(a 'Sin–Exile–Return' passage), there is a reference to the coming of
Jesus Christ. The author of the T12P puts into the Patriarch's mouth all
kinds of quotations of or allusions to Old Testament passages (above
all from the prophetic books) that in the early Church were regarded
as speaking about the coming of Christ. The chapter has a number of
similarities with TLevi 18, another passage that deals with the future
Messiah.

24:1   And after these things a star will arise to you from Jacob in peace,
            and a man will arise from my seed like the sun of righteousness,
                walking with the sons of men in meekness and righteousness
                and no sin whatever will be found in him.
2   And the heavens will be opened to him,
                to pour out the blessing of the spirit of the holy Father,
                and he will pour out the spirit of grace upon you;
3   and you will be sons to him in truth
            and you will walk in his commandments from first to last.
4   This (is) the branch of God Most High,
            and this (is) the fountain unto life for all flesh.
5   Then the sceptre of my kingdom will shine
            and from your root a stem will arise;
6   and in it a rod of righteousness will arise to the nations,
                to judge and to save all who call upon the Lord.

   24:1. The coming of the Messiah. *a star will arise to you from Jacob
in peace, and a man will arise from my seed like the sun of righteousness*:
cp. TLevi 18:3f; TZeb 9:8; from Num. 24:17 LXX, 'a star will arise

from Jacob, and a man will arise from Israel', and Mal. 4:2 (3:20 LXX), 'for you...the sun of righteousness shall rise', cp. Zech. 6:12, passages taken as references to Jesus Christ in the early Church; see Justin, *Apology* 1.32.12ff; *Dialogue* 106.4; 121.2; Origen, *Contra Celsum* 1.59; VI.79, etc. *from my seed*: cp. Num. 24:7; emphasis on the Messiah's descent from Judah. *walking with the sons of men in meekness and righteousness*: cp. TIss 7:7; TDan 5:13; 'walking with men' is an expression frequently used to characterize Jesus' life on earth in early Christian literature. *in meekness and righteousness*: cp. Ps. 45:4; Zech. 9:9; for Jesus' *meekness*, see TDan 6:9; Matt. 11:29; 21:5; 2 Cor. 10:1, etc. *and no sin whatever will be found in him*: cp. Isa. 53:9; PssSol 17:36 (41); 2 Cor. 5:21; Heb. 4:15; 1 Pet. 2:22.

24:2. The outpouring of the Holy Spirit upon Jesus and upon his 'children'. *the heavens will be opened to him, to pour out the blessing of the spirit*: cp. TLevi 18:6f; Mal. 3:10; and the events at Jesus' baptism in the Jordan in Matt. 3:16f and parallels. *the holy Father*: cp. John 17:11; Didache 10:2; Odes Sol 31:5; Origen, *Commentary on John* xx.22, etc. *and he will pour out the spirit of grace upon you*: cp. TLevi 18:11. This phrase refers to Acts 2:1ff, 17ff, 33; and John 15:26; 16:7ff; 14:16f, 26; see also Eusebius, *De ecclesiastica theologia* III, 5f. *the spirit of grace*: cp. Zech. 12:10; and Heb. 10:29; 1 Clement 46:6.

24:3. To receive the spirit from the Messiah implies to be his children and to do his commandments. All this stresses the particular relation between Christ and those who believe in him. *you will be sons to him in truth*: cp. TLevi 18:8. *you will walk in his commandments*: for this expression, cp. Lev. 26:3; 1 Kings 8:61; Hermas, *Similitude* 5:1, 5; and esp. Ezek. 11:20; 37:24. *from first to last*: for this typical Hebrew (OT) expression, cp. 2 Chron. 9:29; 12:15; 16:11, etc.

24:4. *the branch of God Most High*: an allusion to Gen. 49:9 (LXX, 'you have gone up from the branch, my son'), another passage frequently interpreted as referring to Jesus Christ (from the tribe of Judah); see Justin, *Dialogue* 86.4; *Apostolic Constitutions* VI.11.10; Hippolytus, *Benedictio Jacobi* 16; *Antichrist* 8, etc. *the fountain unto life*: cp. the expression 'fountain of life' as used of God in Jer. 17:13 (see also 2:13; Ps. 36:9); the same or similar expressions are used also in connection with Christ: see Justin, *Dialogue* 69.5f; Clement of Alexandria, *Protrepticus* 10 (110.3); Eusebius, *De ecclesiastica theologia* 1.8.20.

24:5–6. These verses introduce a new theme, *viz.*, Jesus' righteous kingship, his judgement, and the salvation of all believers, Jews or Gentiles. *the sceptre*: symbol of power and authority; cp. Num. 24:17. For Jesus as 'sceptre', cp. 1 Clem. 16:2. *of my kingdom*: stresses another theme – Jesus' descent from Judah and Judah's eternal kingship. *will shine*: cp. TLevi 18:4; Isa. 9:2, 'light has dawned upon them', frequently understood as an allusion to the coming of Christ (see, e.g., Matt. 4:15f); see further Justin, *Dialogue* 113.5. *and from your root a stem will arise; and in it a rod of righteousness will arise*: from Isa. 11:1, 'Then a shoot shall grow from the stock of Jesse, and a branch shall spring from his roots', again a passage interpreted christologically in the early Church. *a rod of righteousness*: cp. Ps. 45:6f; and see Heb. 1:8f; Justin, *Dialogue* 38.4. *rod*: symbol of kingship. *to save all who call upon the Lord*: cp. Joel 2:32 (3:5 LXX), 'Then everyone who invokes the Lord by name shall be saved'; Acts 2:21; and esp. Rom. 10:12f, 'there is no distinction between Jew and Greek, because the same Lord is Lord of all, and is rich enough for the need of all who invoke him' (then follows a quotation of Joel 2:32).

Joseph and Aseneth

CHR. BURCHARD

Subject and genre

The Bible says that Joseph, after Pharaoh had made him viceroy of Egypt, married Aseneth (so the LXX), the daughter of Potiphera, priest of On-Heliopolis (Gen. 41:45). Gradually this noble match came to look like a mésalliance. No later certainly than the Maccabaean revolt in the second century BC, Jewish exegetes began to ask themselves what might have happened to allow the Patriarch to wed an idolatrous foreign girl. One of the answers was that Aseneth had turned to the God of Israel beforehand. How this came about is related in the first part, chapters 1–21, of the anonymous romance that we now call 'Joseph and Aseneth' (the original title is not known for certain). Aseneth's conversion is touched off by an unexpected meeting with Joseph, confirmed by an angel from heaven, and followed by a happy wedding. A second part ensues, chapters 22–9. Some years later, after Jacob had settled in Egypt with all of his kin (Gen. 46–7), Pharaoh's first-born son attempted to abduct Aseneth but failed, because some of Joseph's brothers, principally Benjamin and Levi, repelled him.

All this is told at a leisurely pace with a good deal of repetition. There is less action in the story than there might have been. Colourful events inviting narration, such as the marriage feast and the military entanglements of the second part, are stated rather than described. Instead much space is given to dialogues, meditations about what to do, and prayers. The outcome is a text which is a little longer than, e.g., the Gospel of Mark, or, if a non-biblical comparison is preferred, about the length of 'Cupid and Psyche' as told by Apuleius, *The Golden Ass*, Books IV–VI.

No source is known for the narrative as a whole or for major parts of it, but many elements of form and content are traditional. The cast of characters, the general setting, and a number of details come from the biblical story of Joseph (Gen. 37–50), except Pharaoh's first-born son who seems to be modelled upon Shechem, the son of Hamor (Gen. 34). Many other motifs, speech forms, etc., have parallels in the

92

Bible and Jewish literature, or in hellenistic writings such as the Greek erotic novels (Chariton, Xenophon of Ephesus, Longus, Achilleus Tatius, Heliodorus, and, in Latin, Apuleius). Aseneth's conversion may reflect rites or customs that were practised when a person embraced Judaism, but it is hard to tell which. The original Greek of the book draws freely on the vocabulary and idioms of the Septuagint, although unlike TJob it rarely borrows from individual passages, and imitates biblical narration, avoiding subordinate clauses and participial constructions.

In recent years JosAsen has often been labelled as a romance. In addition to the erotic variety, such writings as Ruth, Judith, Tobit, Esther, the Life of Alexander, of Aesop, the apocryphal Acts of various apostles and others have also been characterized as romances. The term thus covers a wide variety. JosAsen certainly has some things in common with Judith or Esther, and other things with the erotic novels. But neither group tells about conversion. To explain the conversion section of our book, 'Cupid and Psyche' and the retransformation of Lucius in Apuleius, Book XI, offer some help, but more so a number of Jewish and Christian texts relating to conversion such as Dan. 4; TJob 2–5; Matt. 16:16–18; Luke 7:36–50; Acts 9:1–19; 26:12–18. It seems best at present, however, not to look too hard for an established sub-type of the romantic genre for JosAsen, but to acknowledge affinities with whatever romance, or group of romances, lends itself to comparison, and not to forget that other writings may have a word to say about its genre, too.

Central message

The central message of the book is twofold. The first part relates what adherence to Judaism means. It means fullness of life including wisdom, health, happiness, public reputation, and a suitable spouse; it goes on past a person's physical death into eternal heavenly rest. The unconverted, on the other hand, live in darkness and are virtually dead. Interestingly enough, Aseneth is not only a model proselyte, the first known in history. She is also promoted to the rank of City of Refuge for all who repent like her. This is to say that fullness of life cannot be achieved solely by turning to God; one must also turn Jewish and rally to the Jews. But whoever does so will be safe forever, body and soul. God and his or her fellow Jews will see to that. This is spelled out in the second part. Of course the author may have had other things in mind, too. His book also teaches the conditions of mixed marriages, and enjoins certain aspects of Jewish ethics.

Origin

JosAsen appears to have originated in the Jewish diaspora of Egypt, no later than *c.* AD 100 and perhaps as early as the first century BC. A sectarian milieu has been suggested: Essenes, Therapeutae, or some unknown form of Judaism shaped in the image of a hellenistic mystery religion. But the book presents Judaism, not a special form distinct from others. According to some scholars, it was written to promote Jewish mission among non-Jews, or Jews, or both. However, Judaism as depicted in JosAsen is not mission-minded. Besides the book never bothers to explain Jewish life. The sabbath, circumcision, the interdiction against pork, the standards of levitical purity, indeed the necessity of keeping the Law, which is fundamental to all forms of Judaism, go unmentioned. So it is safer to assume that JosAsen was meant to be read by Jews as a reminder of the supernatural vitality and lofty morality which were theirs. We should remember, however, that the Egyptian diaspora undoubtedly included many proselytes and attracted 'God-fearing' sympathizers such as we know, e.g., from the Book of Acts.

Textual witnesses

We do not know how well JosAsen was received by Jewish readers. Christianity must have appropriated it at an early date when polytheism was still strong. It was then widely read in the Eastern Church as a book of devotion, sometimes also as a historical source, witness the sixteen extant Greek mss. from the tenth to the nineteenth centuries, as well as the translations into Syriac (sixth century), Armenian (sixth to seventh century?), Ethiopic (lost), Serbo-Slavonic (fifteenth century), Modern Greek (sixteenth century), and Rumanian (seventeenth century?). In the Western Church two Latin versions were made before AD 1200, one of them in England. John Lydgate (*c.* 1370–*c.* 1451) appears to allude to it in the fifth stanza of 'To Mary, the Queene of Heaven'. An unknown cleric rendered it into middle English verse not long after Chaucer (d. 1400). Vincent of Beauvais included a condensed version of the first Latin translation into his world history, *Speculum historiale*, Book I.118–24, completed by AD 1253. This was widely distributed with the *Speculum*. It was often copied and circulated independently. In addition it also found its way into numerous other compilations in many European languages down to the nineteenth century.

The original of JosAsen has, of course, been lost. For its reconstruction we must rely on the sixteen Greek mss. and the versions mentioned above. Most or all of these witnesses have been retouched and abbreviated in one way or another. They fall into several recensions. The oldest text has to be reconstructed from these, a task begun but not yet satisfactorily completed.

Bibliography

The Greek text was first published by P. Batiffol, 'Le livre de la Prière d'Aseneth', in *Studia Patristica*, Paris, 1889–90, and translated into English by E. W. Brooks, *Joseph and Asenath*, London, 1918. This is a Byzantine recension (*a*) which is close to the original in substance but has been rewritten in many places to improve the Greek. A shorter recension (*d*) was published and translated into French by M. Philonenko, *Joseph et Aséneth* (Studia Post-Biblica 13), Leiden, 1968. A provisional critical text based on all the available evidence appeared in *Dielheimer Blätter zum Alten Testament* 14 (1979), pp. 2–53. It was translated into English by the present author in J. H. Charlesworth (ed.), *The Old Testament Pseudepigrapha*, vol. II (forthcoming) (the following selections are taken from this work); and into German, 'Joseph und Aseneth', JSHRZ II 4 pp. 577–735. The Middle English was printed by H. N. MacCracken, 'The Storie of Asneth', *The Journal of English and German Philology* 9 (1910), 224–64 (contains also Vincent's abridgement).

By way of introduction, those who read Greek may consult S. West, 'Joseph and Asenath: A Neglected Greek Romance', *Classical Quarterly* N.S. 24 (1974), pp. 70–81. More Aseneth lore is digested by L. Ginzberg, *The Legends of the Jews*, vol. II, Philadelphia, 1910, pp. 170–8; vol. V, 1925, pp. 336–9, 374–5 *et al.*; V. Aptowitzer, 'Asenath, the Wife of Joseph', *HUCA* I (1924), 239–306. D. Sänger, *Antikes Judentum und die Mysterien. Religionsgeschichtliche Untersuchungen zu Joseph und Aseneth*, Tübingen, 1980, can be recommended for further study (extensive survey of previous research and good bibliography).

INTRODUCTION: CAST OF CHARACTERS
AND SCENE OF ACTION

1:1 And it happened in the first year of the seven years of plenty, in the second month, on the fifth of the month: Pharaoh sent out

2 Joseph to drive around the whole land of Egypt. And Joseph came in the fourth month, of the first year, on the eighteenth of the month into the territory of Heliopolis and was gathering the grain

3 of that region like the sand of the sea. And there was a man in that city, a satrap of Pharaoh, and this (man) was a chief of all the satraps and the noblemen of Pharaoh. And this man was exceedingly rich

and prudent and gentle, and he was a counsellor of Pharaoh,
because he was understanding beyond all the noblemen of Pharaoh.
And the name of that man (was) Pentephres, priest of Heliopolis.

4 And he had a daughter, a virgin of eighteen years, very tall and
handsome and beautiful to look at beyond all virgins on the earth.

5 And this (girl) had nothing similar to the virgins of the Egyptians,
but she was in every respect similar to the daughters of the
Hebrews; and she was tall as Sarah and handsome as Rebecca and

6 beautiful as Rachel. And the name of that virgin was Aseneth. And
the fame of her beauty spread all over that land and to the ends of
the inhabited (world). And all the sons of the noblemen and the
sons of the satraps and the sons of all kings, all of them young and
powerful, asked for her hand in marriage, and there was much
wrangling among them over Aseneth, and they made attempts to
fight against each other because of her.

1–2. These verses key JosAsen to Gen. 41:46–9. The translation
follows the Greek as closely as possible. Words without a Greek
equivalent are bracketed.

2. *Heliopolis*: 'Sun City', Hebrew *'Ōn*, Gen. 41:45, 50; 46:20 (cp.
Jer. 43:13), is now Matarieh, a north-eastern suburb of Cairo. A centre
of the sun god Rê in ancient Egypt, it was all but ruined in JosAsen's
day, but remained a tourist attraction. Plato's visit there was remembered among others (Strabo, *Geography* XVII.1.29). Cp. also
Exod. 1:11 LXX; Apion in Josephus, *Apion* II.2 (10–1).

3–6. Romances start like this, e.g. Chariton, *Chaireas and Callirhoe*
I.1; Xenophon, *Habrocomes and Antheia* I.1; 'Cupid and Psyche', in
Apuleius, *The Golden Ass* IV. 28–9.

3. *Pentephres*: the name of Potiphera appears as Pe(n)tephres in the
Septuagint Gen. 41:45, 50; 46:20. In JosAsen he is both chief priest and
governor of Heliopolis. The book, like Philo, Jos 121; Josephus, *Ant.*
II.6.1 (91), does not identify him with the Potiphar of Gen. 37:36;
39:1, but many Jewish and Christian authors did.

5. *Aseneth*: the Septuagint version of the Hebrew *'Āsenat*, which
goes back to an Egyptian name meaning something like 'Belonging to
(the goddess) Neith'. But was JosAsen aware of this?

Despite her many suitors, Aseneth disdained all men and preferred to
live in seclusion, worshipping countless idols (cp. TJob 2:2–3; ApAb

1:3ff; Xenophon's Antheia and Heliodorus' Charikleia also were priestesses), in a luxurious suite on top of a tower adjoining her father's palace.

JOSEPH'S FIRST VISIT TO PENTEPHRES INDUCES ASENETH TO TURN TO HIS GOD

The narrative proper starts with chapter 3. Joseph arrives in Heliopolis to collect the surplus grain of the region. Pentephres tells Aseneth that he has in mind to give her to Joseph in marriage. She refuses, only to develop a violent passion for him as she sees him entering her father's home adorned like a king. Pentephres introduces her to his guest and asks her to greet him with a kiss.

8:5   And as Aseneth went up to kiss Joseph, Joseph stretched out his right hand and put it on her chest between her two breasts, and her breasts were already standing upright like handsome apples. And Joseph said, 'It is not fitting for a man who worships God, who will bless with his mouth the living God and eat blessed bread of life and drink a blessed cup of immortality and anoint himself with blessed ointment of incorruptibility, to kiss a strange woman who will bless with her mouth dead and dumb idols and eat from their table bread of strangulation and drink from their libation a cup of insidiousness and anoint herself with ointment of destruction.
6   But a man who worships God will kiss his mother and the sister (who is born) of his mother, and the sister (who is born) of his clan and family, and the wife who shares his bed, (all of) who(m) bless
7   with their mouths the living God. Likewise, for a woman who worships God it is not fitting to kiss a strange man, because this is an abomination before the Lord God.'

5. *breasts like apples*: a classical metaphor, e.g. Aristophanes, *Lysistrata* 155. It means no more here than that Aseneth is a mature woman. By ancient standards she is more than marriageable at the age of eighteen (1:4). *who worships God*: Greek, *theosebês*. In JosAsen this adjective characterizes those who worship the one and only God of Israel, not just any man or woman who is a devout follower of his or her god. *bread, cup, ointment*: there are similar statements in 8:9; 15:5; 16:16; 19:5; 21:13–14, 21. Their meaning is disputed. Scholars refer them to (1) the common Jewish provisions as opposed to the pagan,

(2) special Jewish meals celebrated, e.g., to solemnize a conversion, or (3) sacramental meals of a special Jewish group, which may or may not have been identical with their daily meals, cp. e.g. the Essenes 1QS VI.4–6; 1QSa II.17–21, and the Therapeutae in Philo, Vit Cont 37ff; 69ff. If (1) is preferred, one should remember that people's provisions are often summarized as 'bread (or other food), wine (or other beverage), oil', e.g. Ps. 23:5; Philo, Spec Leg I.179; Epictetus, *Dissertations* II.23.5. This formula depends on the triad 'grain, wine, oil' frequently used to describe the produce of the land, e.g. Ps. 104:14–15; Apuleius, *The Golden Ass* IX.33.2. See further 16:16 below. *blessed*: probably by grace said over food and ointment. This was considered as one of the marks that distinguished Judaism from paganism. e.g. SibOr IV.25–6 (cp. 1 Tim. 4:3–4). JosAsen seems to think that 'blessing' gives the bread etc. a supernatural quality which in turn provides everlasting life to those who partake of them. The heathen feed and anoint themselves to death on their 'unblessed' provisions. *bread of life*: cp. John 6:35, 48.

8 And when Aseneth heard these words of Joseph, she was cut (to the heart) strongly and was distressed exceedingly and sighed, and she kept gazing at Joseph with her eyes open and her eyes were filled with tears. And Joseph saw her and had mercy on her exceedingly and was himself cut (to the heart), because Joseph was meek and
9 merciful and fearing God. And he lifted up his right hand and put it upon her head and said, 'Lord God of my father Israel, the Most High, the Powerful One of Jacob, who gave life to all (things) and called (them) from the darkness to the light, and from the error to the truth, and from the death to the life, you, Lord, bless this virgin and renew her by your spirit and form her anew by your hidden hand and make her alive again by your life, and let her eat your bread of life, and drink your cup of blessing, and number her among your people that you have chosen before all (things) came into being, and let her enter your rest which you have prepared for your chosen ones, and live in your eternal life for ever (and) ever.'

9. *all* (things): it is common enough to begin a prayer by invoking the creator, e.g. 2 Kings 19:15; Acts 4:24, also 12:1–2 below. *life*: the three pairs of opposites, darkness and light, error and truth, death and life, are often used in Jewish and Christian writings to draw the line

between true religion and paganism or apostasy, e.g. SibOr Fragment 1.25–34; Philo, Virt 179–80; Luke 15:24, 32; Acts 26:18; Col. 1:12–13; 1 John 3:14 (cp. Poimandres 19–20). *spirit*: on renewal by the spirit see e.g. Rom. 7:6; Tit. 3:5. *form her anew*: conversion according to JosAsen is recreation, or rather creation brought to perfection. The unconverted have never attained the fullness of life intended by the creator for all people and naturally possessed by the Jews. *rest*: as in 15:7; 22:13, and probably Heb. 3:7–4:13, this means a heavenly place of rest rather than a state of body or mind. The idea was developed from Ps. 95:11. According to JosAsen 22:13 the heavenly rest-place is a walled city founded upon rock in the seventh heaven. Those who deserve to go there, like Aseneth, apparently will do so right after death. Unlike Jewish apocalyptic and the New Testament, JosAsen does not say that this world will come to an end and be replaced by a new world.

ASENETH REPENTS AND AN ANGEL ANNOUNCES THAT GOD HAS ACCEPTED HER

Joseph's prayer sends Aseneth fleeing up to her suite in remorse. He then leaves to pursue his corn-gathering, promising to be back a week later. Pentephres and his family go to their country-seat. Alone, Aseneth hurls her idols out of the window and torments herself in sackcloth and ashes for a week. On the morning of the eighth day she encourages herself in two lengthy monologues (chapter 11) to address the God of Joseph. At last she does address him:

12:1 'Lord God of the ages, who created all (things) and gave life (to them), who gave breath of life to your whole creation, who
2 brought the invisible (things) out into the light, who made the (things that) are and have an appearance from the non-appearing and non-being, who lifted up the heaven and founded it on a firmament upon the back of the winds, who founded the earth upon the waters, who put big stones on the abyss of the water, and the stones will not be submerged, but they are like oak leaves (floating) on top of the water, and they are living stones and hear your voice, Lord, and keep your commandments which you have commanded to them, and never transgress your ordinances, but are doing your will to the end. For you, Lord, spoke and they were

brought to life, because your word, Lord, is life for all your
3   creatures. With you I take refuge, Lord, and to you I will shout,
Lord, to you I will pour out my supplication, to you I will confess
my sins, and to you I will reveal my lawless deeds.'

1. *all (things)*: if conversion is (new) creation, to invoke the creator
implies that he can, and will, act anew as such in the present situation.
This clause and the following ones are participial in Greek, elevating
the prayer above the ordinary prose level. They give an idea of how
JosAsen interprets Gen. 1.

2. *non-being*: it is an essential tenet of Jewish and Christian cosmo-
logy that God made the world from nothing, e.g. Rom. 4:17, or from
formless matter, e.g. Gen. 1:2 LXX; Wisd. of Sol. 11:17; 2 Macc.
7:28; Philo, Op Mund. JosAsen seems to side with the latter view. It
corresponds to its interpretation of conversion. *your word is life*:
another cosmological principle. God created and maintains the world
by his word, e.g. Gen. 1; Ps. 33:9; Wisd. of Sol. 9:1; John 1:3, 10.

3. *refuge*: see 15:7 below.

Aseneth then goes on (chapters 12–13) to confess both her idolatry and
her contempt of Joseph, the son of God (see 23:10 below). At the end
she asks to be allowed to become Joseph's handmaid (cp. Luke 15:19).

14:1   And when Aseneth had ceased making confession to the Lord,
behold, the morning star rose out of heaven in the east. And
Aseneth saw it and rejoiced and said, 'So the Lord God listened to
my prayer, because this star rose as a messenger and herald of the
2   light of the great day.' And Aseneth kept looking, and behold
close to the morning star, the heaven was torn apart and great and
3   unutterable light appeared. And Aseneth saw (it) and fell on (her)
face on the ashes. And a man came to her from heaven and stood
4   by Aseneth's head. And he called her and said, 'Aseneth, Aseneth.'
5   And she said, 'Who is he that calls me, because the door of my
chamber is closed, and the tower is high, and how then did he
6   come into my chamber?' And the man called her a second time and
7   said, 'Aseneth, Aseneth.' And she said, 'Behold, (here) I (am), Lord.
8   Who are you, tell me.' And the man said, 'I am the chief of the house
of the Lord and commander of the whole host of the Most High.
Rise and stand on your feet, and I will tell you what I have to say.'

1–8. In form, these verses resemble e.g. Christ's appearance to Saul, Acts 9:3–8. In function, the heavenly man's visit, chapters 14–17, is parallel to Saul's vision referred to in Acts 9:12 and the angel's visit to Cornelius in Acts 10:3–7 (cp. also Apuleius, *The Golden Ass* XI.3–6). The functional counterpart to Acts 9:3–8 in JosAsen is Joseph's entry into Pentephres' house and Aseneth's reaction, chapters 5–6.

3. *man*: JosAsen always calls him so though obviously he is an angel, see verse 8 below. As a rule Jewish angels are male (but cp. 15:7 below).

8. JosAsen shares the common idea that God's reign is organized like a king's. Hellenistic rulers relied essentially on military power and organization. So the chief of the Lord's host is also his grand-vizier and represents him in every respect. Both the Jewish and Christian tradition later call the supreme angel Michael; in earlier texts Michael is one of several chief angels and specifically appointed over Israel, e.g. Dan. 10:13, 21; 12:1. What JosAsen thought the man's name was is unknown because of 15:12x (see below).

The angel tells Aseneth to restore her outward appearance and to come back for further information. She does so with her head veiled.

15:1 And she went to the man into her first chamber and stood before him. And the man said to her, 'Remove the veil from your head, and for what purpose did you do this? For you are a chaste virgin

2a today, and your head is like that of a young man.' And Aseneth removed the veil from her head.

1. Does this mean that virginity makes both sexes equal (cp. 7:7)? Or that women are not inferior to men in Judaism (for a Christian view cp. Gal. 3:28)? It probably does not mean that virgins or women should always go unveiled, as perhaps some Corinthians proposed (1 Cor. 11:2–16).

2b And the man said to her, 'Courage, Aseneth, chaste virgin. Behold, I have heard all the words of your confession and your

3 prayer. Behold, I have also seen the humiliation and the affliction of the seven days of your want (of food). Behold, from your tears and these ashes, plenty of mud has formed before your face.

4 Courage, Aseneth, chaste virgin. For behold, your name was written in the book of the living in heaven; in the beginning of the book, as the very first of all, your name was written by my

5   finger, and it will not be blotted out for ever. Behold, from today,
    you will be renewed and formed anew and made alive again, and
    you will eat blessed bread of life, and drink a blessed cup of im-
    mortality, and anoint yourself with blessed ointment of incor-
6   ruptibility. Courage, Aseneth, chaste virgin. Behold, I have given
    you today to Joseph for a bride, and he himself will be your
    bridegroom for ever (and) ever.'

    2–10. Cp. Apuleius, *The Golden Ass* XI.5–6. Isis announces to Lucius
    that he will be relieved of his asinine form, become human again, and
    be protected by the goddess forever.
    4. This book is a sort of heavenly citizens' register, a common
    Jewish and Christian idea deeply rooted in the Ancient Near East,
    e.g. Exod. 32:32–3; 1QM XII.1–2; Luke 10:20; Rev. 20:12, 15. This
    seems to be in fulfilment of 8:9, 'and number her among your people'.
    5. This again takes up the prayer at 8:9. See further 8:5 above and
    16:16 below.

7   'And your name shall no longer be called Aseneth, but your name
    shall be City of Refuge, because in you many nations will take
    refuge with the Lord God, the Most High, and under your wings
    many peoples trusting in the Lord God will be sheltered, and behind
    your walls will be guarded those who attach themselves to the
    Most High God in the name of Repentance. For Repentance is in
    the heavens, an exceedingly beautiful and good daughter of the
    Most High. And she herself entreats the Most High God for you at
    all times and for all who repent in the name of the Most High God,
    because he is (the) father of Repentance. And she herself is guardian
    of all virgins, and loves you very much, and is beseeching the Most
    High for you at all times and for all who repent, and has prepared
    for them a place of rest in the heavens. And she will renew all who
8   repent and wait on them herself for ever (and) ever. And Repent-
    ance is exceedingly beautiful, a virgin pure and laughing always,
    and she is gentle and meek. And therefore the Most High Father
    loves her, and all the angels stand in awe of her. And I, too, love
    her exceedingly, because she is also my sister. And because she
    loves you virgins, I love you, too.'

7. *City of Refuge*: proselytes often took on a new name, but this is more. Aseneth is given her new name from above like other important figures in the Bible and Jewish literature, e.g. Abraham and Sarah, Gen. 17:5, 15; Jacob, Gen. 32:28; Job, TJob 2:1; Peter, James and John, Mark 3:16–17; Peter, Matt. 16:18. 'City of Refuge' may be reminiscent of Num. 35:27–8. More probably it was suggested by the Septuagint text of Zech. 2:15 (Eng. trans. verse 11), 'and many nations will take refuge with the Lord on that day' (or perhaps Isa. 54:15), which is taken up in the following clause. This is a prophecy on Zion, i.e. Jerusalem in its function as mother-city and representative of Israel (cp. also e.g. Isa. 62:4–12; Jer. 50:5; 4Ezra 9:38ff; Rev. 21). It is here applied to Aseneth the mother of the proselytes. All who seek shelter 'in her', i.e. rally to the Egyptian diaspora whose ancestor she is, will be safeguarded for ever, i.e. endowed with the spiritual heritage sketched in verses 4–5, which was first hers. In both her function and in the imagery employed to express it, Aseneth parallels Abraham the Rock from which Israel was hewn (Isa. 51:1–2; *LAB* 23:4–5), also often portrayed as the first proselyte and missionary, Peter the Rock on which Christ will build his church (Matt. 16:16–18), and the 'Pillar Apostles' of the Jerusalem church (Gal. 2:9, cp. also 4:21–31). *Repentance*: Greek, *metanoia*. She seems to be personified here as an angel (cp. 14:3 above). The idea that angels and other persons in heaven intercede for people is common in Judaism and Christianity; in Hebrews Christ the heavenly high priest performs this office. Repentance and Michael act as a team. She prepares a convert's acceptance: he then ratifies it. *virgins*: this probably has an extended meaning here to include everyone who is like Aseneth; cp. verse 1 above. *place of rest*: see 8:9 above.

Aseneth praises the angel and asks for his name. He answers that the angels' names must remain unknown to men (15:12x). Aseneth proceeds to invite the angel to a meal of bread and old wine (cp. Judg. 13:15–18). He asks for a piece of honeycomb to go with it. As she confesses to have none in her store-room he tells her she will find one there. She does and brings it to him.

16:11 And Aseneth was afraid and said, 'Lord, I did not have a honeycomb in my store-room at any time, but you spoke and it came into being. Surely this came out of your mouth, because its
12 exhalation is like breath of your mouth.' And the man smiled at
13 Aseneth's understanding, and called her to himself, and stretched

out his right hand, and grasped her head and shook her head with his right hand. And Aseneth was afraid of the man's hand, because sparks shot forth from his hand as from bubbling (melted) iron. And Aseneth looked, gazing with her eyes at the man's hand.

14 And the man saw (it) and smiled and said, 'Happy are you, Aseneth, because the ineffable mysteries of the Most High have been revealed to you, and happy (are) all who attach themselves to the Lord God in repentance, because they will eat from this comb. For this comb is spirit of life. And the bees of the paradise of delight have made this from the dew of the roses of life that are in the paradise of God. And all the angels of God eat of it and all the chosen of God and all the sons of the Most High, because this is a comb of life, and everyone who eats of it will not die for ever (and) ever.'

14. *Happy*: same beginning as in the biblical beatitudes, e.g. Ps. 1:1; Matt. 5:3–12; 16:17. The mysteries revealed are probably the supernatural origin of the honeycomb which Aseneth has just recognized (verse 11; cp. Matt. 16:17), and its use as expressed in the following clauses. *eat from this comb*: see verse 16 below. *paradise of delight*: the Septuagint version of the 'Garden of Eden', e.g. Gen. 3:23f. It is in the third heaven according to ApMos 37:5; 3Bar 4:8; 3En 8:1; 2 Cor. 12:1–4. The further description of the honeycomb (cp. also verse 8) shows that it represents manna (cp. Exod. 16:14, 31; Wisd. of Sol. 19:21; SibOr III.746). It is called 'bread from heaven' in other texts, e.g. Ps. 105:40. The angels and the just in paradise are supposed to live on it. *will not die*: cp. John 6:50, 58.

15 And the man stretched out his right hand and broke a small portion off the comb, and he himself ate, and what was left he put with his hand into Aseneth's mouth, and said to her, 'Eat.' And she ate.

16 And the man said to Aseneth, 'Behold, you have eaten bread of life, and drunk a cup of immortality, and been anointed with ointment of incorruptibility. Behold, from today your flesh (will) flourish like flowers of life from the ground of the Most High, and your bones will grow strong like the cedars of the paradise of delight of God, and untiring powers will embrace you, and your youth will not see old age, and your beauty will not fail for

ever. And you shall be like a walled mother-city of all who take
refuge with the name of the Lord God, the king of the ages.'
16x And the man stretched out his right hand and touched the comb
where he had broken off (a portion), and it was restored and filled
up, and at once it became whole as it was in the beginning.

16. *you have eaten*: Aseneth received at last what Joseph had prayed
for in 8:9 and the angel announced in 15:5. But how, if she really ate
honey? The honey is perhaps best explained as a narrative interpretation of what Jewish daily bread is like if blessed properly (see
8:5 above; cp. 1 Cor. 10). It is manna from heaven and conveys everlasting life. Some scholars either take the honey literally and refer it to
a 'honey communion' celebrated on the occasion of a conversion or
regularly, or else take it as a symbol of the Law or of God's word in
general, e.g. Ps. 19:8–11; Philo, Fug. 137–9. The statement about
bread, cup, and ointment must be understood as an interpretation of
what one really receives when he or she partakes of the honey, if this is
taken literally. *mother-city*: see 15:7 above.

The angel then draws a cross which looks like, or is filled with, blood
on the comb with his finger. Thousands of bees rise from the comb and
encircle Aseneth. Other bees which are big like queens rise and build
another honeycomb on Aseneth's lips. The bees eat from it. The angel
sends them up into heaven. Some who try to sting Aseneth fall dead
to the ground. The angel resurrects them and sends them out to the
trees in Aseneth's garden. This is a miracle to confirm the words which
the angel said to Aseneth (cp. 2 Kings 20:8–11; Luke 2:15). Doubtless
it also has a meaning in itself. It may be a symbolical representation of
Aseneth's earthly future, cp. above all chapters 22–9.
   The angel retires to heaven on a fiery chariot like Elijah (2 Kings
2:11). Joseph's return is heralded. Aseneth puts on her bridal gown.
As she bends over a basin to wash her harassed face, she finds that she
has been endowed with supernatural beauty (18:9). So the promises
given to her in 15:5a; 16:16 begin to be fulfilled.

JOSEPH COMES BACK FOR HIS SECOND VISIT, AND
PHARAOH SOLEMNIZES HIS UNION WITH ASENETH

Joseph arrives. Aseneth meets him at the door and tells him what the
angel has said and done.

19:10 And Joseph stretched out his hands and called Aseneth by a
wink of his eyes. And Aseneth also stretched out her hands and ran
up to Joseph and fell onto his breast. And Joseph put his arms
around her, and Aseneth (put hers) around Joseph, and they
kissed each other for a long time and both came to life in their
11 spirit. And Joseph kissed Aseneth and gave her spirit of life, and he
kissed her the second time and gave her spirit of wisdom, and he
20:1 kissed her the third time and gave her spirit of truth. And they
embraced each other for a long time and interlocked their hands
like bonds.

11. Although life is mentioned here again, Joseph does more than
repeat what the angel did to Aseneth in chapter 16. Life is essentially
mediated through blessed food, wisdom and truth (i.e. recognition of
the true God, not truthfulness) through association with a true Jew.

Aseneth seats Joseph on a throne after this, washes his feet, and takes
a seat beside him.

20:6 And her father and mother and her whole family came from
the field which was their inheritance. And they saw Aseneth like
(the) appearance of light, and her beauty was like heavenly beauty.
And they saw her sitting with Joseph and dressed in a wedding
7 garment. And they were amazed at her beauty and rejoiced and
8 gave glory to God who gives life to the dead. And after this they
ate and drank and celebrated.

6. *came*: they had left in 10:1. *beauty*: see 16:16; 18:9 above.
7. *gave glory to God*: apparently Pentephres and his family embraced
Judaism, too (cp. Matt. 5:16; 1 Pet. 2:12). *who gives life to the dead*:
around the turn of the era, this had become a standing by-word for
God, expressing his way with men better than any other, e.g. 2 Macc.
7:22–3; John 5:21; Rom. 4:17; outside Jewish and Christian tradition
Apuleius, *The Golden Ass* XI.16.2.
8. To celebrate a happy occurrence by a meal is an all but universal
custom. Was a meal held to seal a conversion (cp. Luke 15:22–4)? If
blessed food separated the Jews from the non-Jews, the first Jewish
meal of a convert must acquire a special character.

Joseph then goes to Pharaoh and asks him to give him Aseneth for his wife. The king arranges the wedding. In due time Aseneth gives birth to Ephraim and Manasseh (cp. the wedding of Cupid and Psyche in Apuleius, *The Golden Ass* VI.22–4). This takes up Gen. 41:50–2 to steer JosAsen back to the biblical narrative. Before the story goes on Aseneth recapitulates her conversion in a psalm (21:11–21, cp. Exod. 15; Tobit 13; Judith 16).

PHARAOH'S FIRST-BORN SON ATTEMPTS TO ABDUCT ASENETH, BUT BENJAMIN AND LEVI RESCUE HER

22:1 And it happened after this: the seven years of plenty passed and
2 the seven years of famine began to come. And Jacob heard about Joseph his son, and Israel went to Egypt with his whole family, in the second year of the famine, in the second month, on the twenty-first of the month, and dwelt in the land of Goshen.

2. This verse gears chapters 22–9 to Gen. 45:26–46:7. *Goshen*: perhaps the northern part of the county of Heliopolis and adjoining regions.

Joseph and Aseneth go to see Jacob in Goshen. On their way back Pharaoh's first-born son sees Aseneth, is carried away by her beauty, and tries to engage the help of Simeon and Levi to kill Joseph and abduct Aseneth. Simeon flares up and threatens to slay the prince.

23:8 And Levi saw the intention of his heart, because Levi was a prophet, and he was sharp-sighted with (both) his mind and his eyes, and he used to read what is written in the heart of men. And Levi trod with his foot (on) Simeon's right foot and pressed it and
9 (thus) signalled him to cease from his wrath. And Levi said to Simeon quietly, 'Why are you furious with anger with this man? And we are men who worship God, and it does not befit us to
10 repay evil for evil.' And Levi said to Pharaoh's son with frankness, his face cheerful, and there was not the least (bit of) anger in him, but in meekness of heart he said to him, 'Why does our lord speak words such as these? And we are men who worship God, and our father is a friend of the Most High God, and Joseph our

11 brother is like the first-born son of God. And how could we do
    this wicked thing, and sin before our God and before our father
12 Israel and before our brother Joseph? And now, listen to my words.
    It does not befit a man who worships God to injure anyone in any
    way. And if anyone wants to injure a man who worships God,
    that (first-mentioned) man who worships God does not succour
13 him (the injurer), because a sword is not in his hands. And you at
    least guard against speaking any longer about our brother Joseph
    words such as these. But if you insist on this wicked purpose of
    yours, behold, our swords are drawn in our right hands before you.'

8. *prophet*: as e.g. Luke 7:39 (cp. Mark 2:8 par.; John 2:25). Levi
also reads what is in the book of the living, views a person's heavenly
place of rest (22:13, cp. 8:9), and recognizes things that happen at a
distance (26:6). Enjoining moral principles is consistent with his
prophetic role. But unlike the Old Testament prophets, Levi is never
concerned with history present or future.

9. *who worship God*: see 8:5 above. *not ... to repay evil for evil*: the
most important ethical principle in JosAsen; it is repeated in 28:5, 10,
14; 29:3. To illustrate it is one of the objects of chapters 22–9. It has been
taken over by early Christianity (Rom. 12:17; 1 Thess. 5:15; 1 Pet.
3:9), but certainly not from JosAsen. It does not exclude legitimate
self-defence and criminal justice as the narrative shows. Other principles
are introduced by 'it does not befit' in 8:5, 7; 21:1; 23:12; 29:3.

10. Levi lives up to what he has professed; see also 29:1ff below.
friend of the Most High God: a traditional by-word for important
biblical figures, first of all Abraham. Egyptian and Greek tradition
use it, too, e.g. Epictetus, *Dissertations* II.17.29. *son of God*: Joseph has
been so called earlier in 6:3, 5; 13:13; 18:11; 21:4. The expression
does not make him a figure of the Messiah or Saviour. It means that
he is first among God's children (cp. 16:14; 19:8) and a representative,
albeit not the only one, of all the physical and spiritual qualities
possessed by them.

Unshaken, Pharaoh's son engages Dan and Gad, Naphthali and Asher
to help him with his dark purposes. They set up an ambush for
Aseneth in a wadi and surprise her as she drives to her country-seat to
supervise the grape-gathering while Joseph is away distributing corn.
Levi the prophet alarms Joseph's good brothers and they set out
running to rescue their sister-in-law. In the meantime unexpected help

comes from Joseph's youngest brother who has not been mentioned before in the narrative.

27:1 And Benjamin sat at Aseneth's left (hand) in her carriage. And Benjamin was a boy of eighteen years, big and strong and powerful, and there was unspeakable beauty on him, and strength like (that

2 of) a lion cub, and he was fearing the Lord exceedingly. And Benjamin leapt down from the carriage and took a round stone from the wadi and filled his hand and hurled (the stone) at Pharaoh's son and struck his left temple and wounded him with a serious

3 wound. And Pharaoh's son fell down from his horse on the ground,

4 being half-dead. And Benjamin leapt and went up upon the rock, and said to Aseneth's charioteer, 'Give me stones from the wadi.'

5 And he gave him fifty stones. And Benjamin hurled the fifty stones and killed the fifty men who were with the son of Pharaoh. And all the stones penetrated their temples.

1–5. The story of David slaying Goliath 1 Sam. 17 inspired this scene and also 29:2 below.

3. Cp. Luke 10:30 and 29:3–6 below.

Presently Levi and his brothers arrive and kill the other men who have been waiting in the ambush. Dan and Gad, Naphthali and Asher escape and resolve to kill Benjamin and Aseneth before pursuing their flight. Aseneth prays to God, and the swords fall from the villains' hands. They implore her to intercede for them with their brothers who come running up. She barely succeeds.

29:1 And Pharaoh's son rose from the ground and sat up and spat blood from his mouth, because the blood from his temple ran down

2 over his mouth. And Benjamin ran up to him and took his sword and drew it from its sheath, because Benjamin did not have a sword on his thigh, and set about to strike the breast of Pharaoh's son.

3 And Levi ran up to him and grasped his hand and said, 'By no means, brother, will you do this deed, because we are men who worship God, and it does not befit a man who worships God to repay evil for evil nor to trample underfoot a fallen (man) nor to

4 oppress his enemy till death. And now, put your sword back into its place, and come, help me, and we will heal him of his wound;

and if he lives, he will be our friend after this, and his father
5 Pharaoh will be like a father of ours.' And Levi raised Pharaoh's son
from the ground and washed the blood off his face and tied a
bandage to his wound, and put him upon his horse, and conducted
him to his father Pharaoh, and described to him all these things.
6 And Pharaoh rose from his throne and prostrated himself before
Levi on the ground and blessed him.

3–6. Levi's attitude is close to love of one's enemy as taught in the
parable of the Good Samaritan, Luke 10:30–5, and prescribed by Jesus
in Matt. 5:43–8. But it is really an example of royal clemency, a deed
both noble and sensible, serving the interests of both parties. See also
23:9 above.

4. *put your sword back*: cp. Matt. 26:52; John 18:11.
5. *his horse*: Pharaoh's son's horse. Levi is on foot.

7 And on the third day Pharaoh's son died from the wound (caused
8 by the impact) of the stone of Benjamin the boy. And Pharaoh
mourned exceedingly for his first-born son, and from the mourning
he fell ill; and Pharaoh died at a hundred and nine years, and left
9 his diadem to Joseph. And Joseph reigned as king in Egypt for
forty-eight years, and after this he gave the diadem to Pharaoh's
younger offspring who was at the breast when Pharaoh died. And
Joseph was like a father to Pharaoh's younger son in the land of
Egypt all the days of his life.

8. *a hundred and nine years*: Joseph died at a hundred and ten according to Gen. 50:22.

The Book of Jubilees
JAMES C. VANDERKAM

The Book of Jubilees is a narrative work which presents a strongly edited version of most of the biblical material from the story of creation to the account of the Law-giving on Mt Sinai. It claims to be the written form of the revelation which God, through an angel of the presence, granted to Moses on that mountain.

Titles

Ancient writers used several titles for Jubilees, the most frequently attested of which are the following three. (1) *The Book of the Divisions of the Times*: this name derives from the opening words of the text and aptly captures the author's penchant for dating events according to his peculiar chronological system. The title is found in one of the Qumran Scrolls (the Damascus Document (CD) XVI.3) and, in the abbreviated form *The Book of the Divisions* (or just *Divisions*), remains the standard designation for it in Ethiopic. (2) *The Book of Jubilees*: the familiar English title is a transcription of a name which, with minor variations in spelling, appears in some Greek, Syriac and Mediaeval Hebrew references to the book. A jubilee, which the author understood as a 49-year period, serves as the major chronological unit in his calculation of dates. (3) *The Little Genesis*: a number of early Christian writers and, later some Byzantine chronographers referred to Jubilees under this title. It highlights the obvious relationship of the book to Genesis but why the adjective *little* was added is not clear. It has been suggested that it points to Jubilees' detailed treatments of various topics which are simply mentioned or even ignored in Genesis, but, as there are instances in which Genesis offers greater detail, the hypothesis is unconvincing. It is possible that *little* was used pejoratively, though Jubilees enjoyed high esteem in some Christian areas; but it is at least certain that the adjective does not refer to size, since Jubilees and Genesis are approximately the same length.

Textual material

(1) Hebrew: although Hebrew was the original language of the book, it was thought, before the discoveries of the Qumran Scrolls (between 1947 and 1956), that no trace of the original version had survived. Among the scrolls, however, fragments of some twelve manuscripts of Jubilees – all written in Hebrew – have been identified. Fragments of another scroll – also inscribed in Hebrew – were uncovered, it has been reported, during excavations at Masada. Fragments from only seven of the manuscripts have been published; they correspond with parts of 4:7–11, 13–14, 16–17, 29–30; 5:1–2; 12:15–17, 28–9; 21:22–4; 23:6–7, 7–8, 12–13; 27:19–20; 35:8–10; 46:1–3. According to preliminary reports, the unpublished material contains sections of Jub 1–2; 21–3; 25; and 32–40. (2) Syriac: it is possible that Jubilees was translated from Hebrew into Syriac, though no definitive case for this thesis has been made. Virtually the only evidence for it is the fact that an anonymous Syriac chronicle to the year 1234 cites, in various places, some 161 verses of Jubilees. Whether these quotations originated from a Greek or Hebrew base, they are often of text-critical help. (3) Greek: Jubilees was translated from Hebrew into Greek, but no manuscript of this version has been found. One can argue that a Greek version once existed from features of later translations that were made from it and from numerous citations of Jubilees in works of authors who wrote Greek. (4) Latin: from Greek the book was translated into a rather literal Latin. One copy of this version has survived but in it only approximately one-fourth of the text is preserved. The manuscript itself dates from no later than the sixth century AD; it is, therefore, the earliest extended witness to the text of Jubilees. It contains large portions of chapters 13; 15–42; and 45–9. (5) Ethiopic: the Greek version also served as a base for a translation into Classical Ethiopic, and in this language alone the book has survived in its entirety (50 chapters). It is not known when the translation was made, but, as Jubilees enjoyed canonical status in the Abyssinian Church and later among the Falashas (the Black Jews of Ethiopia), it was probably rendered into Ethiopic very early in the Christian history of that land – perhaps by AD 500. At the time of the last critical edition of Jubilees (1895), only four manuscripts were available, but today twenty-seven have been identified. Comparison of their readings with the fragmentary evidence of the earlier versions (especially the Hebrew one) shows that the text of the book has been preserved very carefully in Ethiopic.

Genre, aims of the author, audience

Jubilees belongs in a category of ancient Jewish writings that has been
called the re-written Bible. It follows the scriptural narratives from
Gen. 1 to Exod. 19, but it includes new material that significantly alters
the biblical base. The writer inserted within the biblical framework
a number of passages which express his distinctive views. His procedure resembles that of the writer of 1 and 2 Chron., who also revised
and supplemented a biblical base (1–2 Sam. and 1–2 Kings). The author
of Jubilees composed a re-written version of Genesis and Exodus in
order to bring to the attention of his Jewish contemporaries a number
of points about belief and practice which he considered essential to the
proper relationship between God and his people. This priestly writer
issued a summons to his fellow Jews to observe carefully the divine laws
about sacrifice, festivals, sabbath and the cultic calendar in order to
avert the sort of punishments that God had meted out to their ancestors.
Only by strict obedience to the laws of God could they hope to enjoy
full divine favour. The only extended eschatological passage in the book
(23:13–31) envisages a period of bliss (after a time of disobedience and
great suffering) which will be ushered in by the return of a group
(called 'the children') to intensive study and practice of the divinely
revealed Law. For the writer, Israel was holy, and that sanctity was to
find expression in both an uncompromising adherence to God's Law
and in strict separation from the nations.

Contents, structure and main themes

As noted above, Jubilees largely borrows its contents and structure from
the biblical stories found in Gen. 1–Exod. 19. Almost without exception
it arranges events in their scriptural order and rarely omits major
segments, though some stories (e.g., finding a wife for Isaac) are
radically shortened. Since the textual base from which the author
worked is available for comparison, the reader can easily see which
passages he reproduced without change, which he altered, which he
omitted, and which he added. Naturally the greatest interest attaches
to those passages which the author altered significantly and to those
which he added from extra-biblical sources. If one focuses upon these
sections, the following emphases can be recognized.

(1) Chronology: the editor who was responsible for the final shape
of Genesis and Exodus dated some events by year, numbered month,
and date within the month (e.g. the flood; passover), but the author of

Jubilees enlarged on this interest and also furnished a comprehensive chronological system for the events of sacred history. He divided the year into 364 days – that is, exactly 52 weeks – so that all dates fall on the same day of the week every year. This solar, sabbatarian calendar was supposed to have been revealed to Enoch before the flood. The year begins on the fourth day of the week (the day on which the sun was created), and each quarter or season has three months of 30, 30 and 31 days respectively. The same calendar is attested in 1En 72–82 and in some of the Qumran Scrolls.

The writer's chronological system employs 49-year units called jubilees. These he divided into seven parts of seven years (termed weeks or weeks of years). By means of this system he dated a large number of events. Where appropriate, the numbers on the Jubilee Calculation are shown in the text within square brackets, e.g. at 4:15. For example, the exodus from Egypt occurred in the fiftieth jubilee-period, the second week of years in it, and the second year of that week (= 2,410 years after creation).

(2) Earlier origins for festivals and rites: the Bible first mentions holidays such as the day of atonement or the festival of weeks within the mass of legislation that was given to Moses at Sinai. In Jubilees, too, Moses receives information about them at Sinai, but there the revealing angel tells him that they had been celebrated already in the times of the Patriarchs and in some cases even earlier. The festival of weeks assumes a particularly important position as the festival of covenants (e.g. with Noah and Abraham). Noah is said to have been the first human to observe the festival, but the claim is added that in heaven it had been celebrated since creation (6:18). Similarly, the author pre-dated the annual observance of the day of atonement to the occasion of Jacob's grief at the 'death' of his son Joseph; his mourning is seen as the historical basis for annual commemoration (34:12–19). The same procedure is followed for circumcision. Whereas in Gen. 17 Abraham and his household are the first to undergo the rite, in Jubilees two classes of angels are reported to have been created circumcised (15:27). The writer never explained why he did this, but it seems reasonable to suppose that by pushing the beginnings of these festivals and rites into more ancient times he meant to underscore their significance and to provide a longer list of exemplary worthies who had obeyed God in these ways. Presumably he intended to impress upon his contemporaries the importance of imitating them.

(3) Solving biblical problems: the author was obviously aware that some biblical passages could raise difficulties in the mind of the careful

reader. An example is the fact that, though God warned that Adam and Eve would die the day they ate the forbidden fruit, they continued to live long lives after their disobedience. He solved the problem by redefining the word *day* (4:29–30). The writer was also concerned to salvage the reputations of the Patriarchs – to present them in a more uniformly favourable light than Genesis does. For instance, in Gen. 12:10–20 Abram lies about the identity of Sarai who is then taken by the pharaoh. Though the lie is essential to the story, Jubilees tells the tale but omits Abram's deception. In this way the author mutilated the story but saved the Patriarch's dignity (13:11–15). He even attempted in several passages to save the Lord himself from criticism by ascribing some of his strange actions to the leader of the evil spirits (e.g., the command to sacrifice Isaac (17:15–16)).

(4) Extra-biblical stories about biblical characters: Jubilees expands the biblical narrative at many points with material drawn from elsewhere. The author enlarged the short notice about Enoch in Gen. 5:21–4 into a much more detailed paragraph (4:15–26) and supplemented his base at many other passages, but it is especially the stories about Abraham, Jacob and Levi which undergo noticeable growth. Tales are added about Abram's youth and early distaste for idolatry, about his extraordinarily warm feelings toward Jacob, and about his words of blessing for him. In the expanded Jacob stories one reads about wars fought by him and his sons against the surrounding peoples – and much more. Jubilees assigns to Levi a priestly office, though in the Bible only his descendants several generations removed assume priestly functions.

The passages which are translated below have been selected to illustrate these special emphases in the book. It seemed pointless to reproduce sections which do little more than repeat biblical stories, but each translated passage is preceded by an explanation of its context in the biblical framework and in Jubilees.

Date

One cannot specify precisely when Jubilees was written, but several lines of evidence converge on a time between c. 160 and 150 BC. The oldest surviving manuscript of the book (one of the unpublished ones from Qumran) was copied in approximately 100 BC. As only fragments of it remain, one cannot be certain that it contained the entire book; yet there is no reason to believe that the full book was not finished by that time. The book exhibits many striking affinities with the Qumran literature in important areas (e.g. the cultic calendar), but nothing in the text offers so much as a hint that the writer knew about the Qumran community or the role of the Teacher of Righteousness in founding it. Moreover, one of the most important of the scrolls cites Jubilees as an authority (CD XVI. 3–4). The combination of these data suggests that Jubilees was written before the community was established at Qumran in c. 150 BC. Also, some allusions in the book to other literature offer some help in dating it. In his expanded section about Enoch and elsewhere the writer reveals knowledge of the Book of Dreams (1En 83–90) which must have been written very close to 164 BC. In addition, there may be – and this is highly uncertain – some reflections of events in Maccabaean wars in the author's descriptions of Jacob's battles with his enemies (e.g. 38:1–14). All of these pieces of evidence favour a date after the Maccabaean revolt (167–165/64 BC) and before 150. Some scholars have maintained that Jubilees bears the scars of editorial revision, but no compelling case has been offered in support of this position. The book appears rather to be a unified composition which came from the pen of a priestly author who wrote during the period immediately after the persecutions of Antiochus IV Epiphanes and the subsequent Maccabaean revolt and independence movement. It emanates from a time of readjustment in Judaism and articulates an urgent call for strict obedience to the ancient religion of the Patriarchs and Moses.

Bibliography

The most important studies of Jubilees were written by R. H. Charles. He edited the Ethiopic text and all other available material in *Maṣḥafa Kufālē or the Ethiopic Version of the Hebrew Book of Jubilees* (Anecdota oxoniensia) Oxford, 1895. He translated the book and added rather extensive explanatory notes in *The Book of Jubilees or the Little Genesis*, London, 1902. His translation was re-published virtually without change but with fewer notes in his *The Apocrypha and Pseudepigrapha of the Old Testament*, vol. II, pp. 1–80. A new translation into German is that by K. Berger, 'Das Buch der Jubiläen' in JSHRZ II/3, pp. 271–575.

Some recent monographs on the Book of Jubilees are:

M. Testuz, *Les idées religieuses du Livre des Jubilés*, Geneva/Paris, 1960.

G. L. Davenport, *The Eschatology of the Book of Jubilees* (Studia Post-Biblica 20), Leiden, 1971.

J. C. VanderKam, *Textual and Historical Studies in the Book of Jubilees* (Harvard Semitic Monographs 14), Missoula, 1977.

I am now preparing a new critical edition (using all textual evidence) and an English translation of Jubilees for the SBL Texts and Translations Series.

The following translations are based primarily upon the Ethiopic ✓ manuscripts, but the fragmentary Hebrew, Greek, Syriac and Latin evidence has been consulted wherever it was available. Two excellent Ethiopic manuscripts were used as base texts: British Museum Orient. 485 – a splendid sixteenth-century manuscript which Charles used as the basis for his 1895 edition; and Ṭānāsee 9 (= Kebrān 9) – a fifteenth-century manuscript which is used with the generous permission of Professor E. Hammerschmidt of the University of Hamburg, who made a copy of it available to the writer.

After a prologue which mentions some of the calendrical contents of the book and its setting, the body of the text begins with Moses' ascent of Sinai (see Exod. 24:12, 15–18).

MOSES IS COMMISSIONED TO WRITE

1:1 In the first year of the Israelites' exodus from Egypt [= 2,410], the third month, the sixteenth of that month, the Lord said to Moses: 'Come up to me on the mountain, and I will give you two stone tablets of the Law and of the commandment which I have written so that you may teach them.' (So) Moses went up onto the

2 mountain of the Lord. Then the Lord's glory settled on Mt Sinai,

3 and a cloud overshadowed it for six days. He summoned Moses into the cloud on the seventh day, (where) he saw the Lord's glory

4 as a fire that was burning on the mountaintop. Moses was on the mountain for 40 days and 40 nights. The Lord told him what had happened and also related to him what would occur – the divisions of all times both for the Law and for the testimony. He said to him:

5 'Pay attention to the entire account which I will relate to you on this mountain and write (it) in a book so that their generations may see that I have not abandoned them because of all the evil which they have done in violating the covenant which I am arranging today on Mt Sinai between myself and you for their generations.

6 Thus, when all of these things happen to them, they will know that I have been more faithful than they in all their judgements and in all their deeds. Then they will know that I have indeed been with them.'

1. *third month, the sixteenth of that month*: cp. Exod. 19:1: 'In the third month after Israel had left Egypt, they came to the wilderness of Sinai.' Jubilees adds the specific date in the month; the sixteenth of the third month is the day after the festival of weeks in this calendar.

4–6. revelation to Moses of the past and future is distinguished from the two tablets which God himself had written.

5. *violating*: a slight emendation yields this meaning.

In the remainder of the first chapter the Lord predicts that Israel will stray from the covenant (8–12), suffer captivity (13–14), and only then will repent and return from exile to enjoy rich divine blessings (15–18, 22–25). An angel of the presence is told to dictate to Moses a sacred history which extends from creation to renewal of creation in the last times (26–9). The historical survey begins with the creation story of Gen. 1:1–2:3 (Jub 2:1–17), though a few modifications are made (e.g. creation of the angels on the first day (2:2)). To his account of the Lord's rest on the seventh day the writer appended a special exhortation about the sanctity of the sabbath.

THE SABBATH AND ISRAEL

2:18 He told us – all the angels of the presence and all the angels of holiness (these two important kinds) – to keep the sabbath day

19 with him in heaven and on earth. He said to us: 'I am now separating for myself a nation from my nations, and they, too, will keep the sabbath. I will sanctify the nation for myself and bless it, as I sanctified the sabbath day, and will sanctify it for myself. In

20 this way I will bless it. Then they will be my people and I will be their God. Among all whom I have seen I have chosen the descendants of Jacob. I have recorded them as my first-born son and have sanctified them as mine for ever and ever. I will tell them about the sabbath days so that they may keep sabbath on them from

21 every kind of work.' He made a sign like this on it by which they, too, would keep sabbath with us on the seventh day by eating, drinking and blessing the one who had created everything, as he had blessed and sanctified them as a nation preferred above all the

22 nations, that they should keep sabbath together with us. He made their wishes rise as a pleasant fragrance which is always acceptable

23   in his presence. There have been twenty-two leaders of mankind
     from Adam to him, and twenty-two kinds of works were made
     until the seventh day. The latter are blessed and holy and the
     former, too, are blessed and holy. The one group as well as the
24   other are meant for holiness and for blessing. It was granted to
     these people always to be the blessed and holy ones of the testimony
     and of the first Law just as sanctification and blessing (were pro-
25   nounced) on the seventh day. He created the heavens and the
     earth and every created thing in six days. Then the Lord gave
     a holy festival day to all his works. For this reason he gave com-
     mand regarding it that anyone who should do any work on it was
     to die and also the one who defiled it was surely to die.

   18. *angels of the presence*... *angels of holiness*: in Jubilees these are the
two highest-ranking categories of angels (2:2) who not only keep
sabbath but were also created circumcised (15:27). One of the angels of
the presence (a biblical title; see Isa. 63:9, though NEB reads only
'angel') reveals the contents of Jubilees to Moses (1:27, 29; 2:1, etc.).
For the idea that an angel or angels revealed the Law, see also Acts 7:38;
Gal. 3:19; and perhaps Heb. 2:2.
   19–21. The writer sees parallels between Israel and the sabbath.
The Lord blessed and sanctified both, and keeping sabbath is a means
by which Israel's holiness is marked and through which it finds
expression.
   23. *to him*: all Ethiopic manuscripts except a few late ones are corrupt
here; biblical genealogies, which are followed by Jubilees, make Jacob
the Patriarch of the twenty-second generation. This is also confirmed
by a Greek citation. *twenty-two kinds of works*: in his version of
the creation story the author lists twenty-two different creations of
God.

After more commands regarding the sabbath conclude the second
chapter, chapter 3 relates the story of Adam and Eve, including their
disobedience and expulsion from Eden. Jub 4 continues the biblical
narrative by reproducing the Cain/Abel account (Gen. 4:1–16) and the
genealogy of Gen. 5. The biblical list is thoroughly schematic for most
of the ten men who appear in it, but an expanded section is devoted to
the seventh Patriarch Enoch (Gen. 5:21–4). At this point Jubilees
reflects a far more extensive cycle of Enochic traditions.

ENOCH

4:15   In the second week of the tenth jubilee-period [449–55] Malaleel
took as his wife Dinah, the daughter of Barakeel, the daughter of
his father's brother. She bore him a son in the third week, in the
sixth year [461], and he named him Jared because in his time the
angels of the Lord, who are named the watchers, descended to
✓   earth to teach mankind and to do what is just and right on the
16   earth. In the eleventh jubilee-period Jared took a wife – her name
was Barakah, the daughter of Rasneyal, the daughter of his father's
brother – in the fourth week of this jubilee-period [512–18]. She bore
him a son in the fifth week, in the fourth year of the jubilee-period
[522], and he then named him Enoch. He was the first among man-
17   kind who have been born on the earth to learn the art of writing,
instruction, and wisdom. He wrote in a book the signs of the sky
in accordance with the order of their months so that mankind could
understand the seasons of the years according to the order of each
18   one of their months. He was the first to write a testimony, and he
testified to mankind in the history of the earth. He told the weeks
of the jubilee-periods and made known the days of the years; he
arranged the months and told the sabbaths of the years as we had
19   informed him. What has happened and what will be he saw in a
vision as he slept – how things will turn out for mankind in their
history until the judgement day. He saw everything, understood,
and wrote for himself a testimony and plaed it on the earth con-
20   cerning all mankind and for their history. In the twelfth jubilee-
period, in its seventh week [582–8], he took a wife for himself, and
her name was Edni, the daughter of Daniel, the daughter of his
father's brother. In the sixth year of this week [587] she bore him a
21   son, and he named him Methuselah. He was, moreover, with the
angels of God for six jubilee-periods of years [294 years]. They
showed him everything that was on the earth and that was in the
heavens – the dominion of the sun – and he wrote down every-
22   thing. He testified to the watchers who had sinned with women
because these had begun to get married so that they were becoming

defiled with earthly women. Enoch testified against all of them.
23 He was taken from the company of mankind, and we led him into
the Garden of Eden for greatness and for honour. There he is now
writing down the judgement and condemnation of the world and
24 all the wickedness of mankind. Because of him no flood waters
came upon the land of Eden, for he was placed there as a sign and
to testify against all people so that he recounts all the deeds of history
25 until the judgement day. He burned the pleasing evening incense of
26 the sanctuary before the Lord on the mountain of the south. For
there are four places on earth which belong to the Lord: the Garden
of Eden, the eastern mountain, this mountain on which you [i.e.
Moses] are today – Mt Sinai – and Mt Zion. It will be made holy
in the new creation for the sanctification of the earth. Because of
this the earth will be sanctified from all its uncleanness and from
sin into the history of eternity.

15. *Dinah*: Jubilees supplies names for the wives of all the Patriarchs
while Genesis usually does not mention them. *brother*: the Ethiopic
manuscripts read *sister*, but Syriac and Greek evidence shows that
brother is preferred here and in verses 16 and 20. *Jared*: his name, spelled
yered in Hebrew, is related to the Hebrew verb *yrd* which means *to
descend*. *angels*: these are the 'sons of the gods' of Gen. 6:2, 4. Their
descent to earth and crimes are detailed in Jub 5:1–11.
17. *book*: this is probably a reference to the Astronomical Book of
Enoch (1En 72–82).
19. *What has happened and what will be...wrote for himself a testimony*:
these words may point either to the Enochic Book of Dreams (1En
83–90) or to the Apocalypse of Weeks (1En 93:1–10; 91:12–17).
21. *with the angels of God for six jubilee-periods*: cp. Gen. 5:22:
'Enoch walked with God for three hundred years.' The author understood the plural term for God (*'ĕlōhīm*) as *angels*.
22. Parts of the Book of Watchers (1En 1–36) are summarized
here.
23. *was taken*: cp. Gen. 5:24: 'Enoch was seen no more, because God
had taken him away.'
24. *no flood waters came*: all but a few Ethiopic manuscripts read (*he*)
brought the flood waters, but that reading makes no sense in the context.
The divergence in readings arose from a very easy confusion in Ethiopic
(*'i-maṣ'a* was misread as *'amṣe'a*).

25. *south*: the best Ethiopic reading is *noon*, but a Syriac citation offers the preferable reading *south*.

At the end of his version of the Gen. 5 genealogy, the writer adds a note about the timing of Adam's death. In it he attempts to solve the problem which was raised by Adam's long life after his sin, although the divine threat of Gen. 2:17 was that he would die on the day of his disobedience.

ADAM'S DEATH

4:29 At the end of the nineteenth jubilee-period, in the seventh week in the sixth year of it [930], Adam died. All his children buried him in the land where he had been created. He was the first to be
30 buried in the earth. He lacked 70 years from 1,000 years because 1,000 years are one day in the testimony of heaven. For this reason it was written regarding the tree of knowledge: 'On the day you eat from it you will die.' Therefore he did not complete the years of this day but died during it.

30. *1,000 years are one day*: see Ps. 90:4 and cp. 2 Pet. 3:8. *on the day*: a quotation from Gen. 2:17.

Both Genesis and Jubilees follow with a section (much shorter in Genesis) about the 'sons of the gods' who mated with women and then the flood. In the biblical story (Gen. 6:5–9:17) a few dates appear, but the writer of Jubilees adds more of them and in this way makes the flood story an appropriate peg on which to hang important features of his cultic calendar. In 6:15–22 he dates the divine covenant with Noah to the third month (according to Gen. 8:14 Noah emerged from the ark on the twenty-seventh of the second month; in Jub 6:1 he leaves on the first of the third month) and maintains that the festival of weeks serves as the annual renewal of that pact. Later (6:23–38) he presents the 364-day calendar as if it were structured by events which happened during the flood and warns against failure to employ this revealed system.

THE COVENANT WITH NOAH AND THE FESTIVAL OF WEEKS

6:15 He gave Noah and his children a sign that there would not again
16 be a flood on the earth. He placed a rainbow in the clouds as a sign

of the eternal covenant that flood waters would not again be on

17 the earth to destroy (it) as long as the earth remains. For this reason it has been ordained and written on the heavenly tablets that they should celebrate the festival of weeks during this month – one time each year – to renew the covenant annually.

18 This entire festival was celebrated in heaven from the time of creation until Noah's day – for twenty-six jubilee-periods and five weeks of years [1,309 years]. Noah and his children kept it for seven jubilee-periods and one week of years [350 years] until Noah's death. His children corrupted (it) until Abraham's time

19 and would eat blood. Abraham alone kept it; then his sons Isaac and Jacob kept it until your [Moses'] time. In your day the Israelites had forgotten (it) until I renewed (it) for them at this mountain.

20 Now you command the Israelites to keep this festival throughout their history as a commandment for them that they celebrate the

21 festival one day in the year during this month. For it is (both) a festival of weeks and a festival of first fruits. This festival is twofold and of two kinds, as it is written and inscribed regarding observing

22 it. For I have written in the book of the first Law, in which I wrote for you, that you should celebrate it at each of its proper times one day in the year. I told you about its sacrifices as well so that the Israelites would continually remember to celebrate it during their history – one day each year during this month.

THE REVEALED CALENDAR

23 On the first of the first, the first of the fourth, the first of the seventh, and the first of the tenth month are the memorial days and the days of the seasons. They have been written down at the four divisions of the year and are ordained as an eternal testimony.

24 Noah ordained them for himself as festivals throughout the history

25 of eternity because he held commemorations on them. On the first of the first month he was told to make an ark, and on it, when

26 the earth had become dry, he opened (the ark) and saw the earth. On the first of the fourth month the mouths of the depths of the abyss

below were shut. On the first of the seventh month all the mouths
of the depths of the earth were opened, and the waters began to
27   descend to the depths below. On the first of the tenth month, when
28   the tops of the mountains became visible, Noah rejoiced. Therefore
he ordained them as memorial festivals for himself for ever, and so
29   they are ordained. They were placed on the heavenly tablets:
thirteen weeks for each of them [i.e. the seasons]; (the day which
marks the change) from one to the other is their memorial day:
from the first to the second, from the second to the third, and from
the third to the fourth.
30   All of the days which have been commanded are fifty-two weeks
31   of days; then the entire year is completed. This is how it has been
inscribed and ordained on the heavenly tablets, and there is to be
no transgressing for a single year or year by year.
32   Now you command the Israelites to keep the years by number –
364 days – which constitute a complete year and do not disturb its
seasons from their days or from their festivals, for everything will
turn out in accord with their testimony. Then they will neither
33   leave out a day nor disturb a festival. If they transgress and do not
constitute them [i.e. the years] as they have been ordered, then
all of them will disturb their seasons and even the years will move
one away from the other. They will disturb the seasons as well,
the years will move, and their order will be transgressed. All of the
34   Israelites will forget and not find the way of the years. They will
forget the first of the month, season and sabbath, and will err in all
35   the arrangements of the years. For I myself know and inform you
from now on – not from myself because this is how the book is
written in front of me – the divisions of days have been ordained
on the heavenly tablets so that they may not forget the festivals
of the covenant and pursue, through the festivals of the nations,
36   their errors and their ignorance. There will be people who make
very careful observations of the moon although it disturbs the
37   seasons and is ten days too early from year to year. For this reason
years will come for them when they disturb (them) and make a
day of testimony a worthless one and an impure day a festival.

Everyone will mix them up – holy days as impure ones and impure ✓
ones as holy days. For they will err with respect to the months,
38 sabbaths, festivals and jubilee-period. Therefore I command you
and testify to you that you may testify to them, for after your death
your children will disturb (these arrangements) so that they will
not make the year 364 days only. For this reason they will err with
regard to the firsts of the months, the seasons, the sabbaths and the
festivals. They will eat all sorts of blood and every kind of meat.

17. *festival of weeks*: a pilgrimage festival (later called Pentecost)
which is first mentioned in Exod. 23:16 (for the name see Exod. 34:22).
In Jubilees it is dated to the fifteenth day of the third month and
becomes the central covenantal festival. Later the covenant with
Abraham is dated to this holiday (Jub 15:1–10). The revelation to
Moses also came in the third month.

18. [*1,309*]: in the Jubilees chronology the flood lasted from the
second month of 1308 to the second month of 1309; this period coin-
cided with parts of Noah's six-hundredth and six-hundred-and-first
years. After the deluge he lived 350 years (Gen. 7:11; 8:14; 9:28–29).

21. *festival of weeks. . .festival of first fruits*: both are biblical names for
the festival (see, for example, Exod. 23:16; 34:22).

23. *first of the first* (*month*): the term translated here (*šarqa*) means
new moon, but that can hardly be its significance in Jubilees in which the
moon is irrelevant to calendrical calculations.

33. This is probably a reference to the practice of intercalating months
at intervals into the lunar calendar to bring it into harmony with the
solar year.

36. *ten days too early*: 12 lunar months include 354 days, 10 days
fewer than the 364-day year of Jubilees.

Jubilees devotes large parts of the following chapters to detailed
descriptions of the division of the earth among Noah's descendants.
All boundaries were fixed by oaths. One of the writer's main emphases
in all of this geographical material is to underscore the guilt of Canaan,
Noah's grandson, who is cursed in Gen. 9:25, because he, despite his ✓
oath and against the urgent advice of his relatives, took part of Shem's
territory. This is a rather blatant attempt to justify the later Israelite
conquest of Canaan.

During Noah's lifetime his sons and grandsons brought a complaint
to him that demons were misleading and harming them. The demons

were descendants of the angelic watchers (who had been imprisoned); they were, in effect, the medium for the continuing influence of their evil ancestors. Noah responded to their complaint with a prayer.

NOAH AND THE SPIRITS

10:4 'Now, you bless me and my children so that we may increase,

5 multiply, and fill the earth. You know how your watchers, the fathers of these spirits, acted in my time. So lock up these spirits, too, who have remained alive and take them captive to the place of judgement. Do not let them bring about destruction among the children of your servant, my God, for they are savage and

6 were created for the purpose of destroying. Do not let them rule over the spirits of the living, for you alone know their punishment. Let then have no power over the children of the righteous from now and for ever.'

7, 8 So our God told us to bind all (of them). Then Mastema, the leader of the spirits, came and said: 'Lord, creator, leave some of them in my presence and let them listen to me and do all that I tell them because if some of them are not left for me, it will prove impossible to exercise the authority of my will among mankind. For their purposes are to destroy and mislead before my punish-

9 ment, since mankind's wickedness is very great.' He [i.e. God] said that one-tenth of them should be left in his presence and that he would make nine parts go down to the place of judgement.

10 He told one of us to teach Noah all their medicines because he knew that they would not behave fairly or fight according to the

11 rules. We did as he commanded: we bound all the savage, evil ones in the place of judgement and left one-tenth of them to exercise

12 authority on the earth in the presence of Satan. We told Noah all the medicines for their diseases along with their seductions so that

13 he could effect cures by using the trees of the earth. Noah wrote down in a book everything as we had instructed him with every kind of medicine. So the spirits of the evil ones were prevented

14 from persecuting Noah's children. He gave all of the books that he had written to Shem, his oldest son, because he loved him much more than all his children.

5. *your watchers*: the view that originally these angels were good
finds expression here and in 4:15.

8. *Mastema, the leader of the spirits*: the chief of the angelic forces of
evil is usually called the prince of Mastema, but this verse shows that
Mastema alone can be used to designate him. The name is a Hebrew
noun (*masṭēmāh*) which means *enmity, hostility*. It may be related to the
Hebrew root from which the title *Satan* is derived.

9. *one-tenth*: in this way the writer explains the ongoing influence of
evil on the earth while simultaneously maintaining that God is ultimately in control.

14. *he loved him much more*: see Noah's blessing on Shem (Gen.
9:26–7). Abraham, Isaac, Jacob and all Israel were descendants of Shem.

Jubilees continues with a notice about Noah's death, the story of Babel,
more material about the division of the earth, a hearty curse on the
presumptuous Canaan, and an indication that evil was increasing among
Noah's descendants. Abram is introduced at 11:15 and is the leading
character until chapter 23. Jubilees supplies a number of stories about
his piety already as a youth in Ur of the Chaldees and also mentions
his skill as inventor of a plough that buried seeds in the soil so that
birds could not eat them. His biblical itinerary from Ur to Haran to
Canaan is reproduced, as are his journey to Egypt, the stories about Lot,
and Abram's war against the kings. Chapters 14 and 15 present the
covenants of Gen. 15 and 17; both are dated to the festival of weeks
(Jub 14:10, 20; 15:1). Circumcision was the sign of the latter agreement,
and mention of it allows the writer to elaborate on the extreme
importance of the rite.

CIRCUMCISION

15:23   Abraham did as the Lord had told him. He took his son Ishmael
and all who had been born in his house as well as those he had
purchased – all males in his house – and circumcised the flesh of

24   their foreskins. On this (same) day that Abraham was circumcised,
the men of his household, and all those whom he had purchased

25   from foreigners were circumcised with him. This law is (valid) for
all of history for ever. There is no 'cutting off' of (its) days and no
omitting a single day from the eight for the eternal ordinance is

26   ordained and written on the heavenly tablets. Anyone who is born,
the flesh of whose organ has not been circumcised on the eighth

day, does not belong to the people of the covenant which the Lord concluded for Abraham but belongs to the people (who are meant for) destruction. There is thus no sign on him that he should belong to the Lord; rather he is meant for destruction and for perishing from the earth because he has broken the covenant of the Lord

27 our God. For such was the nature of all the angels of the presence and all the angels of holiness from the time of their creation. In front of the angels of the presence and the angels of holiness he sanctified Israel to be with him and with his holy angels.

28   Now you command the Israelites to keep the sign of this covenant throughout their history as an eternal ordinance. Then

29 they will not be eradicated from the earth. For the commandment has been ordained through a covenant that they should keep it

30 for ever upon all the Israelites. For the Lord did not bring Ishmael, his children, his brothers, or Esau to himself nor did he choose them (just) because they were Abraham's children because he knew

31 them. But Israel he chose to be his people. He sanctified and gathered (them) out of all mankind because there are many peoples and many nations and all belong to him. He gave spirits authority

32 over all to make them stray from following him. But over Israel he gave authority to no angel or spirit; rather, he alone is their ruler. He will guard them and seek their welfare from his angels and his spirits and from all whom he has placed in command so that he may guard and bless them and that they may be his and he

33 theirs from now and for ever. I am telling you now that the Israelites will prove untrue to this ordinance and will not circumcise their sons in accord with this entire law. For in circumcising their children they will omit some of the flesh of their circumcision. All the sons of Belial will leave their sons un-

34 circumcised as they were born. There will be great anger from the Lord against the Israelites because they abandoned his covenant and departed from his command. They have provoked and blasphemed in that they have not performed the ordinance of this sign because they have made themselves like the nations so that they will be removed and eradicated from the earth. They

will have, therefore, no forgiveness or pardon so that he should forgive them and they be pardoned from all the sins of the violation of this eternal (ordinance).

25. *'cutting off' of (its) days*: literally 'circumcision of days' (it is not found in the Latin text). The above translation assumes a play on the word *circumcision* (cp. Paul's pun in Gal. 5:12). An alternate translation is *temporary (law of?) circumcision*.

26. *on the eighth day*: the Ethiopic manuscripts read *until the eighth day*, but 15:12, 14 require that a boy should be circumcised *on* not *by* the eighth day (as does Gen. 17:14 in the Samaritan Pentateuch and in the Septuagint). The faulty Ethiopic text is probably the result of a simple Hebrew confusion.

31–2. These verses are based on Deut. 32:8–9 in the wording known from the Septuagint.

32. *and from all whom he has placed in command*: the best Ethiopic manuscripts have *and from all and from all his commands*. The translation follows an emendation which R. H. Charles suggested, but it remains conjectural.

33. *some of the flesh*: though other translators (e.g. Charles) treated this line as if it referred to omitting circumcision altogether, that makes little sense after the phrase *in circumcising their children*. The literal reading is *from the flesh*, and, as the preposition *from* is often used in Hebrew and Ethiopic in the sense *some of*, the above translation seems preferable.

In chapter 16 the author narrates another promise of a son to Abraham, the tale of Lot and Sodom, the birth of Isaac, and the first festival of tabernacles. He begins chapter 17 with the expulsion of Hagar and Ishmael, but in verses 15–18 he explains the Lord's bizarre command that Abraham should sacrifice his son. His explanation is reminiscent of Job 1: the order to sacrifice Isaac was a test, demanded by an evil angel, of Abraham's faithfulness.

ABRAHAM AND HIS TRIALS

17:15   ...there was a report in heaven regarding Abraham that he
         was faithful in everything he told him and that the Lord loved
   16   him. In every adversity he was faithful. The prince of Mastema
         came and said in God's presence: 'Abraham loves his son Isaac and
         is more pleased with him than with anyone else. Tell him to offer

him as a sacrifice on an altar. Then you will see whether he carries out this order and will know whether he is faithful in everything in which you test him.' The Lord knew that Abraham was faithful
17 in every adversity which he had ordered for him because he had tested him in (the case of) his country and through famine. He had tested him through the wealth of the kings; he had tested him moreover through his wife when she was taken by force, and through circumcision; and he had tested him through Ishmael and
18 Hagar his slave-girl when he had sent them away. In everything in which he had tested him he was found faithful. He did not become impatient nor did he hesitate to act, for he was faithful and one who loved the Lord.

17. Seven trials are listed (counting Hagar and Ishmael as two), all of which the author has drawn from Genesis. Jub 19:8 mentions ten trials which Abraham endured. The additional three include the 'sacrifice' of Isaac, which is described in chapter 18, and the death of Sarah, as the context in chapter 19 indicates (verses 3, 8). The remaining test may have been the second occasion on which Sarah was taken (Gen. 20), but Jubilees omits that story.

Chapter 18 tells of Abraham's aborted sacrifice of Isaac. The journey to and from Mt Zion, where the author locates the altar, and their stay there took seven days. This last point serves to explain the origin of the seven-day festival of unleavened bread. The writer continues in chapter 19 with the death of Sarah, the purchase of Machpelah, Isaac's marriage, and Abraham's third marriage. At this point he introduces Jacob, who is the principal character in the book, and Esau who suffers terribly at the author's hands. The following passage reveals his awareness that in biblical chronology Abraham lived for fifteen years after the births of the twins and that therefore Abraham must have known them. He brings Abraham and Jacob into close contact and adds his authority to Rebecca's preference for her younger son.

ABRAHAM AND JACOB

19:14 As the youngsters grew up, Jacob learned how to write but Esau did not learn how because he was a rustic man and a hunter.
15 He learned about warfare, and everything he did was harsh. Now

16   Abraham loved Jacob but Isaac (loved) Esau. When Abraham saw
     the things Esau did, he knew that through Jacob he would have
     a name and posterity. So he summoned Rebecca and gave her
     orders about Jacob, for he saw that she too loved Jacob much more
17   than Esau. He said to her: 'My daughter, take care of my son
     Jacob because he will take my place on the earth and (will prove to
     be) a blessing among mankind and a cause for boasting for all the
     descendants of Shem. For I know that the Lord will choose him as
18   his own peculiar people out of all who (live) on the face of the
19   earth. Now my son Isaac loves Esau more than Jacob, but I see that
20   you are one who loves Jacob rightly. Further increase your kind-
     ness to him and may your eyes look upon him with love, for he
     will prove a blessing for us upon the earth from now and through-
21   out all the history of eternity. May your hands be strong and your
     heart rejoice in your son Jacob because I love him much more than
     all my children, for he will be blessed for ever and his descendants
22   will fill the entire earth. If one is able to count the sands of the
23   earth, then his descendants too will be numbered. All the blessings
     with which the Lord has blessed me and my descendants are to
24   belong to Jacob and his descendants for all time. Through his
     descendants may my name and the name of my fathers Shem,
25   Noah, Enoch, Malaleel, Enos, Seth and Adam be blessed. They are
     to lay the foundations of heaven, to make the earth firm, and to
     renew the luminaries which are above the firmament.'

26   Then he summoned Jacob before his mother Rebecca, kissed
27   him, blessed him, and said: 'My dear son Jacob whom I love, may
     God bless you from above the firmament. May he give you all the
     blessings with which he blessed Adam, Enoch, Noah and Shem,
     as well as everything he has promised me. Everything that he said
     he would give me may he attach to you and your descendants
28   for ever, like the days of heaven above the earth. May the spirits
     of Mastema not rule over you and your descendants to remove
     you from following the Lord who is your God from now and
29   for evermore. May the Lord God be your father and you his
     first-born son and people for all time. Go in peace, my son.'

15. *Abraham loved Jacob*: this verse is a revision of Gen. 25:28 with the major alteration being that Abraham replaces Rebecca.

18. *peculiar*: both the Ethiopic and Latin versions appear to be corrupt at this point. A Greek citation preserves the correct reading and also allows one to uncover the source of the corrupt readings.

24. For these names see Gen. 5.

25. In Jubilees phrases such as these have an eschatological meaning (see, for example, 1:29).

Chapters 20–3 deal with the last days of Abraham. He gave gifts to all of his children but especially favoured Isaac (Jub 20). To his favourite son he gave final instructions which dealt at some length with sacrificial topics (Jub 21). Then, in harmony with his emphasis on Abraham's affection for Jacob the writer also has Abraham deliver a final speech to him (Jub 22). Chapter 23 begins with Abraham's death (only Jacob was with him at the end) at 175 years. Mention of his age introduces a section which considers the ages of men in different epochs. Though Abraham was the paradigm of virtue he lived only 175 years because his was an evil time. These thoughts launch the author into the most extended eschatological section in Jubilees. In 23:11–25 he describes the evil which will prevail from the present until the judgement, though in verse 16 there is an anticipatory reference to the children's criticizing of their elders. A change comes in verse 26 in which the pivotal event is that the 'children' will begin to study the Law and seek the commandments; 23:27–31 picture the gradual arrival of a time of bliss. Finally people's ages will match those of the Patriarchs who lived before the flood. It should be noted that there is no mention – here or elsewhere in Jubilees – of a Messiah.

EVIL UNTIL THE JUDGEMENT

23:11   All of the generations that will arise from now until the day of the great judgement will age quickly before they complete two jubilee-periods [= 98 years]. Their knowledge will abandon them because of their old age, and all their knowledge will depart.

12   At that time, if a man lives for one and one-half jubilee-periods of years [= 73½ years], they will say of him: 'He has lived for a long time, but most of his days (consisted of) pain, labour, and

13   trouble; there was no peace.' For there is wound upon wound, trouble upon trouble, affliction upon affliction, bad news upon

bad news, sickness upon sickness – and all evil punishments such as these, one after the other: sickness, disaster, snow, hail, hoar-frost, fever, cold, convulsions, famine, death, sword, exile, and

14 every trouble and pain. All of these will befall the evil generation which commits sins on the earth through fornicating pollution, impurity and their abominable actions.

15 Then they will say: 'The lifetimes of the ancients were long – as much as 1,000 years – and good, but now our lives – if one lives a long time – (last) 70 years, and, if one is strong, 80 years. But all are evil, and there is no peace during the time of this wicked generation.'

16 But during that generation the children will find fault with their fathers and elders because of sins, injustice, their speech, the great evils which they commit, and their abandoning the covenant which the Lord had concluded between them and himself so that they would keep (it) and perform all his commands, ordinances and

17 all his laws. There was to be no deviating to the left or right. For all of them have acted wickedly, every mouth utters sin(ful words) and all their deeds are pollutions and abominations. All their ways

18 are impurity, pollution and corruption. Indeed the earth will be destroyed because of all their actions. There will be no produce from the vine nor oil because what they do is (a product of) com-plete disobedience. All of them will be destroyed together – wild animals, cattle, birds and all the fish of the sea – because of mankind.

19 They will quarrel with one another – the young with the old and the old with the young; poor with rich, the lowly with the great, the needy with the ruler – regarding the Law and the covenant, since they have forgotten the commandments, the covenant, the festivals, the months, the sabbaths, the jubilee-periods, and all

20 judgements. They will rise with swords and warfare to direct them into the way, but they will not return until much blood has been poured out on the earth – the one group against the other. Those who escape to safety will not turn from their wickedness into the right way because all of them elevate themselves for cheating and through wealth so that each one takes everything that

belongs to another. They will mention the great name but not
truly or properly. They will defile the holy of holies with the corrupt impurity of their abominations. There will be a great punish-
22   ment from the Lord on the actions of that generation. He will
deliver them to the sword and judgement, to captivity, plundering
23   and devouring. He will arouse against them the gentile sinners who
will show them neither pity nor mercy and who show partiality
to no one, either to the old or the young or to anyone at all. For
they are wicked and powerful (enough) to be more wicked than all
peoples. They will produce chaos in Israel and sin against Jacob.
Much blood will be poured out on the earth, but there will be no
one to gather up (corpses) and no one to bury (them).
24   At that time they will cry out, call, and pray to be rescued from
the power of the gentile sinners, but there will be no one who will
25   rescue. The heads of the children will be white with gray hair. An
infant three weeks old will look as aged as one who is a hundred
years old. Their condition will be destroyed by troubles and
calamities.

RENEWED STUDY OF THE LAW AND
ESCHATOLOGICAL JOY

23:26 In those days the children will begin to study the laws, to seek
27   the commandments, and to return to the right way. (Their) days
will begin to multiply and increase – mankind as well – generation
by generation, day by day, until their lives approach 1,000 years
28   and to more years than there had been days previously. There will
be no one who is old nor anyone who has filled up the number of
29   (his) days for all of them will be infants and children. All of their
days they will complete in peace and joy. They will live, and there
will be no satan nor any evil one who destroys, because all of their
days will be days of blessing and healing. Then the Lord will heal
30   his servants. They will rise and see great peace; he will expel his
enemies. The righteous will see, give thanks, and rejoice en-
thusiastically for ever and ever. They will see all their punishments

31 and curses on their enemies. Their bones will rest in the earth, but their spirits will be very happy. They will know that the Lord is the one who executes judgement and who shows kindness to hundreds and thousands and to all who love him.

32   You, Moses, write down all these words because this is how it is written. They are placed in the testimony of the heavenly tablets for the history of eternity.

12. Cp. Ps. 90:10.

15. Cp. Ps. 90:10.

16. *the children*: this designation reminds one of 1En 90:6–7 in which, in a similar context, a group is presented under the youthful image of lambs among sheep. The people in question are probably the pious ones (*ḥasīdīm*) who are first mentioned in the first half of the second century BC and from whose circles the Qumran community was later to develop. The following verses are best interpreted against the backdrop of events before and during the persecutions of Jews by Antiochus IV Epiphanes and his forces.

27. *than there had been days previously*: the best Ethiopic reading – *and to many years from many days* – is not very clear, but the translation offered appears to give the meaning intended.

28. See Isa. 65:20 for the notion that people will live for a longer time in the new age.

30. *They will rise*: as the context (see verse 31: *Their bones will rest in the earth*) indicates, no resurrection is meant here. Military action may be intended.

31. An immortality of sorts is clearly envisaged but not a physical one.

Chapter 24 contains the Isaac stories of Gen. 26 (to which is added a robust curse on the Philistines in verses 28–32) as well as the episode of Esau's selling his rights of the first-born to Jacob. One reads more of the author's efforts to denigrate Esau for the greater glory of Jacob (Jacob stoutly refused to marry a Canaanite woman though Esau had urged him to do so); there one also finds Rebecca's blessing on Jacob. Chapter 26 relates the story of Isaac's blundering attempt to bless Esau. 26:13–19 provide another example of the writer's willingness to revise a biblical passage to spare one of his heroes from a sin – in this case Jacob's lie about his identity.

JACOB DECEIVES ISAAC

26:13   When 'Jacob' had come in to where his father was, he said:
       'I am your son. I have done as you told me. Come on, sit down
14   and eat from my catch, father, so that you can bless me.' But
      Isaac said to his son: 'How did it happen that you found (it) so
15   quickly, my son?' Jacob replied: 'It was your God who directed
16   (it) in front of me.' Isaac said to him: 'Come here so that I can
      touch you, my son, (to check) whether you are my son Esau or
17   not.' When Jacob had approached his father Isaac, he touched him
18   and said: 'The voice is the voice of Jacob, but the hands are the
      hands of Esau.' He did not recognize him because there had been
      a change from heaven to remove his ability to perceive. Isaac did
      not comprehend because his hands were hairy like Esau's hands so
19   that he could bless him. He said: 'Are you my son Esau?' He
      replied: 'I am your son.' He said: 'Bring (the food) to me, my
      son, and let me eat from your catch, my son, so that I may bless
      you.'

   13. *I am your son*: Gen. 27:19: 'I am Esau, your elder son.'
   19. *I am your son*: Gen. 27:24: 'He said, "Are you really my son
Esau?", and he answered, "Yes."'

Chapters 27–8 tell of Jacob's flight to Mesopotamia, including his
dream at Bethel, and his marriages, children, wealth and troubles with
Laban. In 29 one learns of his return and his later practice of sending
food to his parents four times each year (Esau had stolen their herds).
The events of Gen. 34 – the rape of Dinah, Jacob's daughter, by
Shechem and the slaughter of the Shechemites by Jacob's sons Simeon
and Levi – provide the foundation for Jub 30. The author omits any
reference to circumcision of the men of Shechem and, with other
ancient writers, gives a favourable verdict on the actions of Jacob's sons.
This directly opposes Jacob's view expressed in Gen. 34:30–1 and the
curse which he utters against his two sons in Gen. 49:5–7. Gen. 34:9, 21
report that the Shechemites had proposed intermarriage between themselves and Jacob's clan. Their suggestion provided the writer with an
opportunity to detail his views regarding this subject.

PROHIBITION OF ISRAELITE–GENTILE MARRIAGES

30:5 Therefore no such thing is to be done from now on – namely defiling a daughter of Israel – for in heaven there was ordained against them the punishment that they should exterminate all the men of Shechem with the sword because they had committed a

6 shameful deed in Israel. So the Lord delivered them to the power of Jacob's sons so that they could eradicate them by the sword, execute judgement against them, and so that there should not again be anything of this sort in Israel – to defile an Israelite virgin. If there is in Israel a man who wishes to give his daughter or if there is one who has given his daughter or his sister to any man who belongs to the descendants of the nations, he is surely to die. He is to be stoned because he has done a shameful thing in Israel. The woman is to be burned because she has defiled the reputation of her father's house. She is to be eradicated from Israel.

8 No adulterer or impure person is to be found in Israel throughout all of the earth's history, for Israel is holy to the Lord. Anyone who

9 defiles (it) shall die; he is to be stoned. For thus has it been ordained and written on the heavenly tablets regarding all the descendants of Israel: whoever defiles (it) is to die; he is to be stoned. This law has

10 no end, nor is there pardon or any forgiveness. Rather, the one who has defiled his daughter within all of Istael is to be eradicated because he has given one of his descendants to Molech and has sinned by defiling it.

11 Now you, Moses, command the Israelites and testify to them that they are not to give any of their daughters to the nations nor take any daughters of the nations because it is despicable before the Lord.

   .   .   .   .

17 Because of this I have commanded you: Give this testimony to Israel: 'See how matters turned out for the Shechemites and their children – how they were delivered into the hands of Jacob's two sons who subjected them to a painful death. It was a just

18 action for them and was recorded as a just act for them. Levi's descendants were chosen for the priesthood and as levites to

minister before the Lord, as we always do. Levi and his sons will
be blessed for ever. For he was eager to carry out what was right,
judgement and revenge against all who rose up against Israel.
19 Thus before the God of all, blessing and righteousness have been
placed on the heavenly tablets, in a testimony for him. We our-
20 selves remember the proper actions which the man performed
during his lifetime and at all times of the year. Until 1000
generations will they be placed (on the tablets), and they will come
to him and his descendants after him. He was recorded on the
heavenly tablets as a friend and as an upright person.'

7–10. The regulations given in these verses generally exceed the
requirements of biblical laws. Intermarriage with gentiles auto-
matically involves a defiling of those responsible and of Israel itself
because the nation is to be holy and thus totally set apart. It is a kind of
prostitution and this entails that laws for prostitution apply (see Lev.
21:9: a priest's daughter who becomes a prostitute is to be burned to
death; here the law is extended to every Israelite woman). The writer
also equates intermarriage with giving a child to Molech, a god of the
Ammonites. This permits him to apply biblical sanctions against child
sacrifice to this deity to a man who gives his daughter in marriage to a
gentile – stoning (Lev. 20:1–5). For other biblical passages which deal
with the problem of Israelite–gentile marriages, cp. Ezra 9–10; Neh.
13:23–7; Deut. 21:10–14.

17–20. The author not only contradicts the biblical condemnation of
Levi but grounds the divine selection of him and his descendants as
priests in his zealous slaughter of the Shechemites. Note the similarity
in language between the end of 30:17 and Gen. 15:6.

The Patriarch Isaac is given an opportunity to pronounce a final
blessing in chapter 31. The recipients of his testament are Levi and
Judah, two sons of Jacob from whose descendants would come the
priests and kings of Israel respectively. The contrast between Jacob's
final words for Levi (Gen. 49:5–7) and Isaac's blessing on him in Jub
31:13–17 could hardly be greater, while there is a vague resemblance
between the blessing of Judah by Jacob (Gen. 49:8–12) and Isaac's
words in Jub 31:18–20.

ISAAC BLESSES LEVI

31:12 When the spirit of prophecy descended into his mouth, he
13   took Levi by his right hand and Judah by his left hand. First he

turned to Levi and began to bless him first. He said to him: 'May
the Lord of all – he is the Lord of all ages – bless you and your
children throughout all eternity. May the Lord give to you and
14 your descendants extreme greatness for (your) glory. May he
make you and your descendants, out of all human beings, approach
him to minister in his sanctuary as do the angels of the presence and
the holy ones. Your children's descendants will prove glorious,
15 great and holy as they are. May he make them great for all ages
They will become rulers, princes and leaders of all Jacob's
descendants. They will speak the word of God truthfully, and
they will decide all his judgements justly. They will tell my
ways to Jacob and my paths to Israel. The blessing of the Lord
will be placed in their mouths to bless all the descendants of the
16 beloved one. Your mother has named you Levi, and she has given
you the right name: you will be joined to the Lord and (will be)
a companion for all of Jacob's children. May his table belong to
you. You and your sons are to eat from it. Throughout all of
history may your table be full and your food not lacking for all
17 ages. May all who hate you fall before you. May all your enemies
be eradicated and perish. May the one who blesses you be blessed,
and all peoples who curse you be cursed.'

ISAAC BLESSES JUDAH

31:18 Then he also spoke to Judah: 'May the Lord give you strength
and power to trample on all who hate you. Be a ruler – you
and one of your sons – for Jacob's children. May your name and
your sons' names circulate and move about in all lands and
regions. Then the nations will be frightened at your presence. All
19 the nations will be disturbed and all peoples will be disturbed. In
you is to be the help of Jacob, and in you is to be found the safety
20 of Israel. When you sit on the glorious throne that is rightfully
yours, there will be great peace for all the descendants of the
beloved one's children. The one who blesses you will be blessed
but all who hate and trouble you as well as those who curse you
will be eradicated and perish from the earth and are to be cursed.

12–13. These verses reflect the pre-eminence of priests in Jewish society in the post-exilic period, including the time of the author. In Jub 32:1, 3, 9 Levi is ordained to the priesthood and begins to exercise his office.

14. *descendants extreme greatness for (your) glory*: the best Ethiopic manuscripts read literally *great greatness for glory*; the Latin text has *great descendants to understand his glory*.

15. *princes*: the Ethiopic term could also be translated *judges*.

16. *Levi...joined*: for the play on the name *Levi* see Gen. 29:34, but here the joining refers to Levi and the Lord, unlike Genesis where Leah and Jacob are meant.

18. Some commentators have understood the words *one of your sons* as a reference to a Messiah. If so, this is the only passage in Jubilees to mention one. It seems more likely that the words refer to David or to the one descendant of Judah who happened to be ruling at a particular time.

20. *throne that is rightfully yours*: literally *throne of your righteousness*.

Chapter 32 adds more details about tithes and also describes two visions which Jacob received. In the second an angel showed him seven tablets on which his and his descendants' futures were recorded. Jacob wrote down all of this information. In chapter 33 one reads about Reuben's sin with Bilhah, his father's concubine; to this story the writer adds laws about incest.

In 34:1–9 the author narrates a battle pitting seven Amorite kings against Jacob and his sons. This story is an elaboration of Gen. 48:22 in which the aged and dying Jacob says to Joseph: '"I give you one ridge [*șekem*, understood by the author as Shechem] of land more than your brothers: I took it from the Amorites with my sword and my bow."'

SEVEN AMORITE KINGS FIGHT JACOB AND HIS SONS

34:2 The seven Amorite kings assembled against them to kill them
3   while hiding beneath the trees and to take their cattle as booty. Now Jacob, Levi, Judah and Joseph were in the house with their father Isaac, because his mind had grown sad and they were not able to leave him. Benjamin was the youngest and for this reason stayed
4   with him. The king of Tappuah, the king of Hadashah, the king of Piraton, the king of Shiloh, the king of Gaash, the king of Bethoron, and the king of Mahaneh-soker came as well as all who

were living on this mountain – who were living in the forest of the
5 land of Canaan. Jacob was then told: 'The kings of the Amorites
have now surrounded your sons and have plundered their flocks.'
6 He rose from his house – he, his three sons, all the servants of his
father, and his servants – and went against them with 6,000 men
7 who carried swords. He killed them in the pastures of Shechem,
pursued those who had fled, and killed them with the sword's edge.
He killed Hadashah, Tappuah, Piraton, Shiloh, Mahaneh-soker, and
8 Gaash; and he gathered his flocks. When he had prevailed over
them, he imposed tribute on them: they were to give him as
tribute five products of their land. Then he built Arbel and Timnath-
9 heres. After returning in peace, he established peaceful relations
with them. They became his slaves until he and his sons descended
to Egypt.

3. *Levi, Judah*: these two continue to enjoy prominent roles in
Jubilees.

4. The place names are the Hebrew forms which are most likely
reflected in the Ethiopic and Latin spellings.

The author gives an abbreviated form of the story about Joseph's visit
to his brothers and their sale of him to Ishmaelites who brought him to
Egypt (34:10–11). Jacob's grief upon learning of his son's 'death'
supplied for the writer the historical basis for the annual day of
atonement.

JACOB'S GRIEF AND THE DAY OF ATONEMENT

34:12 Jacob's sons slaughtered a goat and dipped Joseph's coat in the
blood. Then they sent (it) to their father Jacob on the tenth day of
13 the seventh month. He mourned all that night because they had
brought it to him in the evening. He grew feverish with grief at
his death and said: 'A wild animal has eaten Joseph.' All of the
people of his household mourned with him that day; they were
14 distressed and mourning with him all that day. His sons and his
daughter rose to console him, but he was not consoled because
15 of his son. On that day Bilhah heard that Joseph had perished.
As she was mourning for him, she died. She had been living in
Qafratef. And Dinah, his daughter, died after Joseph perished.

16 These three griefs came to Israel in one month. Bilhah was buried
    opposite the tomb of Rachel, and also Dinah, his daughter, was
17 buried there. He kept mourning for Joseph for one year and was
    not comforted, for he said: 'Let me go down to the grave
18 grieving for my son.' Therefore it has been ordained regarding the
    Israelites that they should be distressed on the tenth of the seventh
    month – the time when that (news) which made him weep for
    Joseph reached his father Jacob; and that they should seek pardon
    for themselves on it with a young goat – on the tenth of the
    seventh month, once a year – because of their sins. For they had
    saddened the affection of their father regarding his son Joseph.
19 This day has been ordained for them to become sorrowful on it
    because of their sins and because of all their evils and all their
    errors – so that they should purify themselves on this day once
    a year.

   12. *tenth day of the seventh month*: the date for the day of atonement;
see, for example, Lev. 16:29.
   13. *night*: this is the Latin reading which, in this context, is preferable
to the Ethiopic *day*.
   15. *Qafratef*: this name may reflect the words *Kibrat hā'āreṣ* in Gen.
35:16 (NEB 'some distance', but understood by several ancient commentators as a place name) or it could be a corrupt form of *derek
'eprāthāh* (Gen. 35:19; NEB 'the road to Ephrathah').

Jub 35–8 tell of the final instructions which Isaac and Rebecca gave
their two sons, of the oaths of filial loyalty that Esau and Jacob swore
to one another, and of a disastrous attack by Esau and his sons against
Jacob as he wept for his departed wife Leah. It is possible that the
description of this battle, in which Jacob kills Esau and defeats his sons and
their allies, mirrors campaigns of Judas the Maccabee and his brothers.
   Jub 39–43 present the Joseph stories – a narrative broken only by the
tale of Judah and Tamar (Gen. 38) in chapter 41. Chapter 44 describes
another of Jacob's visions (Gen. 46:1–4) and dates it to the festival of
weeks; it also contains a list of his descendants who went to Egypt. Jub
45 and 46 tell about the reunion between Jacob and Joseph and the
deaths of Jacob and all his children and bring the story as far as the
early chapters of Exodus. Chapter 47 presents the Moses story to the
point at which he is forced to flee to Midian.

THE PRINCE OF MASTEMA OPPOSES MOSES AND ISRAEL

48:1   In the sixth year of the third week of the forty-ninth jubilee-period [= 2,372], you went and lived in the land of Midian for five weeks (of years) and one year [= 36 years]. Then you returned to Egypt during the second week, in the second year of it, in the

2   fiftieth jubilee-period [= 2,410]. You know what he said to you on Mt Sinai and what the prince of Mastema wanted to do to you as you were returning to Egypt on the road when you met

3   (him) at the resting-place. Did he not wish with all his power to kill you and to save the Egyptians from your power because he saw that you had been sent to execute judgement and revenge on

4   the Egyptians? I rescued you from his power. You performed the signs and wonders which you were sent to do in Egypt to the pharaoh, to all his house, to his servants and to his people.

.   .   .   .

9   The prince of Mastema was opposing you and wishing to throw you into the pharaoh's hand. He was helping the Egyptian magicians as they were opposing and performing in front of you.

10   We allowed them to do evil things, but we did not permit healings

11   to be performed by them. The Lord struck them with bad sores; then they were unable to offer opposition because we had ruined

12   them so that they could do no sign at all. But despite all the signs and wonders, the prince of Mastema was not shamed until he summoned up his strength and cried out to the Egyptians to pursue you with all the power of Egypt – with their chariots, their horses,

13   and all the multitudes of the Egyptian people. I stood between the Egyptians and Israel. We rescued Israel from his power and from the power of the people, when the Lord brought them through

14   the middle of the sea as if through dry land. As all the people whom he had led out were pursuing Israel, the Lord our God threw them into the sea – into the depths of the abyss in place of the Israelites, as the Egyptians had thrown their sons into the river. He took revenge on 1,000,000 (men). 1,000 strong and courageous men perished for one nursing child from the children of your people

whom they had tossed into the river. On the fourteenth day, the fifteenth, the sixteenth, the seventeenth, and the eighteenth, the prince of Mastema was fettered and locked up behind the Israelites

16 so that he could not accuse them. On the nineteenth day we freed them to help the Egyptians and to pursue the Israelites. He hardened

17 their hearts and made them stubborn. They were made stubborn by the Lord our God so that he could strike the Egyptians and throw them into the sea. On the fourteenth day we had fettered

18 him so that he would not accuse the Israelites when they were asking for utensils and clothing from the Egyptians – utensils of silver, gold, and copper – so that they could plunder the Egyptians in return for their reducing them violently to slavery. We did not

19 lead the Israelites out of Egypt empty-handed.

1. *land of Midian*: Latin reads *in the land of Med(ian)*; the Ethiopic manuscripts have *there*. *[2,372]*...*[2,410]*: these numbers do not tally with the figure of thirty-six years (which should be thirty-eight years). 2,410 is the year of the Exodus.

2. *prince of Mastema*: some ancient versions of Exod. 4:24 ascribe this action to an angel of the Lord. Here as elsewhere the author credits the prince of evil with a questionable deed that the Bible claims was performed by God (compare 2 Sam. 24:1 with 1 Chron. 21:1 for a precedent). *when you met* (him): this is the Latin reading; the Ethiopic may locate this meeting at a shady tree.

9–18. Any successes of the Egyptian magicians and armies during the plagues and the Exodus are credited to the prince of Mastema's efforts.

13. *I stood*: the Ethiopic manuscripts add *between you* (singular).

14. *courageous*: a form of the word *three* precedes this word in the best Ethiopic manuscripts.

15. *the fourteenth*: the date of passover.

17. *were made stubborn*: another Ethiopic reading involves the same consonants, two of which have been transposed, and means *were thought, planned*.

19. *not*: the context requires a negative but the Ethiopic manuscripts lack it.

Jub. 49 is devoted to the passover and laws for celebrating it, while the last chapter deals with sabbatical periods, jubilees, and especially with regulations for proper observance of the weekly sabbaths (50:6–13).

The Testament (Assumption) of Moses
JOHN J. COLLINS

In 1861 Antonio Ceriani published a fragmentary Latin manuscript which he had found in the Ambrosian Library in Milan and which he identified as the Assumption of Moses. The identification was based on chapter 1 verse 14, which corresponds to a quotation from the Assumption of Moses by Gelasius (*Ecclesiastical History* II.17.17). Gelasius elsewhere (II.21.7) refers to the dispute between Michael and the Devil in the Assumption of Moses. This episode is not found in the manuscript published by Ceriani, but is often referred to in patristic sources and even already in the New Testament in Jude, verse 9. (The allusion is not identified in Jude but is specified in Clement, Origen and other patristic sources.) The Latin manuscript does not refer to the death of Moses or his subsequent assumption at all and, since it is primarily a prophecy delivered before death, it is more properly described as a testament. In fact the Stichometry of Nicephorus and other lists mention a Testament (*Diathēkē*) of Moses immediately before the Assumption, and the dominant opinion of scholars is that Ceriani's text corresponds to the Testament rather than the Assumption. In view of the citations in Gelasius, some have suggested that the Testament and the Assumption were combined in a single book. The surviving Latin text is incomplete, and may have concluded with an account of the assumption of Moses. Origen (*De Principiis* III.2.1) uses the title 'Ascension of Moses' for the document which contains the dispute between Michael and the Devil, i.e. the Assumption of Moses.

There was an extensive literature dealing with the death of Moses in antiquity, in the later Jewish and Samaritan traditions and in Slavonic, Ethiopic and Armenian Church traditions. (For references see J. H. Charlesworth, *The Pseudepigrapha and Modern Research*, pp. 160–3.)

The present work should be distinguished from the Apocalypse of Moses, which is really a recension of the Life of Adam and Eve, and from the Prayer of Moses, which is part of Pseudo-Philo's *Liber Antiquitatum Biblicarum* (19:14–16), see pp. 14f above. There are several mediaeval Jewish documents, in Hebrew, which deal with the Ascension or Assumption of Moses.

The manuscript published by Ceriani is still the only text of this work. It is a palimpsest from the sixth century and is illegible in places. The edition of R. H. Charles in 1897 has not been surpassed. The consensus of scholarship is that the Latin was translated from Greek, but the original was in a Semitic language, most probably Hebrew.

The genre

The work published by Ceriani may be viewed as a re-writing of the last words and demise of Moses in Deut. 31–4. The first chapter contains the announcement of Moses' forthcoming death, the commissioning of Joshua as his successor, and instructions to preserve the books which were being transmitted. All these points are paralleled in Deut. 31. Then in chapters 2–9 there is an extensive review of the history of Israel, indicating a pattern of sin and punishment. Deut. 32 has a schematic review of Israel's history, although the period reviewed is much more limited and the review is not presented as a prediction. Chapter 10 brings the dénouement of history and the exaltation of Israel. Deut. 33, the blessing of Moses, is not eschatological, but may be said to have eschatological implications. Finally, the death and burial of Moses in Deut. 34 was presumably adapted in the lost conclusion of the Latin manuscript. It should be clear that the apocryphal book was not following Deuteronomy rigorously. The essential debt to the biblical book lies in the use of Moses' last words as a context and in the pattern of sin and punishment in the history of Israel.

The testamentary character of the apocryphal book should be clear from the parallels with Deuteronomy. The book is simply the farewell discourse of Moses, framed by the introductory explanation of the circumstances, and, presumably, by Moses' departure at the end. The Testament of Moses is simpler in form than the Testaments of the Twelve Patriarchs, which typically include a narrative about the Patriarch's life, to exemplify a vice or virtue, and a hortatory section. These elements are not found here, but the review of history with an eschatological conclusion is typical of the Testaments, as is the Sin–Exile–Return pattern, which derives from the Deuteronomic view of history. The Testament of Moses has many affinities with apocalyptic literature but is not an apocalypse in form. The decisive difference lies in the manner of revelation. An apocalypse always involves a mediating angel (or other supernatural figure) who interprets symbolic visions or guides the visionary on a heavenly tour. Here Moses is the giver of revelation, not the recipient. The affinities of the Testament with the apocalyptic writings lie in the *ex eventu* (after the fact) prophecy of history and the transcendent eschatology in chapter 10.

A theology of history

The Testament of Moses seeks to demonstrate a theology of history, according to which God created the world on account of his people, although this design is hidden from the Gentiles (1:12–13). The history itself falls into two cycles. The first, in chapters 2–4, covers the period down to the Babylonian exile. What is remarkable here is that the southern tribes view their exile as punishment for the sin of the northern tribes, even though it is admitted that some southern kings broke the covenant. The sin of the northern tribes lies in their breach with the Jerusalem temple. The second cycle begins with the restoration after the exile and concludes with another time of wrath and persecution. This time a man named Taxo from the tribe of Levi takes his seven sons and resolves to die rather than transgress the Law. Then the kingdom of God is ushered in and Israel is exalted to the stars. In Chapter 12 Moses adds some explanatory comments to console Joshua. The departure of Moses should not cause great anxiety because God has foreseen and provided for the entire course of history. Those who transgress the commandments will suffer at the hands of the Gentiles, but those who observe them will prosper.

The theology of the Testament may be categorized as a thoroughgoing 'covenantal nomism': salvation comes through membership of the Jewish people, and this membership requires observance of the commandments. It is remarkable that the Deuteronomic theology of reward and punishment is maintained even in the light of the persecution of the righteous in chapters 7–9. The strong emphasis on the solidarity of all the people in the first cycle of history gives way to a distinction between those who observe the Law and those who do not in chapter 12. The most significant variation on the basic covenantal nomism is found, however, in the story of Taxo. In the time of persecution, a righteous man can turn the tide of history by purifying himself and submitting to death rather than break the law. The reason is that God will 'avenge the blood of his servants' as promised in Deut. 32:43. The paradigm of Deut. 32 is invoked explicitly in the story of the martyrs in 2 Macc. 7:6 and implicitly in 1 Macc. 2:37. Taxo is exceptional in so far as he deliberately sets out to provoke the divine vengeance by innocent death.

Unity and date

In its present form the Testament of Moses must be dated around the turn of the era, since there is a clear allusion to the partial destruction of the temple in the campaign of Varus in 4 BC (TMos 6:8–9). The document shows no awareness of the final destruction of AD 70. Scholarly opinion is divided as to whether chapters 5–6, which develop the course of history through the first century BC were part of the original document or a later insertion. These chapters clearly refer to the Hasmoneans, Herod and the campaign of Varus. Yet the final persecution, in chapter 8, is strongly reminiscent of the persecution under Antiochus Epiphanes. R. H. Charles attempted to resolve this anomaly by re-arranging the chapters so that 8–9 stood before 5–6. This proposal is unacceptable since the logic of the book demands that the divine intervention in chapter 10 should follow directly on the most severe persecution and especially on the episode of Taxo and his sons. The specificity of the account of the persecution in chapter 8 suggests that this is an account of the author's time, rather than a stereotyped eschatological scenario. In this case we must assume that chapters 5–6 were inserted to update the book. The account of the persecution then becomes an eschatological scenario in the revised document. Support for the theory of a second redaction can be found in 10:8 where the phrase 'the wings of the eagle' is an addition, and may allude to the pulling down of the golden eagle over the temple gate shortly before the campaign of Varus (Josephus, *Ant.* xvii.6.3 (155–7).

Purpose

The Testament of Moses serves a twofold purpose. On the one hand, it assures the Law-abiding Jews that the world is created for them, even though this design may be hidden in the present. On the other hand it encourages non-violent resistance. The way to usher in the kingdom of God is not through militant action, but through purification, scrupulous observance of the Law, and martyrdom. The latter point is reinforced through the implicit contrast between Taxo and Mattathias, father of the Maccabees. Both Taxo and Mattathias (in 1 Macc. 2) come from priestly families, invoke the Law and their fathers and urge their sons to die for the Law. Significantly, however, Taxo has seven sons, the perfect number, while Mattathias has only five. Mattathias looks to Judas for vengeance, but Taxo looks to God. The style of action represented by Taxo is in evident contrast to that of Mattathias, and is rather

reminiscent of the martyrs in the cave in 1 Macc. 2:31-8. The contrast
with Mattathias would surely have been obvious at the turn of the
era when 1 Maccabees was in circulation, and when the militant
factions in Judaism remembered the Maccabees as heroes (it is significant
that two of the rebel leaders in the time of Varus were named Judas and
Simon; Josephus, *Ant.* XVII.10.5-6 (271-7)). However, the contrast
may have been apparent already at the time of the Maccabaean rebellion.

Provenance

Despite occasional attempts to ascribe the Testament to the Essenes
or some other party, we have no adequate basis for such an attribution.
The strong covenantal nomism of the work does not suggest sectarian-
ism. The only hint of sectarian provenance is the statement in 4:8 that
after the restoration the 'two tribes' will be sad and lament because they
cannot offer sacrifices to the God of their fathers. This verse may imply
a rejection of the second temple, but it is possible that it refers to those
of the southern tribes who remained in exile, and so could not offer
sacrifices with any frequency.

Bibliography

The basic edition, translation and commentary is still that of R. H. Charles, *The
Assumption of Moses*, London, 1897. See also his treatment in *The Apocrypha and
Pseudepigrapha of the Old Testament*, vol. II, pp. 407-24. Text, French translation
and extensive introduction are provided by E -M. Laperrousaz, *Le Testament
de Moïse* (Semitica 19), Paris, 1970.

Recent introductions and annotated translations are E. Brandenburger,
'Himmelfahrt Moses', JSHRZ v/2, pp. 57-84 and J. Priest, 'The Testament of
Moses', in J. H. Charlesworth (ed.), *The Old Testament Pseudepigrapha*, vol. I,
pp. 919-34. For discussion see G. W. E. Nickelsburg (ed.), *Studies on the Testament of Moses* (SCS 4), Missoula, 1973.

Some noteworthy articles are:
J. Licht, 'Taxo, or the Apocalyptic Doctrine of Vengeance' *JJS* 12 (1961),
pp. 95-103;
A. Yarbro Collins, 'Composition and Redaction of the Testament of Moses 10'
HTR 69 (1976), pp. 179-86;
D. R. Schwartz, 'The Tribes of As. Mos. 4:7-9', *JBL* 99 (1980), pp. 217-23.

THE COMMISSIONING OF JOSHUA

1 (1) [It came to pass in the one hundred and twentieth year of the life
   of Moses] 2 which is the two thousand five hundredth year from

the creation of the world... 6 that he summoned Joshua the son of Nun, a man acceptable to the Lord... 8 that he should lead the people into the land which had been given to their fathers[a] 9 so that it should be given to them through the covenant and oath which he pronounced in the tabernacle to give it through Joshua... 11 Thus says the Lord of the world. 12 For he created the world on account of his people 13 but he did not begin to make this design of creation manifest from the beginning of the world so that the nations might be condemned by it and condemn themselves in humiliation by their disputes. 14 Accordingly, he devised and invented me, who have been prepared from the beginning of the world to be the mediator of his covenant. 15 And now I make clear to you that the time of the years of my life is completed and I pass over to the sleep of my fathers, even in the presence of all the people. 16 But grasp this writing so that you may know how to preserve the books which I will give you, 17 which you will put in order and anoint with cedar oil and place in vessels of clay in the place which he made from the beginning of the creation of the world, 18 so that his name would be invoked until the day of repentance in the visitation with which the Lord will visit them at the completion of the end of days.

a Reading *patribus* for *ex tribus.*

1. This verse is supplied from Deut. 31:2.

2. There is considerable variation in the dating of Moses' death in the Jewish writings of this period. Verses 3–5 provide further editorial specification of the setting. Verse 3 is illegible.

9. Here and in 5:1 the Latin *de* with the accusative seems to reflect the Greek *dia.*

12. Compare 4Ezra 6:55: 'All this I have spoken before thee, O Lord, because thou hast said that for our sakes thou hast created this world.' Also 4Ezra 7:11; 2Bar 14:19; 15:7; 21:24.

13. Charles translates 'he was not pleased' assuming that the Hebrew *hōʾīl* was misunderstood.

14. This verse is cited by Gelasius. In rabbinic literature the name of the Messiah was said to exist before the creation of the world. In the Similitudes of Enoch pre-existence is attributed to 'that Son of Man' (1En 48:2–3).

16. Presumably the Pentateuch.

17. Jerusalem, or Zion which was said to be the starting-point of creation in some rabbinic sources (b.Yoma 54b).

18. The temple was expected to stand until the eschatological time. For the idea of eschatological repentance compare SibOr 4:65–7. In Luke 1:16–17 this repentance is associated with Elijah. Compare Mal. 4:5–6 (Hebrew 3:23–4).

THE REVIEW OF HISTORY: FIRST CYCLE

2 1 Through you they will enter the land which he decreed and promised to give to their fathers... 3 for five[a] years after they enter their land, and thereafter they will be ruled by leaders and kings for eighteen years and for nineteen years ten tribes will break off...

3 1 In those times a king from the east will come upon them and cavalry will cover their land 2 and he will burn their settlement with fire, together with the holy temple of the Lord 3 and he will evict the whole people and take them to his native land, and he will take the two tribes with him. 4 Then the two tribes will call upon the ten tribes... 5 'Just and holy is the Lord, for you sinned and we equally are led away with you, with our children...'

4 1 Then one will enter who is over them, and will stretch out his hands and kneel and pray for them... 5 Then God will remember them because of the covenant which he made with their fathers, and he will manifest his mercy also in those times 6 and he will prompt the king to have mercy on them and send them to their own land and country. 7 Then some parts of the tribes will go up and come to their appointed place, renew the place and fortify it. 8 But the two tribes will remain in their prescribed faith, sad and lamenting because they cannot offer sacrifices to the Lord of their fathers. 9 And the ten tribes will increase and multiply[b] among the Gentiles, in the time of the tribes.

a The number is supplied on the basis of Josh. 14:7, 10. Cp. Josephus, *Ant.* v.1.19 (68).
b Reading *multiplicabunter* for *devenient*, to complement *crescent*, increase. Also *nationes* for *natos*.

2:3. Each year represents a reign or ruler. The eighteen years represent fifteen judges (including Joshua, Abimelech and Samuel) and the first three kings. The nineteen years are the nineteen kings of Israel from Jeroboam to Hoshea.

2:7–9 acknowledge that some kings of Judah will break the covenant, but the text is corrupt.

3:5. The two southern tribes (Judah and Benjamin) imply that they are punished because of the sins of the northern ten. Compare 2Bar 77:4. In 3:11–13 the tribes are said to remember that Moses foretold all this when he called heaven and earth to witness (i.e. Deut. 32).

4:1. The *one who is over them* is usually identified as Daniel (cp. Dan. 9), but the identification is not compelling. Ezra has also been proposed. It may be that the Testament intended to refer to an official leader such as the High Priest or possibly to an angel.

4:2. The pattern is familiar from the Deuteronomic history. The prayer opens the way for God's mercy beause of the covenant.

4:6. The king in question was Cyrus of Persia.

4:7. The place is Jerusalem, not just the temple.

4:8. It is not entirely clear whether the two tribes represent the people of Judah after the exile or rather the descendants of the old southern kingdom who remained in the exile. In the former case, the verse would imply rejection of the second temple. Rejection of the temple cult may also be implied in 1En 89:73.

4:9. *In the time of the tribes* is obscure. Charles suggests 'the time of their captivity', but this requires a radical alteration. The phrase marks the end of the discussion of the tribes in this document.

THE REVIEW OF HISTORY: SECOND, POST-EXILIC, CYCLE

5 1 And when the times of condemnation approach and vengeance arises through kings who share in their crimes and punish them 2 they also will be divided as to the truth. 3 Therefore it came to pass: 'They will depart from justice and succumb to iniquity and defile with pollutions[a] their house of worship' and that 'they will fornicate after foreign gods'. 4 For they will not follow the truth of God, but some will defile the altar with the very gifts they offer to the Lord. They are not priests, but slaves born of slaves...

6 1 Then kings will arise, ruling over them, and they will be called priests of the Most High God. They will assuredly act impiously from the Holy of Holies. 2 An insolent king will succeed them,

who will not be from the race of priests, an impetuous and perverse man. He will judge them as they deserve... 7 And he will beget sons who will rule[b] for shorter periods, succeeding him. 8 Cohorts will come into their territory,[c] and a powerful king of the west and he will conquer them. 9 He will take captives and will burn part of their temple with fire and he will crucify some around their settlement.

a *inquinationibus* for *in genationibus*.
b The text is fragmentary and corrupt. Read *dominarent* for *donarent*.
c *in partes eorum cohortes venient* for *in pares eorum mortis venient*.

5:1. The kings in question are presumably the Seleucids, especially Antiochus Epiphanes. Compare 2 Macc. 4:16: 'The very people whose manner of life they emulated, and whom they desired to imitate in everything, became their enemies and oppressors.'

5:2. The reference is to the division in the Jewish community prior to the Maccabaean revolt.

5:3. The quotations are not precise but are patchworks of biblical phrases.

5:4. The polemic is against the hellenizing priests prior to the Maccabaean revolt. At least Menelaus was not from a priestly line. The charge of fornicating after foreign gods is more appropriate for these priests than for any others in the post-exilic period. The passage goes on to describe their corruption as judges. Josephus, *Ant.* XIII.10.5 (292) says that John Hyrcanus was told by a Pharisee to give up the high-priesthood because his mother was a captive under Antiochus Epiphanes, and some scholars see an allusion to this episode here.

6:1. The Maccabees and their descendants, who usurped the high-priesthood but were from a priestly family.

6:2. Herod, who ruled from 39 BC to 4 BC. The following verses say that he will kill young and old and cause great fear.

6:7. Herod's kingdom was divided between Archelaus, who ruled Judaea from 4 BC to AD 6, Antipas, who became tetrarch of Galilee and ruled from 4 BC to AD 39 and Philip, who was tetrarch of the remoter areas such as Trachonitis and Panias from 4 BC to AD 34. Since the Testament claims that they ruled for shorter periods than Herod it must have been written before the death of Philip.

6:8. There was widespread opposition to the succession of Archelaus. Augustus sent a procurator, Sabinus, to enforce Herod's will. He was forced to call in Varus, legate of Syria, for support. A massacre ensued.

Some of Sabinus' soldiers set fire to the temple. Varus crucified 2,000 Jews. See Josephus *Ant.* XVII.8.4–10.10 (200–98), *War* II.1.1–3.3 (1–79).

THE PERSECUTION

8 1 A [second]ᵃ vengeance and wrath will come upon them such as has not occurred among them from the beginning until that time, when he will stir up against them the king of the kings of the earth and a ruler with great power, who will crucify those who confess their circumcision. 2 Those who conceal itᵇ he will torture and hand over to be led, bound, into prison. 3 Their wives will be given to the gods among the Gentiles and their youngᶜ sons will be operated on by doctors to bring forward their foreskins.ᵈ 4 Those among them will be punished by tortures, fire and sword and they will be forced to carry in public their polluted idols, which are as polluted as those who keep them. 5 They will likewise be forced by their tormentors to enter their secret place and they will be forced with goads to blaspheme the word with insults, finally after this the laws and that which they have on their altar.

a *Altera*, second, is only partly legible, but is supplied by analogy with 9:2.
b *Celantes* for *necantes*, killing.
c The word *pueri* is duplicated.
d *acrobistiam* for *acrosisam*.

1. Compare Dan. 12:1. The first vengeance was the Babylonian exile. God will stir up Antiochus Epiphanes against the Jews. The title 'king of kings' is used for Nebuchadnezzar in Ezek 26:7 and Dan. 2:37 and for Artaxerxes in Ezra 7:12.

Josephus, *Ant.* XII.5.4 (256) says that Jews were crucified under Antiochus Epiphanes, but this is not reported in the books of Maccabees. Crucifixion was a typical Roman form of punishment, but it originated in the east and could have been used by Antiochus. There is no doubt that Antiochus forbade circumcision.

3. 2 Macc. 6:4 mentions fornication and prostitution in the temple court. This may have had pagan cultic significance. 1 Macc. 1:15 says that the hellenizers had their circumcision surgically disguised before the outbreak of the persecution.

4. 2 Macc. 6:7 says that Jews were compelled to march in the procession of Dionysus, wearing ivy wreaths.

5. The *secret place* is the holy of holies.
The *word* is the divine name.
For the custom of swearing by the gift on the altar see Matt. 23:18.

TAXO

9 1 Then on that day[a] there will be a man of the tribe of Levi whose name will be Taxo, who having seven sons will say to them and propose: 2 'See, my sons, behold a second cruel, unclean vengeance has come upon the people, a merciless development, surpassing[b] the first. 3 For what nation or what country or what people of sinners against the Lord, which committed many crimes, has suffered such evils as have afflicted us? 4 Now, therefore, my sons, listen to me, for you see and know that neither our parents nor their ancestors tempted God so as to transgress his commands. 5 For you know that this is our strength and this we will do. 6 Let us fast for three days and on the fourth day let us enter a cave which is in the field and let us die rather than transgress the commandments of the lord of Lords, the God of our fathers. 7 For if we do this and die our blood will be avenged before the Lord.'

a *die* for *dicente*.   b *eminens* for *eminent*.

1. Taxo, Greek *taxōn*, means 'orderer' or regulator (Hebrew *meḥōqēq*). For his seven sons, compare 2 Macc. 7 and contrast the five sons of Mattathias.

2. The Latin, *eminens principatum*, is a garbled rendering of the Greek (probably *hyperechōn tēn archēn*).

3. Compare 4Ezra 3:31–5, where Ezra complains 'Have the deeds of Babylon been better than those of Sion?'

4. This claim could scarcely apply to the whole people, but at most to a faithful remnant.
Note the contrast with 3:5, where distress is still a punishment for sin. In the story of Taxo innocence is crucial. God is moved to act not by prayer but by innocent suffering. In all parts of TMos human initiative is required to precipitate the action of God.

6. It is not clear whether suicide is intended or merely submission to death like the martyrs in 1 Macc. 2:31–8.

7. Deut. 32:43. The martyrs in 1 Macc. 2 also appeal to Deut. 32 indirectly by invoking heaven and earth.

THE DIVINE INTERVENTION

10. (1) And then his kingdom will appear in all his creation
        and then the Devil will come to an end
        and sadness will be taken away with him.

     (2) Then the hands of the messenger will be filled
         who is appointed on high,
         who will immediately avenge them on their enemies.

     (3) For the heavenly one will rise[a] from the throne of his kingdom
         and will go forth from his holy habitation
         with anger and wrath on account of his sons

     (4) and the earth will tremble and it will be shaken to its limits,
         and the high mountains will be brought low
         and the hills will be shaken and fall...

     (6) and the sea will retreat to the deep...

     (8) Then you, Israel, will be happy
         and you will ascend above the necks and wings of the eagle
         and [the days][b] will be fulfilled

     (9) and God will exalt you
         and cause you to remain in the heaven of the stars,
         the place of their habitation,

     (10) and you will look from on high and see your enemies on
          earth
          and you will recognize them and rejoice
          and give thanks and confess your creator.

     (11) But you, Joshua son of Nun, keep these words and this book

     (12) for from my death, assumption, to his coming there will be
          250 times.

> a The word *exurget*, rise, is only partly preserved.
> b 'the days' are supplied to fill out the last line.

2. The messenger is an angel, presumably Michael (cp. Dan. 12:1; 1QM 17:7). Compare also the figure of Melchizedek in 11Q Melch. Filling the hands is an Old Testament idiom for consecration.

3–7. These verses constitute a divine warrior hymn. The biblical precedents are found in such passages as Deut. 33; Hab. 3; Mic. 1:3–4.

Eschatological use of this motif is found in 1En 1. For the disruption of nature in verses 4–6 compare Mark 13:24–5. On the disappearance of the sea in verse 6 compare Rev. 21:1.

8. Deut. 33:29 provides the point of departure for this verse: 'Happy are you, people of Israel.' The Greek rendering of that verse concludes 'and you will mount on their neck'. Since the Latin line is too long and breaks the rhythm, it appears that the reference to the wings of the eagle is an addition. It may have been prompted by the tearing down of the golden eagle outside the temple shortly before the death of Herod (Josephus, *Ant.* xvii.6.3 (155–7)).

9. Exaltation to the stars (i.e. to the angelic host) figures in a number of apocalyptic writings. The clearest example is 1En 104:2 ('you will shine like the lights of heaven...and the gate of heaven will be opened to you') and 104:6 ('for you shall be associates of the host of heaven'.) Compare Dan. 12:3.

10. Charles emends 'earth' to Gehenna, but this is not necessary.

12 The term 'assumption' is apparently an insertion in apposition to death, and may have been occasioned by the combination of the Testament and the Assumption of Moses. 250 times must be taken as 250 weeks of years or 1,750 years.

MOSES' FINAL DISCOURSE

12 3 Joshua, do not despise yourself but be confident and attend to my words. 4 God created all the peoples who are in the world[a] and us also, and he foresaw them and us from the beginning of the creation of the world and to the end of the age. Nothing has been neglected by him, even to the least thing, but he foresaw all...

8 I say to you Joshua, not because of the piety of this people will you eradicate the nations. 9 All the firmament of the dome of heaven is made and approved by God and is under the ring[b] of his right hand. 10 Accordingly, those who do and fulfil the commandments will increase and follow a good path. 11 But the good things which have been predicted will be lacking for those who sin and neglect the commandments and they will be punished by the nations with many torments. 12 For it cannot be that he will totally eradicate and destroy them. 13 For God who foresaw all

things for ever will go forth and his covenant is established and the oath which...

a *orbe terrarum* for *ore terrarum*.   b *annullo* for *nullo*.

In chapter 11 Joshua expresses his distress at Moses' imminent departure.
8. Compare Deut. 7:7: Israel's success is not due to its greatness.
Ezek, 36:22, 32: God does not act for the sake of Israel but for his name.
10–11. Compare 3Bar 15–16, which emphasize individual rewards and punishments but also suggest that sinners are punished 'by a people that is no people' (compare Deut. 32:21). The Gentiles, then, serve a purpose by punishing sinners.

The Psalms of Solomon

M. DE JONGE

Title

'Psalms of Solomon' is the title given to a collection of eighteen psalms
preserved in Greek and Syriac but in all probability originally composed in Hebrew. All but the first have a superscription which mentions
Solomon as author, but nothing in these songs warrants an ascription
to the famous son of David. They are not even pseudepigraphical in
the usual sense of the word. The psalms proper do not hint at any connection with Solomon and the circumstances in which he reigned.
They need not have originated at the same time and may have been
composed by more than one author. At a certain moment they were
brought together to be used in assemblies of pious Jews (mentioned
e.g. in 8:23f; 17:16, 32, 43) for meditation, prayer, instruction, perhaps
also to be sung (see the superscriptions of Psalms 10, 14, 16 and 17). To
give them some authority the collector(s) attached Solomon's name to
the individual psalms and to the collection. After all he was reported to
have composed 1,005 songs (1 Kings 4:32 (5:12). This is the number
in the Hebrew text; the LXX has 5,000) and the regular Psalter contained
only two psalms bearing Solomon's name (Pss. 72, 127). The fact that
Psalms 17 and 18 in this collection hope for a wise and pious king from
the family of David may have suggested the connection with David's
successor. In the Syriac tradition the Psalms were handed down together
with (and after) 42 Odes of Solomon, an entirely different collection of
hymns.

Form and content

The PssSol show many similarities, both in form and content, with the
psalms contained in the Bible. With regard to vocabulary and ways of
expression they are clearly dependent on them as well as on the prophetic and Wisdom books of the Old Testament. A number of psalms
are typical thanksgiving psalms; in others lament prevails (so PssSol 8
and 17 below); again others may be called hymns (see, partly, PssSol 3
and 18). In the psalms both 'I' and 'we' are found; the one who prays,

praises, laments or meditates, formulates his reflections on God's dealings with the pious and the sinners, with Israel and the nations, speaks on behalf of and to a group of believers. As to genre and form the psalms are not always consistent and within individual psalms unexpected changes occur. This is typical also for other late Jewish psalms, as S. Holm-Nielsen (following H. Ludin Jansen) has emphasized (see bibliography).

A few themes are central; above all God's righteousness, as revealed in his dealings with mankind and his treatment of the wicked and the pious. Looking back on recent events which bewildered and distressed the pious, the psalmists try to discover God's hand and they exhort God's servants to thank him: 'Worthy to be praised is the Lord who judges the whole earth in his righteousness!' (8:9, cp. 34). There is an essential difference between the righteous and the sinners (see e.g. PsSol 3). The righteous stumble, depart from God's ways and God chastens them. The sinners neglect God's warnings and punishment and will be destroyed while 'those who fear the Lord will rise to eternal life' (3:16). This means that the pious, while distressed and scattered over the entire earth (17:16–20) may confidently await God's help – and also God's final and definitive intervention. Particularly PssSol 11, 17 and 18 give voice to 'eschatological' expectations.

The sinners are, in the first place, non-Jews who do not observe God's commandments, but who are used as instruments of God for the punishment of his people (PssSol 2, 8, 17). But sinners are also found in Israel and their transgressions are the reason for God's intervention. The pious are painfully aware of a split within the community of the believers and of the necessity to seek for the true observation of God's law.

Date and place of provenance

The PssSol were, if not written, at least redacted and collected for use in a certain group. Because of the connections with the Wisdom books of the Old Testament one may think of circles of pious men coming together in private houses and synagogues to search the Scriptures and to discern the signs of the times. There are no typical apocalyptic elements nor sectarian tendencies (as in the Qumran sect that produced its hymns, the *Hodayot*; see also the volume by M. A. Knibb in this series), nor need we think of exclusive use in Wisdom circles. A number of scholars have advocated Pharisaic origin, but we know too little of the tenets of the Pharisaic movement in the first century BC to be quite sure.

This leads us to the question of the date. The PssSol do not describe

historical events, but reflect them. They are clearly against the Hasmoneans, who did not discharge their priestly duties in a proper way
(1:8; 8:11–13, 22) and usurped the highpriesthood (8:11) as well as
royal authority (17:5f). Psalm 8 clearly describes Pompey's entry into
Jerusalem in 63 BC, together with the events leading up to and following
it (verses 15–21; cp. 17:7–14). Ps. 2:1f mentions his capture of the city
together with his pollution of the temple (so also 17:13f). Psalm 2
pictures him first and foremost as a proud and insolent sinner who
does not observe the limits set to him as instrument of the Lord and
disregards God's strength and judgement (cp. verses 23–37). The author
of this psalm prays for deliverance and is shown how the insolent
transgressor lies slain on the mountains of Egypt without anyone to
bury him (2:26f). Although the language is traditional we may see
here a reference to Pompey's death in Egypt in 48 BC.

Because of the concentration on Jerusalem and the temple the place
of origin is very probably Jerusalem or some place in Judaea.

What these historical references mean for the origin of the other
psalms – which may include earlier and later psalms – and for the
bringing together and final redaction of the collection, is not clear.
Because there are no hints at the reign of Antigonus in Jerusalem (40–37),
nor at that of Herod the Great (37–4), scholars usually assume that the
collecting took place before 40 BC.

Witnesses to the text

Eleven Greek manuscripts are known, dating from the tenth to the
sixteenth century. A Syriac version, made from the Greek, exists in
four manuscripts; two of these are manuscripts of the Psalms and the
Odes, the other two give only the text of Ps. 16:6–13. Ps. 3:1–6 are
quoted, in a different translation, in the margin of a manuscript of the
Hymns of Severus (for details see below). The Greek is clumsy, the
vocabulary is relatively limited and stereotyped. Many passages read
like a (too literal) translation from a Semitic original, and virtually all
who have studied the PssSol have assumed a Hebrew original. Particularly the sudden changes between present, future and aorist in a
number of psalms can be explained as awkward renderings of Hebrew
verbs. At what date the translation from Hebrew into Greek was made,
cannot be determined. PssSol are mentioned in the list of contents of the
fifth-century Codex Alexandrinus of the Greek Bible, and they are
often found in LXX-codices together with books such as the Wisdom
of Solomon and Sirach (Ecclesiasticus).

Bibliography

The standard edition is still that of O. von Gebhardt, *Die Psalmen Salomos* (TU 13, 2), Leipzig, 1895, based on eight mss. A new edition by R. B. Wright has been announced, but so far only R. R. Hann's *The Manuscript History of the Psalms of Solomon* (SBL Septuagint and Cognate Studies Series 13, Chico, Ca., 1982) is available. It should be consulted for details of the readings of all eleven manuscripts known at present. PssSol can be consulted very conveniently in the LXX-editions of H. B. Swete, *The Old Testament in Greek*, vol. III, Cambridge (from the second edition (1899) onwards) and of A. Rahlfs, *Septuaginta*, vol. II, Stuttgart, 1935. Swete uses von Gebhardt's eight manuscripts; Rahlfs closely follows von G.'s edition.

The Syriac version was edited by W. Baars in *The Old Testament in Syriac acc. to the Peshitta Version*, vol. IV, 6, Leiden, 1972. The independent fragment can be found in R. Harris–A. Mingana, *The Odes and Psalms of Solomon*, vol. II, Manchester, 1920, pp. 433f. On the Odes see also J. H. Charlesworth, *The Odes of Solomon*, Second edition, Missoula, 1977.

English translations of PssSol are those by G. B. Gray in *The Apocrypha and Pseudepigrapha of the Old Testament*, vol. II, pp. 625–52 and by R. B. Wright in J. H. Charlesworth (ed.), *The OldTestamentPseudepigrapha,*vol. II (forthcoming).

A modern German translation (with instructive notes) is that by S. Holm-Nielsen in JSHRZ IV/2, pp. 49–112. In French we have the translation (with an elaborate commentary) by J. Viteau in his *Les Psaumes de Solomon*, Paris 1911.

The most recent monograph dealing with the theology of PssSol is J. Schipphaus, *Die Psalmen Salomons* (ALGHJ 7), Leiden, 1977. On late Jewish psalmody see H. Ludin Jansen, *Die späjüdische Psalmendichtung*, Oslo, 1937.

On the selections

In the following, translations are given of PssSol 1 and 18 (the first and the last psalm in the collection and, as such, in strategic positions), and of Psalm 3 that gives a 'timeless' description of the righteous and the sinner. Next, of Psalm 8 that reflects on recent events, as does Psalm 17 (well-known for its expectation of a new king, Son of David and anointed of the Lord).

The verse numbers are those of von Gebhardt/Rahlfs. Those of Swete (going back to H. E. Ryle and M. R. James in their edition of 1891) are given in brackets.

PSALM I

1 (1) I cried to the Lord in utter distress,
       To God when sinners assailed.

2 (2) Suddenly the alarm of war was heard before me;
      'He will hear me, for I am full of righteousness.'

3 (3) I thought in my heart that I was full of righteousness,
      Because I prospered and had become rich (fem. !) in children.

4 (4) Their wealth spread over the whole earth
      And their glory to the end of the earth.

5 (5) They were exalted to the stars,
      And they said (that) they would not fall.

6 (6) But they became insolent in their prosperity,
      And they could not bear (it).

7 (7) Their sins were in secret.
      And even I had no knowledge of them.

8 (8) Their transgressions exceeded those of the nations before
      them.
      They polluted the holy place (or: things) of the Lord
      with pollution.

1. *I cried*: probably Jerusalem (or the congregation of the true
Israelites in Jerusalem) pictured as a woman (see verse 3; cp. Isa. 49:14,
20; 54; Bar 4:30–5:9). *sinners*: clearly non-Jews.

2. *the alarm of war*: explained in the following psalm, to which Ps 1
(which lacks a title and a proper ending) is an introduction; cp. also
8:1–13. It is important to note that this psalm now heads the whole
collection and sets the tone for it.

3–8. The impending crisis reveals that not all believers are righteous
and faithful. Clearly the faithful are speaking.

6. *could not bear* (*it*): translation uncertain, cp. Jer. 20:9 LXX.

8*a*. A theme also found in 2:9; 8:13; 17:15.

8*b*. Pollution of the temple and/or 'the holy things': cp. 2:3; 8:12,
22.

PSALM 3

A Psalm of Solomon. Concerning the righteous.

1 (1) Why do you sleep, (my) soul, and do not praise the Lord?
      Sing (plur.) a new hymn for the Lord who is worthy
      to be praised.

2 (2) Sing (sing.) and be wakeful in wakefulness for him,
      For good is a psalm for God from a glad heart.

3 (3) The righteous remember the Lord at all times,
      With thanksgiving and declaration of the righteousness
      of the Lord's judgements.

4 (4) The righteous does not belittle it when he is chastened
      by the Lord,
      At all times his good will is before the Lord.

5 (5) If the righteous stumbles, he holds the Lord righteous,
      If he falls he watches for what God will do for him;
  (6) He keeps a steady watch for whence his deliverance
      will come.

6 (7) The steadfastness of the righteous (is) from God their
      deliverer
      In the house of the righteous (sing.) sin does not dwell
      upon sin.

7 (8) The righteous continually searches his house,
      To remove completely all unrighteousness resulting
      from his error.

8 (9) He makes atonement for (sins of) ignorance by fasting
      and humbling his soul,
  (10) And the Lord purifies every pious man and his house.

9 (11) When the sinner stumbles, he curses his life,
      The day of his birth and his mother's travail.

10 (12) He adds sins to sins in his life;
  (13) He falls – bad is his fall, and he will stand up no more.

11   The destruction of the sinner is for ever,
  (14) And (the Lord) will not remember him when he visits
      the righteous.

12 (15) This is the portion of the sinners for ever.
  (16) But those who fear the Lord will rise to eternal life,
      And their life (will be) in the light of the Lord and will
      come to an end no more.

1–4. Note the combination of singular and plural.
2. *in wakefulness for him*: or: 'against the time he awakes'?
3b. A major theme in PssSol (cp. 8:7f; 17:10; 18:3), here applied to
God's dealings with individuals.

4*a*. *when he is chastened*: cp. e.g. 8:26, 29; 17:42, 18:4, 7.

5–8. In Greek aorists and presents alternate. Obviously the typical case of a righteous man is compared to that of a typical sinner in verses 9–10.

5*c*. Cp. Ps. 121:1; 123: 1.

6. *steadfastness*, Gr. *alètheia* opp. to 'sin' (*hamartia*) in the next clause.

8. *humbling his soul*: this must be the meaning of the incorrect *tapeinōsei psuchèn*.

9–10. See on 5–8.

9*b*. Cp. Jer. 20: 14f; Job. 3:3f.

10*b*. *bad is his fall*: Gr. *hoti* cannot be translated with 'that' or 'because'; it is emphatic, as the Hebrew *ki*.

11–13. Note how the mention of the sinner who does not stand up after his fall (cp. verse 5) leads to the theme of the resurrection of the righteous, cp. 13:11; 14:10 in contrast to the eternal destruction of the sinners (cp. 2:31; 14:9; 15:10, 12f).

PSALM 8

Of Solomon. To victory.

1 (1) Distress and sound of war has my ear heard,
        the sound of a trumpet announcing slaughter and calamity.
2 (2) The sound of a numerous people as of a very strong wind,
        As a storm with much wind sweeping through the desert.
3 (3) And I said to my heart: where will God judge it?
4 (4) A sound I heard (moving) to Jerusalem, the city of holiness,
        (5) My loins were broken when I heard it;
5 (6) My knees were paralysed, my heart was afraid,
        My bones were shaken like flax.
6 (7) I said: They direct their ways in righteousness!
7   I summed up the judgements of God since the creation of
            heaven and earth.
        And I held God righteous in his judgements which have
            been from of old.
8 (8) God laid bare their sins in the full light of the sun.
        All the earth came to know the righteous judgements of
            God.

9   (9) In secret places underground were their transgressions,
            provoking (him) to anger;

    (10) Son consorted with mother and father with daughter.

10 (11) They committed adultery, each with his neighbour's wife,
            They made covenants about these things with one another,
            under oath.

11 (12) They plundered God's sanctuary, as if there were no heir to
            vindicate it.

12 (13) They trod on the altar of the Lord (coming) from all sorts
            of impurity,
            And with menstrual blood they defiled the sacrifices, as
            (if they were) common flesh.

13 (14) They left no sin undone, wherein they did not do more
            than the nations.

14 (15) Therefore God mixed for them a spirit of error,
            He made them drink a cup of undiluted wine that they
            might become drunk.

15 (16) He brought him who is from the end of the earth, who
            smites mightily.

    (17) He decreed war against Jerusalem and against her land.

16 (18) The leaders of the land went to meet him with joy;
            They said to him: Blessed be your way! Come and enter
            (plur.) with peace.

17 (19) They smoothed rough ways before his entry;
            They opened the gates to Jerusalem, crowned its walls.

18 (20) He entered as a father the house of his sons, with peace,
            He established his feet in great safety.

19 (21) He captured her fortresses and the wall of Jerusalem,

    (22) For God led him in safety, while they erred.

20 (23) He destroyed their leaders and everyone wise in counsel,
            He made the blood of the inhabitants of Jerusalem flow
            away like water of impurity.

21 (24) He led away their sons and daughters whom they had
            begotten in defilement.

22 (25) They did according to their impurity, even as their fathers.

(26) They defiled Jerusalem and the things sanctified to the
     name of God.

23 (27) But God has shown himself righteous in his judgements
        among the nations of the earth,

(28) And the pious ones of God are as innocent lambs in their
     midst.

24 (29) Worthy to be praised is the Lord who judges the whole
        earth in his righteousness.

25 (30) Behold now, O God, you have shown us your judgement
        in your righteousness,

(31) Our eyes have seen your judgements, O God.

26   We have justified your for ever honourable name,

(32) For you are the God of righteousness, judging Israel
     with chastening.

27 (33) Turn, O God, your mercy upon us
        And have pity upon us.

28 (34) Reassemble the dispersion of Israel with mercy and
        goodness

(35) For your faithfulness is with us.

29   And we stiffened our necks,
        But you are our chastener.

30 (36) Do not neglect us, O our God,
        That the nations may not swallow us up, as if there were
        no deliverer.

31 (37) Yes, you are our God from the beginning,
        And on you is our hope, O Lord.

32 (38) And we shall not depart from you,
        For good are your judgements upon us.

33 (39) For us and our children (is your) good pleasure for ever,
        O Lord, our saviour, we shall be shaken never more.

34 (40) Worthy to be praised is the Lord in his judgements, with
        the mouth of the pious ones,

(41) And blessed be Israel by the Lord for ever.

Superscription: *To victory*: does not seem apposite. Perhaps Gr.
nikos = *neikos* 'quarrel, strife'.

1–13. Cp. PsSol 1.

3. The question is somewhat awkward. It has been suggested that the original Hebrew meant: 'Surely, God will judge us.'

6–13. The sins of important groups of Jews in Jerusalem, including the priests (verses 11f).

11*b*. Probably referring to the Hasmoneans who had usurped the office of High Priest – unlawfully according to the author.

13. Cp. 1:8; 2:9.

14–21. Pompey marches towards Jerusalem and takes the city.

14. Cp. Isa. 19:14; 29:9f; 51:17–23.

15*b*. *He decreed*: subject God (see 15*a*) or Pompey (see 16*a*).

16–18. Josephus, *Ant.* xiv.3.1–3 (37–47); *War* 1.6.3–4 (128–32) describes how Aristobulus, Hyrcanus and the people plead their cause before Pompey at Damascus: the Hyrcanus party, particularly, ask him to intervene – *War* 1.6.5 (133). The latter opens the gates of Jerusalem at Pompey's approach – *Ant.* xiv.4.2 (58–60); *War* 1.7.2 (142–4). Verse 17*b* may, however, refer to the fortifications on the way to Jerusalem, evacuated by Aristobulus under pressure of Pompey; cp. *Ant.* xiv.3.4 (48–53); *War* 1. 6.5 (135–7).

16. *Blessed*: lit. 'desired', but compare Jer. 20:14 LXX with the Hebrew of that verse.

19–21. Pompey uses force – according to Josephus against the party of Aristobulus that occupied the temple – *Ant.* xiv.4.2–5 (60–79); *War* 1.7.3–7 (145–58). Verse 21 refers to Aristobulus' family (and others?) brought to Rome, cp. *Ant.* xiv.4.5 (79); *War* 1.7.7 (158).

22–4. Again: God's judgement, recognized as righteous (cp. verse 7f; 3:3; 17:10), has disclosed the many sins among the Israelites who are called to serve him.

25–31. The psalm ends with a prayer for deliverance that goes beyond the actual situation reflected in the preceding verses. Note the emphasis on chastening (verses 26, 29; see 3:4*a*) and the prayer for the return of the dispersed Israelites (cp. PssSol 11; 17:26, 31, 44).

34. Corresponds with 24 the end of the first section. Note the (additional) reference to the pious and to God's blessing for Israel.

PSALM 17

A psalm of Solomon with a song. For the king.

1 (1) Lord, you yourself are our king for ever and ever,
        For in you shall our soul glory.

2 (2) And what is the time of man's life on earth?
    In accordance with his time is also his hope in it.

3 (3) We shall hope in God, our saviour,
    For the might of our God is for ever with mercy,

  (4) And the kingdom of our God is for ever over the nations
      in judgement.

4 (5) You, O Lord, chose David king over Israel,
    And you swore to him concerning his seed for ever,
    That his kingship would never fail before you.

5 (6) But for our sins sinners rose up against us,
    They attacked us and thrust us out, (people) to whom
      you did not promise (anything),

  (7) They grabbed with violence, and did not glorify your
      honourable name.

6   In glory they put on the kingly diadem instead of their
      (true) honour.

  (8) And they made desolate the throne of David in arrogance
      leading to change.

7   But you, O God, will cast them down and will take away
      their seed from the earth,

  (9) In that there rose up against them a man who was alien to
      our race.

8 (10) In accordance with their sins you will retaliate upon
      them, O God,
    So that it befalls them according to their works.

9 (11) God will not pity them;
    He sought out their seed and let not one of them go free.

10 (12) Faithful is the Lord in all his judgements which he performs
      on the earth.

11 (13) The lawless one stripped our land of its inhabitants,
    They destroyed young and old and their children together.

12 (14) In his anger (...) he sent them away to the west
    And the rulers of the land (he exposed) to derision,
      and he did not spare them.

13 (15) Being alien the enemy acted insolently

And his heart was estranged from our God.

14 (16) And all things that he did in Jerusalem
(were such) as also the nations in their cities (do) for their
gods.

15 (17) And in the midst of the mingled nations the sons of the
covenant surpassed them;
There was no one among them who did mercy and
truth in Jerusalem.

16 (18) Those who loved the assemblies of the pious fled from them,
Like sparrows they flew out from their nest.

17 (19) They wandered in deserts to save their souls from evil,
And precious in the eyes of those who lived abroad was
a soul saved from them.

18 (20) Over the whole earth were they scattered by lawless men.
For the heaven withheld the rain from dripping upon the
earth.

19 (21) Springs were stopped (that sprang) perennial(ly) out of
the depths and from high mountains,
For there was none of them that did righteousness and
justice.

20   From their ruler to the least of them (they were) in all sorts
of pain,

(22) The king in transgression, the judge in disobedience, and the
people in sin.

21 (23) Behold, O Lord, and raise up unto them their king, the son of
David,
At the time you have (fore)seen, O God, to rule over Israel
your servant.

22 (24) And gird him with strength, to shatter unrighteous rulers,

(25) Purge Jerusalem from the nations that trample (her) in
destruction.

23 (26) With wisdom, with righteousness to drive out sinners from
the inheritance,
To destroy the arrogance of the sinner as a potter's vessels.

24   With a rod of iron to shatter all their substance,

(27) To destroy the godless nations with the word of his mouth,

25   (So that) at his threat nations will flee from his presence,
And to reprove sinners with the thought of their heart.

26 (28) He will assemble a holy people that he will lead in
righteousness
And he will judge the tribes of the people made holy by
the Lord its God.

27 (29) He will not allow unrighteousness to encamp in their
midst any longer,
Nor will dwell with them any man who knows evil.

(30) For he will know them, that all are sons of their God.

28   And he will divide them according to their tribes upon
the land,

(31) And neither sojourner nor alien will dwell with them
any more.

29   He will judge peoples and nations in the wisdom of his
righteousness.

[Diapsalma]

30 (32) And he will have the peoples of the nations to serve him
under his yoke;
And he will glorify the Lord in the sight of the whole
earth,

(33) And he will purify Jerusalem by holiness as of old.

31 (34) (So that) nations will come from the end of the earth to
see his glory,
Bringing as gifts her sons who are exhausted,

(35) And to see the glory of the Lord with which God has
glorified her.

32   And he (will be) a righteous king over them, instructed
by God,

(36) And there is no unrighteousness among them in his days.
For all are holy, and their king an anointed (of the) Lord.

33 (37) For he will not put his trust in horse and rider and bow,
Nor will he multiply for himself gold and silver for war,

And he will not gather confidence from a multitude
for the day of battle.

34 (38) The Lord himself is his king, the hope of him who is
strong through hope in God,
And he will have mercy on all the nations in fear before
him.

35 (39) For he will smite the earth with the word of his mouth
for ever,

(40) And he will bless the people of the Lord in wisdom with
gladness.

36 (41) And he will be pure from sin so that he may reign over a
great people,
Rebuke rulers and remove sinners by the power of his
word.

37 (42) And he will not be weak in his days with regard to
his God,
For God has made him strong with holy spirit,
And wise in the counsel of understanding with strength
and righteousness.

38 (43) And the blessing of the Lord will be with him in strength
And he will not be weak.

39 (44) His hope (will be) in the Lord. And who will be powerful
against him?

40   (He will be) strong in his works and mighty in the fear of
God,

(45) Shepherding the flock of the Lord in faithfulness and
righteousness,
And he will allow none among them to become weak in
their pasture.

41 (46) In equity he will lead all of them,
And there will be no arrogance among them, so that
any one among them would be oppressed.

42 (47) This is the majesty of the king of Israel that God has
acknowledged
To raise him up over the house of Israel, to chasten it:

43 (48) His words are more refined than the finest gold,
In the assemblies will he judge the tribes of a sanctified
people.

(49) His words are as the words of holy ones in the midst of
sanctified peoples.

44 (50) Blessed those who will live in those days
To see in the assembling of the tribes the good things of
Israel which God will accomplish.

45 (51) God will hasten upon Israel his mercy.
He will deliver us from the uncleanness of unholy enemies.

46 The Lord himself is our king for ever and ever.

1–3. God is praised as king – also in the concluding verse 46. This
kingship is directly connected with that of David and his descendants
(see verses 4–6, 21f, 34).

2. *in it*: i.e. the time, or *in him* i.e. man.

4. See 2 Sam. 7; Pss. 72, 89, 132, etc. and many prophecies concerning the house of David.

5–6. Probably refers to the Hasmonean house that eventually
usurped royal authority.

6. *instead of their (true) honour*: translation highly uncertain. Another:
'because of their arrogance'. *in arrogance leading to change*: reading
allagmatos with some mss. Other mss. *alalagmatos* leading to the
translation 'in tumultuous arrogance'.

7–14. Again a reference to what Pompey did in Jerusalem. cp.
PssSol 2 and 8.

7–9. Alternation of future and aorist; perhaps on purpose: in what
God did through Pompey the final destruction of the sinners in the
future has begun.

10. Cp. 3:3; 8:7f, 23f.

11a. Pompey, though God's instrument, is not only 'alien to our
race' (verse 7) but also 'the lawless one' (cp. 2:1); 'his heart was
estranged from our God' (verse 13).

11b. Note the plural.

12a. *In his anger*: Gr. reads 'in the anger of his beauty' which must
be either corrupt or a mistranslation, perhaps of *'appau* ('his fury') as
yāpyō ('his beauty'). *to the west*: cp. note on 8:21.

13–14. Cp. 2:28–31! Josephus describes how Pompey entered the
temple – *Ant.* XIV.4.4 (71–3); *War* 1.7.6 (152f); cp. 2:2f.

15–20. The sins of the 'sons of the covenant' (15, 18–20) and the dispersion of 'the assemblies of the pious' (16–17).

15. Cp. 2:9; 8:13.

16–17. Josephus, *Ant.* XIII.14.2 (383) mentions the exile of 8,000 opponents of Alexander Janneus; in XIV.2.1 (21) he tells that during the civil war between Aristobulus and Hyrcanus 'the Jews of best repute left the country and fled to Egypt'. Compare the pious ones mentioned in 1 Macc. 2, the exile of the Qumran community and the repeated gathering of people around prophets in the desert in the first century AD.

17a. *to save their souls*: or 'to save their lives' (from harm).

17b. *from them*: i.e. the sinners; or 'of them' i.e. the pious.

18b–19a. Cp. 1 Kings 17f; Hag. 1:10f; Ecclus. 48:3; AsMos 10:6; 4Ezra 6:24.

20. *to the least of them*: the Greek *kai laou elachistou* must be wrong; it is suggested that '*am* (people) is a misreading of '*ad* (to). So also Syr.

21. Here begins a prayer for the coming of the true son of David, that continues to the end of the psalm. It incorporates a great number of elements traditionally connected with the expectation of the ideal Davidic king. The total picture (not necessarily quite consistent!) is, of course, the author's own. Two features are dominant: (a) He will free Israel from its enemies, the people in dispersion will return and the nations will serve God and him. (b) He will serve the Lord as the ideal pious, obedient and wise man and unrighteousness will be banished from the country. It is wrong to speak of a 'political' Messiah, or a warrior-king; the ideal of a righteous king and a righteous Israel stands in the centre (see verses 26–7, 32, 36–7, 43).

21b. *have (fore)seen*: following the reading *ides* (*eides*); cp. Gen 22:8, 14 LXX for this meaning of the verb.
to rule: the subject may be God or the king; cp. on verses 1–3.

22–5. All verbs, with the exception of *gird* and *purge* in verse 22 are in the infinitive. The emphasis is on the destruction of the godless enemies, by God through the king.

23b–4a. Cp. Ps 2:9.

24b. Cp. Isa 11:4 LXX. See also verse 35.

26. *He will assemble*: cp. verses 31, 44; 8:28 and PsSol 11.
a holy people: see verses 32, 43 and cp. Deut. 7:6; 14:2, 21; Dan. 12:7.

27c. *sons of their God*: Deut. 14:1; Hos. 1:10; Isa. 54:13.

28a. Cp. Ezek. 37:15–28; 47:13.

28*b*. Cp. Isa. 52:1; Joel 3:17.

29. Cp. Isa. 11:1–5; Ps. 72.

Diapsalma Cp. 18:6; it is the Greek translation of *sèlah*, used very often in the book of Psalms. The meaning and function of the Hebrew term are uncertain, but the LXX understood it as marking a break. There is, however, no break at this point.

30. Cp. Ps. 2:8; 72:11; Zeph. 3:9; Dan. 7:14.

31. Cp. Ps. 72:9–11; Isa. 2:2–4; 49:22f; 60:2–7; 66:18–21.

32. See verses 26–7. Note the parallelism between *instructed by God* and *an anointed (of the) Lord*; the latter expression is a qualification rather than a title (see also on 18:1). Gr. reads *christos kurios*; cp. Lam. 4:20 LXX and the use of *kurios* in Ps. 110:1; Ecclus. 51:10 LXX. In PsSol 18:5 (cp. superscription and verse 7) clearly the well-known expression 'anointed of the Lord' is presupposed. The reading *kurios*, found in all witnesses, may go back to a Christian scribe (cp. Luke 2:11; Isa. 45:1 quoted in Barn 12:11).

33. Cp. Deut. 17:16f.

34*a*. Cp. on verses 1–3. Verses 34–41 repeat and emphasize a number of points raised before.

34*b*. *he will have mercy*: cp. verses 30–1.

35. *he will smite*: the author does not feel any contradiction with the preceding clause; cp. Ps. 2:10–12 after 8–9.

37. Cp. Isa. 11:1–5.

40. Cp. Ezek. 34; 37:24 and Isa. 49:9.

42–5. Conclusion and summing up.

42. *that* . . . : the relative points back to 'majesty'. *acknowledged* lit. *known*, cp. Jer. 1:5; Hos. 3:5. *to chasten it*: see 18:7 and on 3:4*a*. Or does the verb mean here: 'to lead'?

43. Cp. verses 26–7; 32. *holy ones*: probably angels in heaven are meant.

44. See on verse 26.

45. Though knowing that it is God who determines the right time (verse 21), the author hopes for deliverance in the near future.

PSALM 18

A psalm of Solomon. Again about the anointed of the Lord.

1 (1) Lord, your mercy is over the works of your hands for ever,
   (2) Your goodness over Israel with a rich gift.

2   Your eyes look upon them (i.e. the works), and none of
them will be wanting;

(3) Your ears listen to the prayer of a poor man in expectation.

3   Your judgements (are) upon the whole earth with mercy,

(4) And your love is towards the seed of Abraham, the sons of
Israel.

4   Your chastening is upon us as on a first-born, only-begotten
son

(5) To turn back the obedient soul from folly in ignorance.

5 (6) May God cleanse Israel against the day of mercy in
blessing,

Against the appointed day when he brings forth his
anointed one.

6 (7) Blessed those who will live in those days,

To see the good deeds of the Lord that he will perform
for the coming generation,

7 (8) Under the rod of the chastening of the Lord's anointed
in his fear of God,

In the wisdom of the spirit, of righteousness and strength;

8 (9) To direct (every) man in works of righteousness in the fear
of God,

To establish them all before the Lord.

9 (10) A good generation in the fear of the Lord in the days of
mercy!

[Diapsalma]

10 (11) Great is our God and glorious, dwelling in the highest;

(12) Who has ordained the lights of heaven in (their) course for
fixed seasons from day to day

And they did not turn aside from the way you have
appointed them.

11 (13) In the fear of God is their way every day,

From the day God created them and for ever.

12 (14) And they have not gone astray since the day he created them,

Since the generations of old they have not left their ways;

Unless God commanded them by the order of his servants.

Superscription. *the anointed of the Lord* cp. verse 5, 7. Here, and in this psalm in general the expression has become a title: in Ps 17 he speaks about the future king (superscription!)who is an anointed of the Lord (verse 22). Psalm 18 repeats elements from earlier psalms (including Ps 17, see verses 5–10) and may only have been added at the final redaction of the collection.

3*a*. See on 3:3*b*.

3*b*. *the sons*: Gr. 'the son', which is clearly impossible.

4*a*. *chastening*: see on 3:4*a*.

4*b*. *folly in ignorance*: cp. 3:8.

5*a*. *May God cleanse*: cp. 3:8; 17:22, 33.

6. Cp. 17:44.

7*a*. Cp. 17:24, 42.

7*b*. Cp. 17:35, 37 dependent on Isa. 11:2f.

9. The sentence is in the nominative and marks the ending of this (part of) the psalm. The *diapsalma* stands here in the right place.

10–12. These verses form a short hymn of praise which concludes the collection. One late manuscript (sixteenth century) adds here: 'Psalm of Solomon 19'. These verses deal with a well-known theme: God's power as revealed in the order observed by the heavenly bodies, cp. Gen. 1:14–19; Isa. 40:26; Ps. 8:4; 104:19; 147:4 and in later literature Bar 3:33–5; Wisd. of Sol. 13:1f; Ecclus. 43:1–12; 1En 41:3–9 and 1QH 1:9–13.

12*a*. *Unless God commanded*, etc.: cp. Josh. 10:12–14; Isa. 38:8.

The Martyrdom of Isaiah

MICHAEL A. KNIBB

The Ascension of Isaiah

The Martyrdom of Isaiah is a Jewish work which has come down to us as part of a larger Christian composition known as the Ascension of Isaiah. The Ascension consists of three separate writings: (1) the Martyrdom itself (the basic material in AscenIs 1:1–3:12 + 5:1–16). (2) An account of a vision seen by Isaiah (AscenIs 3:13–4:22) to which the title the Testament of Hezekiah has sometimes been given. The contents of this Christian writing are summarized below on p. 190. (3) A Christian work known as the Vision of Isaiah (AscenIs 6–11), which describes Isaiah's journey through the seven heavens. While in the seventh heaven he sees the descent to earth, life, death, resurrection and ascension of the Lord. It is this account of Isaiah's journey, or ascension, through the heavens which gives the title to the whole work. Here, however, we are only concerned with the Martyrdom of Isaiah.

Textual history

The textual history of the Martyrdom, like that of the Ascension as a whole, is complex; for full details see the introduction to the translation of this work in J. H. Charlesworth (ed.), *The Old Testament Pseudepigrapha*, vol. II. The Martyrdom was apparently composed in Hebrew, but no trace of this has survived. It was subsequently translated into Greek, while the Christian portions of the Ascension were composed in Greek; of this Greek version only a fragment covering 2:4–4:4 is known to exist. Translations from this Greek version into Ethiopic, Latin (Lat.[1]) and Coptic are known, but it is only in Ethiopic that a complete text of the Ascension has been preserved. (For chapters 6–11 there also exist a second Latin translation (Lat.[2]) and a Slavonic translation, and it appears that this part of the Ascension at one time had an independent existence.) The following translation of the Martyrdom is based on the Ethiopic version since this provides the only complete text; but account has also been taken of the Greek version (covering 2:4–3:12 of the Martyrdom) and of the Latin (covering 2:14–3:12 of the Martyrdom). The fragmentary Coptic evidence is only alluded to in the case of 3:5. Reference should also be made here to the Greek Legend which is sometimes mentioned in the notes. The Greek Legend is a work based on the Ascension of Isaiah in which the material in the Ascension has been totally recast. Most of the textual evidence is conveniently gathered together in the edition of R. H. Charles, *The Ascension of Isaiah*, London, 1900.

Content of Martyrdom of Isaiah. Its genre

In the opening scene of the Martyrdom we are told how Hezekiah, towards the end of his life, summoned his son Manasseh in order to instruct him, and how on that occasion Isaiah foretold, to Hezekiah's distress, that Manasseh would ignore his father's commands and bring about the death of Isaiah (1:1–13). The remainder of the narrative recounts the fulfilment of this prophecy. After Hezekiah's death Manasseh served Satan and made Jerusalem a place of apostasy where divination, fornication, adultery, and the persecution of the righteous all flourished (2:1–6). As a result of this Isaiah and his followers withdrew from Jerusalem, first to Bethlehem, and then to a mountain in a desert place (2:7–11). At this point we are introduced to the false prophet Belkira who was instrumental in causing the death of Isaiah (2:12a), but the narrative is interrupted to describe the fate of another prophet who was martyred for his faithfulness to God, Micaiah the son of Imlah (2:12b–16). The narrative then describes Belkira's accusation of Isaiah and the latter's arrest (3:1–12), and finally the execution of Isaiah (5:1–16).

The Old Testament does not tell us when or how Isaiah died, and the story of the Martyrdom must be regarded as the pious invention of the author or of those responsible for the tradition on which he was drawing. It does seem clear, however, that the Old Testament provided the major source of inspiration for the story. Thus the narrative may be regarded as an elaboration of what is said about the wickedness of Manasseh in 2 Kings 21:1–18, and in particular of the statement in 21:16, 'Manasseh shed so much innocent blood that he filled Jerusalem full to the brim.' It takes over the contrast that is implicit in the Old Testament between the good Hezekiah and the wicked Manasseh. Further, many details in the narrative are drawn from, or based on, the Old Testament, as may be seen from the notes.

The Martyrdom belongs to the genre of the legend. The Old Testament contains a number of prophetic legends (cp. e.g. the stories about Elisha in 2 Kings 4; 6:1–7, 8–23, or the legendary narratives about the siege of Jerusalem in 701 which record the significant role played by Isaiah (2 Kings 18:17–19:37; Isa. 36:2–37:38)). But the closest parallel to the Martyrdom of Isaiah is to be found in the martyr legends of the Old Testament and the Apocrypha: the stories about Daniel and his three companions (Dan. 3 and 6) and the accounts of the martyrdom of Eleazar and of the mother and her seven sons (2 Macc. 6:18–7:42). Stories such as these were told in order to encourage Jews to remain faithful to God in the face of persecution, but unlike the somewhat older stories of Dan. 3 and 6, it is recognized both in the martyr legends of 2 Maccabees and in the Martyrdom of Isaiah that the cost of remaining faithful will indeed be death. In the case of the Martyrdom the message is underlined by the inclusion of the story of Micaiah (2:12b–16). Beyond these general considerations it is difficult to suggest a precise date or setting. The story is almost certainly of Palestinian origin and belongs in the intertestamental period; it is apparently alluded to in Heb. 11:37, and this suggests that it was composed not later than the first century AD. It has been suggested that it goes back ultimately to the time of the persecution of Antiochus Epiphanes (167–164 B.C.), and this may well be so. But it is possible that it reflects the circumstances of some other persecution, and the fact that it is an Israelite king, Manasseh, who is responsible for Isaiah's death might suggest that we should think in terms of a persecution of a group of pious Jews by Jewish rulers. The Martyrdom of Isaiah does not contain the kind of evidence for there to be any certainty on this matter.

The material translated here as belonging to the Martyrdom (1:1–3:12 + 5:1–16) provides a reasonably coherent narrative. Within the material there are some obvious signs of Christian editing, notably in 1:2b–6a, 7, 13; 2:9; 5:1a, 15–16; these passages stem from the final editor of the complete book and serve in part to link the different sections of the Ascension together. It should, however, be observed that it cannot simply be assumed that the material left after the excision of these passages constitutes the original Jewish Martyrdom of Isaiah. The possibility of Christian reworking of what appears to be Jewish material needs to be kept in mind.

Demonology

One very important element in the Martyrdom of Isaiah is its demonology. The leader of the forces of evil, who has at his disposal a host of subordinate angels (2:2; cp. 5:9), is called variously 'Sammael' (cp. 1:8), 'Beliar' (cp. 1:8) and 'Satan' (cp. 2:2), the three names being used interchangeably. These names are used frequently, but two others also occur: Matanbukus (see 2:4 and 5:3) and Malkira (see 1:8). The latter name occurs as an additional name of Sammael and means in Hebrew 'king of evil'.

Both Beliar (1:9; 3:11; 5:1) and Sammael (2:1) are said to dwell in the heart of Manasseh, and it is under the inspiration of Beliar/Sammael that Manasseh has Isaiah put to death. The false prophet Belkira likewise acts as the agent of the leader of the forces of evil and in 5:4–10 appears as the devil himself in human form. The name of this false prophet is given in a wide variety of forms in the different versions (the evidence is set out in full in *The Old Testament Pseudepigrapha*, vol. II), but all these forms appear to derive ultimately from a Hebrew *beḥīr-ra'*, 'the elect of evil'. In the following translation, despite the variety of evidence in the Ethiopic manuscripts and the other versions, the name has been given consistently as 'Belkira', since this is the form in the Ethiopic version – on which the translation is based – which comes closest to *beḥīr-ra'*. One variant spelling of the name should, however, be noted. The variants in some places point back to Malkira, 'king of evil', as the name of the false prophet. We have seen that this name occurs in 1:8 as an additional name of Sammael. The fact that it also occurs as a variant for the name of the false prophet may in part be attributed to error by the copyists, and in part to the fact that the false prophet appears in chapter 5 as Beliar himself in human form.

Consideration of the demonology of the Martyrdom indicates that it is appropriate to talk of a dualistic theology. Behind Isaiah, his fellow prophets and followers, stands God himself; over against them are ranged Manasseh and his court, and Belkira and the other false prophets, the earthly representatives of the spiritual forces of evil. This dualistic theology has been compared to that of the Qumran writings (see especially 1QS III. 13–IV.26), and the view has been advanced that the Martyrdom is a Qumran work, or even that it provides a veiled history of the Qumran community and its leader, the Teacher of Righteousness. The idea that we have to do with a veiled history of the Qumran community seems rather unlikely, and although there are general similarities between the dualistic theology of the Martyrdom and that of the Qumran writings, the fact that the distinctive language and theological emphases of the Scrolls are lacking in the Martyrdom makes it seem unlikely that it should be regarded as a Qumran work. No trace of the Martyrdom has been found among the Qumran writings.

Bibliography

R. H. Charles, *The Ascension of Isaiah*, London, 1900.
R. H. Charles, 'The Martyrdom of Isaiah', in *The Apocrypha and Pseudepigrapha of the Old Testament*, vol. II, pp. 155–62.
M. A. Knibb, 'The Ascension of Isaiah', in J. H. Charlesworth (ed.), *The Old Testament Pseudepigrapha*, vol. II (forthcoming).
D. Flusser, 'The Apocryphal Book of *Ascensio Isaiae* and the Dead Sea Sect', *Israel Exploration Journal* 3 (1953), 30–47.
E. Hammershaimb, 'Das Martyrium Jesajas', in JSHRZ II/1, pp. 15–34.

HEZEKIAH SUMMONS MANASSEH

1:1　In the twenty-sixth year of his reign Hezekiah king of Judah
2　summoned Manasseh his son, for he was his only son. He summoned him in the presence of Isaiah, the son of Amoz, the prophet, and in the presence of Josab the son of Isaiah, in order to hand over to him the words of righteousness which the king himself had seen,
3　and (the words concerning) the eternal judgements, and the torments of Gehenna, and the prince of this world, and his angels,
4　and his authorities, and his powers, and the words concerning faith in the Beloved which he himself had seen in the fifteenth
5　year of his reign during his sickness. And he handed to him the written words which Samnas the secretary had written out, and also those which Isaiah the son of Amoz had given to him, and to the prophets also, that they might write out and store up with him what he himself had seen in the house of the king concerning the judgement of the angels, and concerning the destruction of this world, and concerning the robes of the saints and their going out, and concerning their transformation and the persecution and
6　ascension of the Beloved. In the twentieth year of the reign of Hezekiah Isaiah had seen the words of this prophecy and had handed them to Josab his son. And while (Hezekiah) was giving
7　his commands, with Josab the son of Isaiah standing by, Isaiah said to Hezekiah the king, and not only in the presence of Manasseh did he say (it) to him, 'As the LORD lives whose name has not been transmitted to this world, and as the Beloved of my Lord lives, and as the Spirit which speaks in me lives, all these

commands and these words will have no effect on Manasseh your son, and through the deeds of his hands, tormented in body, I will

8 depart. And Sammael Malkira will serve Manasseh and will do everything he wishes, and he will be a follower of Beliar rather

9 than of me. He will cause many in Jerusalem and Judah to desert the true faith, and Beliar will dwell in Manasseh, and by his hands

10 I will be sawn in half.' And when Hezekiah heard these words, he wept very bitterly, and tore his robes, and threw earth on his

11 head, and fell on his face. And Isaiah said to him, 'Sammael's plan against Manasseh is complete; there will be no benefit to you from

12 this day.' And Hezekiah thought in his heart that he would kill

13 Manasseh his son, but Isaiah said to Hezekiah, 'The Beloved has made your plan ineffective, and the thought of your heart will not come about; for with this calling have I been called, and the inheritance of the Beloved will I inherit.'

The opening chapter tells how Hezekiah summoned his son Manasseh in order to instruct him, and how, on this occasion, Isaiah foretold both Manasseh's wickedness and his own death at the hands of Manasseh. The original (Jewish) narrative has been subjected to Christian re-working, evident in verses 2b–6a, 7 and 13.

1. *the twenty-sixth year*: i.e. three years before his death (cp. 2 Kings 18:2). Although the chapter is not an account of a death-bed scene as such, Hezekiah's words do have someting of the character of a testament (see above, pp. 71–2, for the discussion of the genre of T12P).

2a. *Josab*: i.e. Shear-jashub, cp. Isa. 7:3.

2b–6a. These verses come from the Christian editor and serve in part to link together the different sections of the complete book, the Ascension of Isaiah. Verses 5b–6a, referring to a vision of Isaiah, clearly allude to chapters 6–11; verses 2b–5a, referring to a vision seen by the king, have been taken to allude to the interpolated section 3:13-4:22, but this is less certain. The *Opus Imperfectum*, an incomplete work on Matthew attributed to the sixth century, appears to preserve an earlier version of the scene in chapter 1; according to this work Hezekiah summoned Manasseh to give him, not revelations about the future, but commands (cp. verses 6b, 7) about the fear of God, and about how he should rule.

3. *and the prince of this world*: correction; Eth. 'which is the eternal

place of punishment', or similar. *angels...authorities...powers*: cp.
1 Pet. 3:22; Eph. 6:12.

4. *the Beloved*: a title used for Jesus throughout the whole book (cp.
Mark 1:11; 9:7; Matt. 12:18); the occurrences within the Martyrdom
(1:4, 5, 7, 13; 5:15) all stem from the Christian editor. *his sickness*: cp.
2 Kings 20:1–11; Isa. 38; 2 Chron. 32:24. The idea that Hezekiah
experienced a vision at the time of his sickness is perhaps based on
the tradition that he was given 'a sign' (2 Kings 20:8; 2 Chron.
32:24).

5. *Samnas*: i.e. Shebna, cp. 2 Kings 18:18, etc. *had written out*: these
words imply that Hezekiah dictated the content of his vision to
Samnas. *the robes of the saints*: the heavenly robes which the saints put on
after death, mentioned frequently in the Christian portions of the
Ascension, are a symbol of their transformed state; cp. Rev. 6:11; 7:9,
13–14; 2 Cor. 5:1–4. *and their going out*: i.e. their departure from this
life. But in the light of Greek Legend 1:2 the text should perhaps be
emended, 'and concerning the going out, and the transformation, and
the persecution and ascension of the Beloved'. The 'going out' in this
case is the descent of the Beloved through the seven heavens (10:7–31,
not included here).

7. *As the* LORD *lives*: the common Old Testament oath formula,
cp. e.g. 1 Sam. 14:39, 45. *and as the Beloved...in me lives*: Christian
editorial addition.

8. *Sammael*: according to Jewish tradition Sammael was originally
one of the chief archangels, but after inciting the serpent to tempt Eve
he became the leader of the Satans. It is as leader of the forces of evil
that he is mentioned in the Ascension where his name seems to be
merely another name for Beliar. *Malkira*: this name means in Hebrew
'king of evil'; it is used here as an additional name for Sammael, but
elsewhere occurs as a variant form of Belkira, the name of the opponent
of Isaiah (cp. 2:12, and see above, p. 181). *Beliar*: a variant form of the
name Belial, cp. e.g. 2 Cor. 6:15; TLevi 3:3; 1QS 1.18.

9. *He will cause many...to desert the true faith*: cp. 2 Kings 21:9;
2 Chron. 33:9. *I will be sawn in half*: the tradition that Isaiah was sawn
in half is apparently alluded to in Heb. 11:37.

10. A description of the conventional signs of distress, cp. 2 Sam.
13:19, 31; Job 2:12.

13. *and the inheritance of the Beloved will I inherit*: this clause, like the
mention of 'the Beloved' earlier in the verse, stems from the Christian
editor. As an heir of the Beloved, Isaiah's fate is to be one of suffering;
cp. Rom. 8:17.

MANASSEH'S WICKED REIGN

2:1 And it came about that after Hezekiah had died, and Manasseh had become king, (Manasseh) did not remember the commands of Hezekiah his father, but forgot them; and Sammael dwelt in
2 Manasseh and clung closely to him. And Manasseh abandoned the service of the LORD of his father, and he served Satan, and his
3 angels, and his powers. And he turned the house of his father which had been in the presence of Hezekiah away ⟨from⟩ᵃ the words of
4 wisdom and the service of the LORD. Manasseh turned them away so that they served Beliar; for the angel of iniquity who rules this world is Beliar, whose name is Matanbukus. And he rejoiced over Jerusalem because of Manasseh, and he strengthened himᵇ in causing apostasy, and in the iniquity which was disseminated in Jerusalem.
5 And sorcery and magic, augury and divination, fornication and adultery,ᶜ and the persecution of the righteous increased through Manasseh, and through Belkira,ᵈ and through Tobiah the Canaanite,
6 and through John of Anathoth, and through Zaliq Neway. And the rest of the acts, behold they are written in the book of the kings of Judah and Israel.

a Correction based on Greek Legend 3:3.
b Correction, apparently supported by Greek; Eth. 'and he held him firmly'.
c and adultery: Greek omits.
d and through Belkira: Greek omits.

The description of Manasseh's reign is built up from the description of his wickedness in 2 Kings 21:1–18 and 2 Chron. 33:1–9; there is no mention of the story of his repentance and reform found in 2 Chron. 33:12–16 and reflected in the Prayer of Manasseh.

1. *Manasseh...forgot*: in the Hebrew original there was a play on words linking the name Manasseh with the verb 'to forget' (*nāšāh*); cp. Gen. 41:51.

4. *the angel of iniquity who rules this world*: cp. John 12:31; 14:30; 16:11; 2 Cor. 4:4; Eph. 2:2. *Matanbukus*: another name for Beliar, the Hebrew original of which perhaps means 'gift of desolation'; see also 5:3.

5. *the persecution of the righteous*: cp. 2 Kings 21:16. *and through Belkira*: lacking in the Greek, and probably an addition here. *Tobiah the*

Canaanite...John of Anathoth...Zaliq Neway: the origin of this list of
names is unknown. For the third Greek has 'Zadok, the overseer of the
works'; Eth. 'Zaliq Neway' is perhaps a corruption of an expression
meaning 'the overseer of the works'.

6. Cp. 2 Kings 21:17; 2 Chron. 33:18.

ISAIAH WITHDRAWS FROM JERUSALEM

2:7   And when Isaiah the son of Amoz saw the great iniquity which
      was being committed in Jerusalem, and the service of Satan,
      and his wantonness he withdrew from Jerusalem and dwelt in
 8   Bethlehem of Judah. And there also there was great iniquity; and
      he withdrew from Bethlehem and dwelt on a mountain in a desert
 9   place. And Micah the prophet, and the aged Ananias, and Joel, and
      Habakkuk, and Josab his son, and many of the faithful who believed
      in the ascension into heaven, withdrew and dwelt on the moun-
10   tain. All of them were clothed in sackcloth, and all of them were
      prophets; they had nothing with them, but were destitute, and
11   they all lamented bitterly over the going astray of Israel. And they
      had nothing to eat except wild herbs (which) they gathered from
      the mountains, and when they had cooked (them), they ate (them)
      with Isaiah the prophet. And they dwelt on the mountains and on
      the hills, for two years of days.

   8. *on a mountain*: the narrative has possibly been influenced by
the story of Elijah, 1 Kings 19:1–8. *in a desert place*: the wilderness
was a traditional place of refuge, cp. e.g. Judg. 20: 47; 1 Macc.
2:27–30.
   9. *Micah the prophet...Joel, and Habakkuk*: these prophets are presented as contemporaries of Isaiah, but only Micah can clearly be
regarded as such. However, although the book of Joel is commonly
assigned to the post-exilic period, in Jewish tradition the prophet was
thought to have lived in the eighth century, as the placing of his
prophecy between those of Hosea and Amos indicates. *the aged Ananias*:
it is not known who is meant. *who believed in the ascension into heaven*:
so Eth.; Greek 'who believed that (he) had ascended into heaven'.
A reference to the ascension of Isaiah (so apparently Greek) makes no
sense here, but a reference to the ascension of Jesus, or of believers, is

equally out of place. Textual corruption or Christian editorial revision seems likely.

10. *sackcloth:* rough clothes seem to have been the traditional dress of prophets, cp. 2 Kings 1:8; Zech. 13:4; Matt. 3:4.

11. *wild herbs:* cp. the story of the group of prophets during a famine, 2 Kings 4:38–9.

THE STORY OF ZEDEKIAH AND MICAIAH

2:12   And after this, while they were in the desert, there was a certain man in Samaria named Belkira, of the family of Zedekiah the son of Kenaanah, the false prophet, whose dwelling (was) in Bethlehem[a]. And Zedekiah[b] the son of Kenaanah, who was the brother of his father, was the teacher in the days of Ahab, king of Israel, of the four hundred prophets of Baal. And he struck and abused

13   Micaiah, the son of Amida, the prophet. And he was abused by Ahab, and Micaiah was thrown into prison with Zedekiah the prophet; they were with Ahaziah the son of Alamerem Balalaaw.

14   And Elijah the prophet from Tishbe in Gilead reproved Ahaziah and Samaria, and he prophesied concerning Ahaziah that he would die on his bed of sickness, and Samaria[c] would be given into the hand of Shalmaneser,[d] because he had killed the prophets of the

15   LORD. And when the false prophets who (were) with Ahaziah the son of Ahab[e] and their teacher Jalerias from mount Joel

16   heard – now he was a brother of Zedekiah – when they heard, they persuaded Ahaziah the king of Aguaron and ⟨killed⟩[f] Micaiah.

a Greek 'Bethany'.
b *Zedekiah:* so Greek; Eth. 'Hezekiah'.
c *and Samaria:* so Greek; Eth. 'in Samaria'.
d Correction; Eth. 'Leba Naser', or similar; Greek 'Alnasar'.
e Greek 'Alam'.
f *killed:* so Greek Lat.[1]; Eth. omits.

We are now introduced for the first time to Belkira, the adversary of Isaiah (the reference to him in 2:5 is suspect). But the narrative is then briefly interrupted to describe the fate of another prophet who suffered for his faithfulness to God, Micaiah son of Imlah (cp. 1 Kings 22:1–28).

12. *Belkira*: the name appears in various forms in the versions, but seems to go back ultimately to a Hebrew *beḥīr-ra'*, 'the elect of evil'. *Zedekiah the son of Kenaanah*: cp. 1 Kings 22:11. *And Zedekiah...was the brother of his father*: i.e. Zedekiah was the uncle of Belkira. The author ignores or is unaware of the chronological difficulties involved in this supposed relationship inasmuch as the story of Micaiah's clash with Zedekiah belongs some one hundred and fifty years before the time of Isaiah. *the four hundred prophets of Baal*: the writer has confused the four hundred prophets mentioned in 1 Kings 22:6 with the four hundred and fifty prophets of Baal mentioned in 1 Kings 18:19, 22; some Ethiopic mss. omit 'of Baal'. *And he struck*: cp. 1 Kings 22:24. *Amida*: the various forms of this name in the Ethiopic and Greek are corruptions of 'Imlah', cp. 1 Kings 22:8.

13. *And he*: apparently Micaiah. *and Micaiah was thrown into prison*: cp. 1 Kings 22:26–8. *with Zedekiah the prophet:* so Eth., but there is nothing in the Old Testament to suggest that Zedekiah was thrown into prison with Micaiah; Greek 'and he was with Zedekiah the false prophet'. It is difficult to know how to explain Eth. and Greek, and also the following statement that Micaiah and Zedekiah were 'with Ahaziah'; it is possible that the text is corrupt for 'the people of Zedekiah the false prophet were with Ahaziah'. Underlying verses 13*b*–16 is an otherwise unknown tradition about the fate of Micaiah in the reign of Ahaziah (cp. 1 Kings 22:51–2 Kings 1:18), but many details are obscure. *Alamerem Balalaaw*: so Eth.; Greek 'Ala[m] in Semmōma', but the manuscript is damaged. The text is corrupt and perhaps read originally 'Ahab in Samaria'.

14. *And Elijah the prophet from Tishbe in Gilead*: cp. 1 Kings 17:1. *prophesied concerning Ahaziah that he would die on his bed of sickness*: cp. 2 Kings 1:1–8. *and Samaria would be given into the hand of Shalmaneser*: Elijah's prophecies contain no mention of Shalmaneser, but for the fall of Samaria see 2 Kings 17:1–6.

15. *Jalerias*: so Eth.; Greek 'Iallarias'; Lat.[1] 'Gamarias'; no such false prophet is known in the Old Testament. *Joel*: so Eth.; Greek 'Islal'; Lat.[1] 'Efrem'. 'Mount Ephraim' (cp. e.g. Josh. 17:15, 'the hill-country of Ephraim') was probably the original reading; it is possible that 'Israel' was substituted for 'Ephraim', and that the existing Greek and Ethiopic forms are corruptions of this.

16. *now he*: so Lat.[1], the reference correctly being to Jalerias/Gamarias; Greek and Eth. by mistake add the name of Isaiah's opponent (Greek 'Becheir⟨a⟩'; Eth. corrupt 'Ibkira', or similar). *Aguaron*: so Eth.; Greek Lat.[1] 'Gomorrah', used here as a contemptuous name for

Samaria (cp. 3:10; Isa. 1:10; Jer. 23:14). Eth. 'Aguaron' is perhaps a corruption of 'Ekron' – Ahaziah is king of Ekron because he consults the god of Ekron (2 Kings 1:1–16). *and killed Micaiah*: the Old Testament does not mention the execution of Micaiah.

ISAIAH IS ACCUSED

3:1 And Belkira[a] discovered and saw the place of Isaiah and of the prophets who were with him, for he himself dwelt in the district of Bethlehem, and he was a follower of Manasseh. And he prophesied lies in Jerusalem, and there were many from Jerusalem

2 who joined with him, but he himself was from Samaria. And it came about, when Shalmaneser[b] the king of Assyria came and captured Samaria, and took the nine[c] tribes into captivity, and led

3 them to the provinces[d] of the Medes and the rivers of Gozan,[e] that this youth escaped and came to Jerusalem in the days of Hezekiah king of Judah, but he did not walk in the ways of his Samaritan

4 father because he feared Hezekiah. And he was found in the days

5 of Hezekiah speaking words of iniquity in Jerusalem. And the servants of Hezekiah accused him, and he escaped to the district of

6 Bethlehem and persuaded... And Belkira accused Isaiah and the prophets who (were) with him, saying, 'Isaiah and the prophets who (are) with him prophesy against Jerusalem and against the cities of Judah that they will be laid waste, and also (against) Benjamin that it will go into captivity, and also against you, O lord king, that you will go (bound) with hooks and chains of

7, 8 iron. But they prophesy lies against Israel and Judah. And Isaiah

9 himself has said, "I see more than Moses the prophet." Moses said, "There is no man who can see the LORD and live." But Isaiah

10 has said, "I have seen the LORD, and behold I am alive." Know, therefore, O king, that they (are) false prophets.[f] And he has called Jerusalem Sodom, and the princes of Judah and Jerusalem he has declared (to be) the people of Gomorrah.' And he brought many

11 accusations against Isaiah and the prophets before Manasseh. But Beliar dwelt in the heart of Manasseh and in the heart of the princes of Judah and Benjamin, and of the eunuchs, and of the king's

councillors. And the words of Belkira pleased him very much,
12 and he sent and seized Isaiah.

> a So Greek Lat.¹; Eth. corrupt, 'and Belkira. And he discovered'.
> b So Lat.¹; Eth. 'Alagar Zagar', or similar; Greek 'Algasar'.
> c So Eth.; Greek Lat.¹ 'nine and a half'.
> d So Eth.; Greek 'mountains'; Lat.¹ 'mountain'.
> e So Greek Lat.¹; Eth. 'Tazon'.
> f So Eth.; Greek Lat.¹ 'that he is a liar'.

The narrative of the martyrdom is resumed from 2:12a; it tells first
how Belkira, a native of Samaria, came to be living in Bethlehem
(verses 1–5), and then recounts his accusation of Isaiah (verses 6–12).

2. *when Shalmaneser...captured Samaria*: cp. 2 Kings 17:1–6;
18:9–11.

5. *and persuaded*: so Eth., but text defective; Greek 'and they persuaded'; Lat.¹ omits; Coptic 'he persuaded Belch [ira'. The fragmentary
Coptic evidence confirms an earlier proposal that the missing object of
the verb was Belkira; the subject was either the false prophets (cp. the
plural verb in the Greek) or Beliar (cp. the singular verb in Eth. and the
Coptic). The point in any case is that Belkira was persuaded to accuse
Isaiah.

6. *that you will go (bound) with hooks and chains of iron*: based on what
is said about Manasseh in 2 Chron. 33:11.

9. *There is no man who can see the* LORD *and live*: cp. Exod. 33:20.
I have seen the LORD: cp. Isa. 6:1.

10. *he has called Jerusalem Sodom, and the princes of Judah and Jerusalem
...Gomorrah*: cp. Isa. 1:10.

The narrative of the martyrdom is interrupted at this point by an
account of a vision which Isaiah is held to have experienced earlier in
his life; Beliar is said to be angry with Isaiah because of the vision, and
hence in the present form of the complete book the vision serves to
explain why Isaiah was martyred. The content of the vision (3:13–
4:22, not presented here) is manifestly Christian; 3:13 summarizes
chapters 6–11, but otherwise the vision refers to the life and death of
the Beloved, the corruption of the Church, the reign of Beliar, and the
second coming of the Lord. The narrative of the Martyrdom is
resumed in chapter 5.

THE EXECUTION OF ISAIAH

5:1 Because of these visions, therefore, Beliar was angry with Isaiah,
and he dwelt in the heart of Manasseh, and he sawed Isaiah in half

2 with a wood saw. And while Isaiah was being sawn in half, his
accuser Belkira stood by, and all the false prophets stood by,
3 laughing and (maliciously) joyful because of Isaiah. And Belkira,
through Mekembekus, stood before Isaiah, laughing and deriding.
4 And Belkira said to Isaiah, 'Say, "I have lied in everything I have
5 spoken; the ways of Manasseh are good and right, and also the
6 ways of Belkira and those who are with him are good."' And he
7 said this to him when he began to be sawn in half. And Isaiah
was in a vision of the Lord, but his eyes were open, and he saw them.

8 And Belkira spoke thus to Isaiah, 'Say what I say to you, and
I will turn their heart and make Manasseh, and the princes of
9 Judah, and the people, and all Jerusalem worship you.' And Isaiah
answered and said, 'If it is within my power to say, "Condemned
10 and cursed be you, and all your hosts, and all your house!" For
there is nothing further that you can take except the skin of my
11 body.' And they seized Isaiah the son of Amoz and sawed him in
12 half with a wood saw. And Manasseh, and Belkira, and the false
prophets, and the princes, and the people, and all stood by looking
13 on. And to the prophets who (were) with him he said before he
was sawn in half, 'Go to the district of Tyre and Sidon, for for me
14 alone the LORD has mixed the cup.' And while Isaiah was being
sawn in half, he did not cry out, nor weep, but his mouth spoke
15 with the Holy Spirit until he was sawn in two. Beliar did this to
Isaiah through Belkira and through Manasseh, for Sammael was
very angry with Isaiah from the days of Hezekiah, king of Judah,
because of the things which he had seen concerning the Beloved,
16 and because of the destruction of Sammael which he had seen
through the Lord, while Hezekiah his father was king. And he did
as Satan wished.

1. *Because of these visions*: an allusion to 3:13-4:22. The first half of
this verse was composed by the editor of the complete book in order
to link 3:13-4:22 with the Martyrdom. *a wood saw*: i.e. a saw to cut
wood. But the underlying Hebrew expression is ambiguous, and in the
Greek Legend and other works it was taken to mean 'a wooden saw',
a saw made out of wood. Cp. Heb. 11:37.

3. *through Mekembekus*: one Eth. ms. has 'and Mekembekus', and this reading is grammatically easier because the following verbs are plural. But the plural forms may be corrupt. 'Mekembekus' is another name for Beliar; it appears to be a corruption of 'Matanbukus' (2:4), but it has been regarded by one scholar as the original form of the name and to have meant in the underlying Hebrew 'he who creates weeping'. Under the inspiration of Mekembekus (i.e. Beliar) Belkira mocks Isaiah.

4–10. Belkira tempts Isaiah.

4. *Belkira*: so one Eth. ms., cp. verse 8; other mss. 'Beliar'. Since Belkira is presented in this section as Beliar himself in human form, it is perhaps hardly surprising that the names should be confused in the manuscripts.

7. Perhaps emend to read, 'and (although) his eyes were open, he did ⟨not⟩ see them'; cp. 6:10 (not presented here).

8. There are some similarities with the temptation of Jesus, cp. Matt. 4:8–10; Luke 4:5–8.

9. *and all your hosts*: it is here perhaps that it is most obvious that Belkira is presented as the devil in human form, with his 'hosts' of evil spirits at his disposal, cp. 2:2. In the corresponding passage in the Greek Legend (3:18) Isaiah answers, 'Accursed be you, O Melchias the false prophet, O devil.'

11–14. The death of Isaiah.

13. *the district of Tyre and Sidon*: it is not clear why this particular region (cp. Matt. 15:21) should be mentioned. It has been suggested that the tradition of Elijah's association with Sidon (1 Kings 17:7–24) may have influenced the author. *the cup*: a symbolic term for the vocation of martyrdom to which Isaiah was called, cp. Mark 10:38–9; 14:36.

15–16. An editorial addition which, like verse 1*a*, serves to link 3:13–4:22 with the narrative of the Martyrdom. *And he did as Satan wished*: the subject is either Manasseh or Belkira.

The Syriac Apocalypse of Baruch

A. F. J. KLIJN

The *Syriac Apocalypse of Baruch* (2Bar) belongs to a group of pseud-epigrapha written under the name of Baruch. Other writings of this group are the *Apocryphal Book of Baruch* (Baruch), the *Greek Apocalypse of Baruch* (3Bar) and the *Rest of the Words of Baruch* (4Bar), also called *Paraleipomena Jeremiou* (PJ). The last two works were written in the first centuries AD and show considerable Christian influence. (See also the introduction to the *Paraleipomena Jeremiou*, pp. 213–16.)

In the Old Testament Book of Jeremiah Baruch is mentioned several times. He is a faithful servant of the prophet Jeremiah, acting as his secretary (36:4 and 45:1–2) and representative (36:8 and 13–14). He is called 'the scribe' (36:26–7 and 32). In the present work Baruch receives information about the future which he has to reveal to Jeremiah and others (5:5, cp. 2:1). With Enoch and Ezra he has become one of the most famous apocalyptic figures in Judaism.

Documentary evidence

Until recently the Apocalypse of Baruch was only known from a Syriac manuscript dating from the sixth or seventh century AD. Since the beginning of this century two fragments have come to light in Greek (12:1–13:2 and 13:11–14:3) from the fourth or fifth century. Small fragments of the text, again in Syriac, have been discovered in lectionaries of the Jacobite Church. However, no fewer than thirty-six manuscripts of the letter at the end of this work (78:1 till the end) are known because it once belonged to the canon of Scriptures in the Syriac speaking Church.

Not long ago the entire work was discovered in an Arabic manu-script on Mount Sinai. This text differs in many details from the Syriac which we already knew before. Nevertheless the Arabic translation appears to be a free rendering of an original Syriac version. This means that the contents are not very helpful in determining the original text of the somewhat corrupt Syriac translation.

The Syriac text has been edited by S. Dedering, in: *The Old Testament*

in Syriac according to the Peshiṭta Version, vol. IV, 3, Leiden, 1973, pp. i–iv
and 1–50. For the final letter, however, one still has to use M. Kmosko,
Epistola Baruch Filii Neriae, in: Patrologia Syriaca, vols. 1 2, Paris, 1907,
pp. 1208–37.

Genre, aims and audience

The work belongs to Jewish apocalyptic literature although it was used
in the early church. They are responsible for a number of interpolations.
It is however, difficult to identify all these interpolations accurately.
The work was originally written in Aramaic or Hebrew and it was
translated into Greek, obviously by a Christian. From this language
the text was translated into Syriac as can still be seen from the title of
the work.

The work appears to have been written after the fall of Jerusalem in
AD 70, like 4Ezra, an apocalypse with which it has a number of points
in common, and the Paraleipomena Jeremiou in which Baruch also is an
important figure. The work tries to give an answer to the burning
question why God allowed his temple to be destroyed. The answer is
that God himself sent his angels to destroy his sanctuary and that the
time of this tribulation will be short. In other words, the destruction of
the temple is God's final act before the day of judgement on which the
enemies of Israel will be punished and God's people will be vindicated.
Although, as the Apocalypse indicates, nothing is left but God and the
Law, Israel may expect to be rescued from its enemies.

The Apocalypse purports to have been written for the people as a
whole living both in and outside Jerusalem. Those living outside
Jerusalem receive the work accompanied by a letter which is attached
to it at the end.

Contents

The contents of this writing are as follows:

1:1–8:5: Baruch is allowed to know that Jerusalem will be destroyed.
This is, however, not done by the enemies but by God's angels.
9:1f: Baruch fasts for seven days.
10:1–12:4: Baruch's lamentation.
12:5: Baruch fasts for seven days.
13:1–20:5: Questions and answers on the usefulness of being righteous
and having a long life. Exhortation not to think about corruption.
21:1: Baruch fasts for seven days.
21:2–34:1: Questions about the future with the answer that God will
    complete the works he resolved upon. Announcement of twelve

disasters. The coming of the Messiah. Resurrection and final judgement. Baruch speaks to the people.

35:1: Baruch in the Holy of Holies.

35:2–46:7: A vision about a forest, a vine and a fountain followed by its interpretation. Answer to the question who will be living to see all this. Baruch speaks to the people.

47:1f: Baruch fasts for seven days.

48:1–77:26: Baruch's prayer. He understands that everything has been destined by God. Question about the condition of the righteous in the coming world. Vision of the clouds and its interpretation. Prayer of thanksgiving. Baruch speaks to the people.

78:1–87:1: Letter to the nine and a half tribes.

The contents show a clear structure. Each part ends with Baruch's fasting and prayer. The nucleus of this work consists of three visions which are explained and followed by an address to the people.

The author used already existing traditions. To these belong his story about the destruction of Jerusalem by angels and the three visions. The contents of the visions he applies to the situation in his own time. He succeeded in writing a work of tolerable unity in spite of his use of traditional material.

The selection chosen here comprises about one fifth of the entire work. The fragments are chosen to give an impression of the variety of themes used by the author.

Date and provenance

As mentioned above, the work was written after the fall of Jerusalem in AD 70. An exact date cannot be given but it is generally accepted that it was written at the very beginning of the second century. The original language was Hebrew or Aramaic. The place of origin must have been Jerusalem or its environment.

Bibliography

Apart from the editions of the Syriac text mentioned above translations exist in English by R. H. Charles, '2 Baruch, or the Syriac Apocalypse of Baruch', in *The Apocrypha and Pseudepigrapha of the Old Testament*, vol. II, pp. 470–526, and by A. F. J. Klijn in J. H. Charlesworth (ed.), *The Old Testament Pseudepigrapha*, vol. I, pp. 615–52; in German by V. Ryssel, 'Die Syrische Baruchapokalypse', in E. Kautzsch, *Die Apokryphen und Pseudepigraphen des Alten Testaments*, Vol. II, pp. 404–46, and by A. F. J. Klijn, 'Die syrische Baruch-Apokalypse', in JSHRZ v/2, pp. 103–91; and in French by P. Bogaert, *Apocalypse de Baruch*, Vols. I and II (SC 144 and 145), Paris, 1969.

The Book of the Apocalypse of Baruch the Son of Neriah translated from the Greek into Syriac

1:1 And it happened in the twenty-fifth year of Jeconiah, the king of
Judah, that the word of the Lord came to Baruch, the son of Neriah,

2 and said to him:

'Have you seen all that this people are doing to me, the evil
things which the two tribes which remained have done – more than

3 the ten tribes which were carried away into captivity? For the
former tribes were forced by their kings to sin, but these two have

4 themselves forced and compelled their kings to sin. Behold, therefore, I shall bring evil upon this city and its inhabitants. And it will
be taken away from before my presence for a time. And I shall
scatter this people among the nations that they may do good to the

5 nations. And my people will be chastened, and the time will come
that they will look for that which can make their times prosperous.

2:1 This, then, I have said to you that you may say to Jeremiah and
all who are like you that you may retire from this city. For your
works are for this city like a firm pillar and your prayers like a
strong wall.'

3:1 And I said: 'O Lord, my Lord, have I therefore come into the

2 world to see the evil things of my mother? No, my Lord. If I have
found grace in your eyes, take away my spirit first that I may go to

3 my fathers and I may not see the destruction of my mother. For
from two sides I am hard pressed: I cannot resist you, but my soul

4 also cannot behold the evil of my mother. But one thing I shall say
in your presence, O Lord: Now, what will happen after these

5 things? For if you destroy your city and deliver up your country
to those who hate us, how will the name of Israel be remembered

6 again? Or how shall we speak again about your glorious deeds?

7 Or to whom again will that which is in your Law be explained? Or
will the universe return to its nature and the world go back to its

8 original silence? And will the multitude of the souls be taken away

9 and will not the nature of man be mentioned again? And where is all that which you said to Moses about us?'

4:1 And the Lord said to me: 'This city will be delivered up for a time. And the people will be chastened for a time. And the world

2 will not be forgotten. Or do you think that that this is the city of

3 which I said: "On the palms of my hands, I have carved you"? It is not this building that is in your midst now; it is revealed with me, that was already prepared from the moment that I decided to create Paradise. And I showed it to Adam before he sinned. But when he transgressed the commandment, it was taken away from

4 him – as also Paradise. After these things I showed it to my servant

5 Abraham in the night between the portions of the victims. And again I showed it also to Moses on Mount Sinai when I showed him

6 the likeness of the tabernacle and all its vessels. Behold, now it is

7 preserved with me – as also Paradise. Now go away and do as I command you.'

5:1 And I answered and said: 'So then I shall be guilty in Zion that those who hate you will come to this place and pollute your sanctuary and carry off your heritage into captivity and rule over those whom you love. And then they will go away again to the land of their idols and boast before them. And what have you done to your great name?'

2 And the Lord said to me: 'My name and my glory shall last unto eternity. My judgement, however, shall assert its rights in its own

3 time. And you shall see with your eyes that the enemy shall not destroy Zion and burn Jerusalem, but that they shall serve the Judge

4 for a time. You, however, go away and do all that I have said to you.'

5 And I went away and took with me Jeremiah and Adu and Seriah and Jabish and Gedaliah and all the nobles of the people. And I brought them to the valley of Kidron and told them all that had

6 been said to me. And they raised their voices and they all lamented.

7 And we sat there and fasted until the evening.

6:1 Now it happened on the following day that, behold, an army of the Chaldeans surrounded the city. And in the evening I, Baruch,

2   left the people, went outside, and set myself by an oak. And I was
    grieving over Zion and sighed because of the captivity which had
3   come upon the people. And behold, suddenly a strong wind lifted
4   me and carried me above the wall of Jerusalem. And I saw, and
    behold, there were standing four angels at the four corners of the
5   city, each of them with a burning torch in his hands. And another
    angel came down from heaven and said to them: 'Hold your torches
6   and do not light them before I tell you. Because I was sent first to
    speak a word to the earth and then to deposit in it what the Lord,
7   the Most High, has commanded me.' And I saw that he descended
    in the Holy of Holies and that he took from there the veil, the holy
    ephod, the mercy seat, the two tables, the holy raiment of the
    priests, the altar of incense, the forty-eight precious stones with
    which the priests were clothed, and all the holy vessels of the
8   tabernacle. And he said to the earth with a loud voice: 'Earth,
    earth, earth, hear the word of the mighty God, and receive the
    things which I commit to you, and guard them until the last times,
    so that you may restore them when you are ordered, so that
9   strangers may not get possession of them. For the time has arrived
    when Jerusalem will also be delivered up for a time, until the
    moment that it will be said that it will be restored for ever.' And
    the earth opened its mouth and swallowed them up.
7:1   And after these things I heard this angel saying to the angels who
    held the torches: 'Now destroy the walls and overthrow them to
2   their foundations so that the enemies do not boast and say: "We
    have overthrown the wall of Zion and we have burnt down the
3   place of the mighty God."' And they restored me to the place
    where I stood before.

In the *heading* the title is given. The translator informs his readers about
his copy, which was written in Greek.

1:1. *Jeconiah* (see Jer. 24:1) is also known as Jehoiachin and according
to 2 Kings 24:8 became king of Judah in his eighteenth year, i.e.
597 BC (cp. 2 Chron. 36:9). Three months later, king Nebuchadnezzar
came to Jerusalem and carried him away to Babylon (2 Kings 24:12).
Contrary to 2 Kings 24:9 Jeconiah was 'kind and just' according to

Josephus, *Ant.* x.7.1 (100). *Baruch, the son of Neriah.* See the Introduction.

1:2. *two tribes...ten tribes.* The commonly accepted tradition speaks about the exile of the ten tribes and their return to the land, cp. 2 Kings 11:35, Josephus, *Ant.* XI.5.2 (133) and b.Sanh. 110ᵇ. In the present work, however, there is also mention of the nine and a half tribes, see 62:5; 77:19 and 78:1. This is also found in 4Ezra 13:40 in some oriental versions. No satisfactory explanation had been given for the idea of nine and a half tribes having gone into exile. One can only assume that half of the tribe of Benjamin was supposed to have been taken captive by the Assyrians.

2:1. *For your works are for this city like a firm pillar*: cp. Gen. 18:28–33.

3:3. *For from two sides I am hard pressed*: cp. Phil. 1:23. This may be a Christian interpolation because it is absent in the Arabic version.

3:7. For *universe* the Syriac text reads *decoration*. This can be explained from the original Greek word *kosmos*, which has both meanings.

4:2 *On the palms of my hands I have carved you*; cp. Isa. 49:16.

4: 3–7. The heavenly tabernacle was shown to Moses (Exod. 25:9 and 40), but according to later Jewish tradition the temple was created before the world and was also shown to Adam and Abraham.

4:3. *is revealed with me.* This means that in the present the temple is only revealed with God, i.e. in heaven.

4:4. *in the night...the victims*, cp. Gen. 15:6–17.

5:1. *So then I shall be guilty in Zion.* The translation is not certain. Baruch may be guilty because he left the city, cp. 2:1.

5:5. The name *Adu* (NEB Iddo) is found in Ezra 8:17 and Neh. 12:16; *Seriah* is a brother of Baruch according to Jer. 51:59 and 61; the name *Jabish* is not found in the Old Testament, but Gedaliah occurs often, cp. Jer. 38:1 and 40:14.

6:3. The word *wind* in Syriac can also be rendered by *spirit*.

6:6. *and then to deposit in it.* In 2 Macc. 2:5–7 it is said that Jeremiah hid the tabernacle and other implements until the time that God would gather his people again.

6:7. the *forty-eight stones* are unknown. About twelve stones, cp. Exod. 28:21.

7:3. This sentence usually gives some difficulties to modern translators because the Syriac version is not entirely clear. However, this translation can be defended and is in agreement with the Arabic version.

The enemies enter the city (8:1–9:2) after which Baruch laments 'Blessed is he who was not born' (10:6). He is, however, certain that Babylon will not always be prosperous (10:1–12:5). Standing on Mount Zion Baruch hears a voice saying that the nations will be judged (13:1–12), but Baruch has doubts about the profit of being righteous (14:1–19). The answer is that this life may be evil but the future is unmeasurable (15:1–20:6). In a prayer Baruch asks when this future will be and when corruption will end (21:1–26). The beginning of the answer on this question is:

22:1 And it happened after these things that, behold, the heaven was opened, and I saw and strength was given to me, and a voice was
2 heard from on high which said to me: 'Baruch, Baruch, why are
3 you disturbed? Who starts on a journey and does not complete it? Or who will be comforted making a sea voyage unless he can reach
4 a harbour? Or he who promises to give a present to somebody – is
5 it not a theft unless it is fulfilled? Or who sows the earth – does he not lose everything unless he reaps its harvest in its own time?
6 Or he who plants a vineyard – does the planter expect to receive
7 fruit from it, unless it grows until its appointed time? Or a woman who has conceived – does she not surely kill the child when she
8 bears untimely? Or he who builds a house, can it be called a house, unless it is provided with a roof and finished? Tell this to me first.'
23:1, 2 And I answered and said: 'No, Lord, my Lord.' And he answered and said to me: 'Why, then, are you disturbed about that which you do not know and why are you restless about that of
3 which you do not possess any knowledge? For as you have not forgotten men who exist and who have passed away, I remember
4 those who will come. For when Adam sinned and death was decreed against those who were to be born, the multitude of those who would be born was numbered. And for that number a place was prepared where the living ones might live and where the dead
5 might be preserved. No creature will pass again unless the number that has been appointed is completed.'

23:5. *unless the number that has been appointed is completed*, cp. Rev. 6:11.

At the end horror will seize the inhabitants of the earth (23:6–24:4).
Baruch asks whether the tribulation will last a long time (26:1). Then
begins the first vision with the words:

27:1   And he answered and said to me: 'That time will be divided
       into twelve parts, and each part has been preserved for that for
2   which it was appointed. In the first part: the beginning of
3, 4   commotions. In the second part: the slaughtering of the great.
5   In the third part: the fall of many into death. In the fourth part:
6   the drawing of the sword. In the fifth part: famine and withholding
7–9   of rain. In the sixth part: earthquakes and terrors. In the eighth
10   part: a multitude of ghosts and the appearances of demons. In the
11   ninth part: the fall of fire. In the tenth part: rape and much violence.
12, 13 In the eleventh part: injustice and unchastity. In the twelfth part:
14   disorder and a mixture of all that has been before. These parts of
       that time will be preserved and will be mixed, one with another,
15   and they will minister to each other. For some of these parts will
       withhold a part of themselves and take from others, and will
       accomplish that which belongs to them and to others; hence,
       those who live on earth in those days will not understand that it is
       the end of times.'

27:8. The seventh part is absent. In the Arabic text 25:4–29:3 is
missing.

27:13–15. No specific calamities are mentioned in these verses. The
situation is described as disorderly because the calamities are mixed.
This is explained in 15: *some...will withhold a part of themselves and
take from others.* This will cause disturbances on earth. Those who do
not understand it are taken by surprise, cp. Mark 4:11–12.

After these calamities, Baruch wants to know particulars (28:4–7) and
receives the following answer:

29:1   And he answered and said to me: 'That which will happen at
       that time bears upon the whole earth. Therefore, all who live will
2   notice it. For at that time I shall only protect those found in this land
3   at that time. And it will happen that when all that which should
       come to pass in these parts has been accomplished, the Anointed One
       will begin to be revealed. And Behemoth will reveal itself from its

place, and Leviathan will come from the sea, the two great monsters which I created on the fifth day of creation and which I shall have kept until that time. And they will be nourishment for all who are

5 left. The earth will also yield fruits ten thousandfold. And on one vine will be a thousand branches, and one branch will produce a thousand clusters, and one cluster will produce a thousand grapes,

6 and one grape will produce a *cor* of wine. And those that are hungry will enjoy themselves and they will, moreover, see marvels every

7 day. For winds will go out in front of me every morning to bring the fragrance of aromatic fruits and clouds at the end of the day to distil

8 the dew of health. And it will happen at that time that the treasury of manna will come down again from on high, and they will eat of it in those years because these are they that will have arrived at the consummation of time.

30:1 And it will happen after these things when the time of the appearance of the Anointed One has been fulfilled and he returns

2 with glory, that then all who sleep in hope of him will rise. And it will happen at that time that those treasuries will be opened in which the number of souls of the righteous were kept, and they will go out and the multitudes of the souls will appear together, in one assemblage, of one mind. And the first ones will enjoy themselves

3 and the last ones will not be sad. For they know that the time has

4 come of which it is said that it is the end of times. But the souls of the wicked will the more waste away when they shall see all these

5 things. For they know that their torment has come and that their perdition has arrived.'

31:1 And it happened after these things that I went to the people and said to them: 'Assemble to me all our elders and I shall speak words

2, 3 to you.' And they all assembled in the valley of the Kidron. And I began to speak and said to them: 'Hear, O Israel, and I shall speak to you, and you, O seed of Jacob, pay attention and I shall teach

4 you. Do not forget Zion but remember the distress of Jerusalem.

5 For, behold, the days are coming that all that has been will be taken away to be destroyed, and it will become as though it had not been.

32:1 You, however, if you prepare your minds to sow into them the

fruits of the law, he shall protect you in the time in which the
2 Mighty One shall shake the entire creation. For after a short time,
the building of Zion will be shaken in order that it will be rebuilt.
3 That building will not remain, but it will again be uprooted after
4 some time and will remain desolate for a time. And after that it is
necessary that it will be renewed in glory and that it will be per-
fected into eternity.'

29:3. *the Anointed One* or: Messiah.
29:4. *Behemoth...Leviathan*. In Job 7:12 and Ps. 148:7 sea monsters
are mentioned and Isa. 27:1 mentions Leviathan. Both appear together
in 4Ezra 6:49–52 and 1En 60:7ff; see also Strack–Billerbeck IV/2,
pp. 1156–61.
29:5. The same expectation can be found with the early Christian
author Papias (about 150 in Asia Minor) who is known for his mil-
lenarian ideas, cp. Irenaeus, *Adversus haereses* V, 33, 3–4. A *cor* is approximately 100 gallons.
30:1. The presence of the Messiah on earth is limited, cp. 40:3.
30:2–3. Cp. 1 Thess. 4:15–17.
32:2–4. The passage speaks about the destruction of the temple in
587 BC, the rebuilding of the temple after the Babylonian exile, the
destruction in 70 AD and, finally, about the time of the eternal temple.

The people are afraid that Baruch will leave them but he promises them
that he will return (32:8–34:1). The second vision given to Baruch is
about a forest, a vine, a fountain and a cedar (35:1–37:1). The trees
are rooted out and only the vine and the cedar are left. Finally the
cedar is sent into eternal torment. The vine is growing and all around
it is a valley with flowers. After Baruch's prayer (38:1–4) he receives
the explanation which begins as follows:

39:1 And he answered and said to me: 'Baruch, this is the explanation
2 of the vision that you have seen. As you have seen the great forest
3 surrounded by high and rocky mountains, this is the word: Behold,
the days will come when this kingdom that destroyed Zion once
will be destroyed and will be subjected to that which will come
4 after it. This again will also be destroyed after some time. And
another, a third, will rise and also that will possess power in its own
5 time and will be destroyed. After that a fourth kingdom arises
whose power is harsher and more evil than those that were before it,

and it will reign a multitude of times like the trees on the plain, and
it will rule the times and exalt itself more than the cedars of Lebanon.

6   And the truth will hide itself in this and all who are polluted with
unrighteousness will flee to it as the evil beasts flee and creep into

7   the forest. And it will happen when the time of its fulfilment is
approaching in which it will fall, that at that time the dominion of
my Anointed One which is like the fountain and the vine, will be
revealed. And when it has revealed itself, it will uproot the multi-

8   tude of its host. And that which you have seen, namely the tall
cedar, which remained of that forest, and with regard to the words
which the vine said to it, which you heard, this is the meaning.

40:1   The last ruler who is left alive at that time will be bound,
whereas the entire host will be destroyed. And they will carry him
on Mount Zion, and my Anointed One will convict him of all his
wicked deeds and will assemble and set before him all the works of

2   his hosts. And after these things he will kill him and protect the rest

3   of my people who will be found in the place that I have chosen. And
his dominion will last for ever until the world of corruption has
ended and until the times which have been mentioned before have

4   been fulfilled. This is your vision and this is its explanation.'

39:3–5. The idea of four kingdoms is found for the first time in
Dan. 7. It is taken over by later apocalypses. Here it refers to Babylon,
Persia, Greece and Rome.

40:3. Also here (cp. 30:1) the time of the Messiah on earth seems to
be limited. *the times. . .fulfilled*, cp. Gal. 4:4.

After some questions and answers about the apostates and the believers
(41:1–43:3), Baruch speaks to the people (44:1–47:2). Next follows a
long prayer (48:1–25) of which the beginning and the end are:

48:1   And it happened after seven days that I prayed before the

2   Mighty One and said: 'O Lord, you summon the coming of the
times, and they stand before you. You cause the display of power
of the worlds to pass away and they do not resist you. You arrange

3   the course of the periods and they obey you. Only you know the
length of the generations and you do not reveal your secrets to

4   many. You make known the multitude of the fire and you weigh

5   the lightness of the wind. You investigate the end of the heights
6   and you scrutinize the depths of darkness. You command the
     number which will pass away and which will be preserved. And
     you prepare a house for those that will be.'

22   'In you we have put our trust, because, behold, your Law is with
     us and we know that we do not fall as long as we keep your
23   statutes. We shall always be blessed; at least, we do not mingle with
24   the nations. For we all are a people of the Name, we who received
     one Law from One. And that Law that is among us will help
     us and that excellent wisdom which is in us will support us.'

   48:6. *And you prepare a house*: cp. John 14:2 and 2 Cor. 5:1–2.
   48:24. *one Law from One*: cp. 85:14 and Eph. 4:4–6.

A number of questions and answers follows about the destiny of men
at the end of time (48:25–52:7). Interesting are the following:

49:1   'And further, I ask you, O Mighty One; and I shall ask grace
2   from him who created all things. In which shape will the living live
     in your day? Or how will remain their splendour which will be
3   after that? Will they, perhaps, take again this present form, and will
     they put on the chained members which are in evil and by which
     evils are accomplished? Or will you perhaps change these things
     that have been in the world, as also the world itself?'
50:1   And he answered and said to me:'Listen, Baruch, to this word
     and write down in the memory of your heart all that you shall
2   learn. For the earth will surely give back the dead at that time;
     it receives them now in order to keep them, not changing anything
     in their form. But as it has received them so it will give them back.
3   And as I have delivered them to it so it will raise them. For then
     it will be necessary to show those who live that the dead are living
4   again and that those who went away have come back. And it will
     be that when they have recognized each other, those who know
     each other at this moment, then my judgement will be strong, and
     those things that have been spoken of before will come.
51:1   And it will happen after this day which he appointed is over, that

both the shape of those who are found to be guilty as also the glory of those who have proved to be righteous will be changed.'

49:2. *In which shape will the living live in your day?* The question and the answer are about the same subject as dealt with in 1 Cor. 15:32–49.

49:3. *chained members*, or literally: members of bonds. The body being corruptible is supposed to imprison man on earth.

The third vision is about a cloud which rains pure and black water in accordance with the history of mankind and, in particular, Israel. This happens twelve times. Finally it will rain exceedingly black water and pure water again. This will be attended with lightning (54:1–12). Baruch asks for an explanation of this vision (54:1–22), which is given to him by the angel Ramael (55:1–74:4). From this section are taken:

56:1 'But now, since you have asked the Most High to reveal to you
2 the explanation of the vision which you have seen, I have been sent to say to you that the Mighty One has let you know the course of times, namely those which have passed and those which in this world will come to pass, from the beginning of his creation until the end, (the times) which are known by deceit and by truth.
3 For as you saw a great cloud which came up from the sea and went and covered the earth, this is the length of the world which the Mighty One has created when he took counsel in order to create
4 the world. And it happened when the word had gone out from him, that the length of the world was standing as something small and it was established in accordance with the abundance of the intelligence
5 of him who let it go forth. And as you first saw the black waters on the top of the cloud which first came down upon the earth; this is
6 the transgression which Adam, the first man, committed. For when he transgressed, untimely death came into being, mourning was mentioned, affliction was prepared, illness was created, labour accomplished, pride began to come into existence, the realm of death began to ask to be renewed with blood, the conception of children came about, the passion of parents was produced, the loftiness of
7 men was humiliated and goodness vanished. What could, therefore,
8 have been blacker and darker than these things? This is the beginning of the black waters which you have seen...

57:1 And after these you saw the bright waters; that is the fountain of Abraham and his generation, and the coming of his son and the son of his son and of those who are like them...

58:1 And the third black waters you have seen; that is the mingling of all sins that the nations committed afterwards, after the death of those righteous men, and the wickedness of the land of Egypt, in which they acted wickedly in the oppression with which they 2 oppressed their sons. But also these perished at the end.

59:1 And the fourth bright waters which you have seen; that is the coming of Moses, and of Aaron, and of Miriam, and of Joshua, the son of Nun, and of Caleb, and all those who are like these...

60:1 And the fifth black waters which you have seen poured down; those are the works which the Amorites have done, and the invocations of their incantations which they wrought, and the wickedness of their mysteries and the mingling of their pollutions...

61:1 And the sixth bright water you have seen; this is the time in 2 which David and Solomon were born. And at that time the building of Zion took place, and the dedication of the sanctuary...

62:1 And the seventh black water you have seen; that is the perversion of the ideas of Jeroboam who planned to make two golden calves...

63:1 And the eighth bright waters you have seen; that is the righteousness and the integrity of Hezekiah, King of Judah, and the grace which came upon him...

64:1 And the ninth black waters you have seen; that is the wickedness that existed in the days of Manasseh, the son of Hezekiah...

66:1 And the tenth bright waters you have seen; that is the purity of the generation of Josiah, the king of Judah, who was the only one in his time who subjected himself to the Mighty One with his whole heart and his whole soul...

67:1 And the eleventh black waters you have seen; that is the disaster which has befallen Zion now...

68:1 And the twelfth bright waters you have seen; this is the word. 2 For there will come a time after these things and your people will fall into such a distress so that they all together are in danger of

3   perishing. They, however, will be saved, and their enemies will fall
4, 5   before them. And to them will fall much joy one day. And at that
time, after a short time, Zion will be rebuilt again, and the offerings
will be restored, and the priests will again return to their ministry.
6   And the nations will again come to honour it. But not as fully as
7   before. But it will happen after these things that there will be a fall
8   of many nations. These are the bright waters you have seen.

69:1   With regard to the last waters you have seen, which are blacker
than all those preceding, which came after the twelfth, those which
were brought together, they apply to the whole earth...

70:7   The Most High will then give a sign to those nations that he has
prepared before, and they will come and wage war with the rulers
8   who will then remain. And it will happen that everyone who saves
himself from the war will die in an earthquake, and who saves
himself from the earthquake will be burned by fire, and who saves
himself from the fire will perish by famine...

72:1   Now, hear also about the bright waters which come at the end
2   after these black ones. This is the word. After the signs have come of
which I have spoken to you before, when the nations are moved
and the time of my Anointed One comes, he will call all nations,
3   and some of them he will spare, and others he will kill. These things
4   will befall the nations which will be spared by him. Every nation
that has not known Israel and that has not trodden down the seed
of Jacob will live...

73:1   And it will happen that after he has brought down everything
which is in the world, and he has sat down in eternal peace on the
throne of the kingdom, then joy will be revealed and rest will
appear.'

59:1. *Moses*, cp. Exod. 2:10; *Aaron*, cp. Exod. 4:14–15; *Miriam*,
cp. Exod. 15:20; *Joshua*, cp. Deut. 31:14ff; *Joshua...Caleb*, cp. Num.
14:38.
60:1. *Amorites*, cp. Josh. 24:18.
61:2. *dedication of the sanctuary*, cp. 1 Kings 8:1ff.
62:1. *Jeroboam*, cp. 1 Kings 12:25–33.
63:1. *Hezekiah*, cp. 2 Kings 16:20.

64:1. *Manasseh*, cp. 2 Kings 21:1–2.

66:1. *Josiah*, cp. 2 Kings 22:1.

68:1–6. This chapter speaks of the time after the destruction of the first temple and the rebuilding of the second temple. During the time of the second temple the final tribulations will take place.

72:2–73:1. Here the subject is the Messianic kingdom.

Baruch thanks God for the explanation (75:1–8). Then he is ordered to speak to the people (76:1–5). In this address he says (77:1–10):

77:5, 6   'And, behold, you are here, with me. If, therefore, you will
make straight your ways, you will not go away as your brothers
7   went away, but they will come to you. For he is merciful whom
you honour, and he is gracious in whom you hope, and true so that
8   he will do good to you and not evil. Have you not seen what has
9   befallen Zion? Or do you think that the place has sinned and that
it has been destroyed for this reason, or that the country has done
10   some crime and that it is delivered up for that reason? And do you
not know that because of you who sinned the one who did not
sin was destroyed, and that because of those that acted un-
righteously, the one that has not gone astray has been delivered up
to the enemies?'

The people ask Baruch to write a letter to the brothers in Babylon (77:11–17).

77:13   'For the shepherds of Israel have perished, and the lamps which
gave light are extinguished, and the fountains from which we
14   used to drink have withheld their streams. Now we have been
left in the darkness and in the thick forest and in the aridness of the
15   desert.' And I answered and said to them: 'Shepherds and lamps
and fountains came from the Law and when we go away, the Law
16   will abide. If you, therefore, look upon the Law and are intent
upon wisdom, then the lamp will not be wanting and the shepherd
17   will not give way and the fountain will not dry up. Nevertheless,
I shall also write to your brothers in Babylon, as you have said to
me. I shall send it by means of men. Also I shall write to the nine
and a half tribes, and send it by means of a bird.'

Baruch writes the two letters of which only the contents of the one
to the nine and a half tribes is given (78:1–87:1). First he tells them
about the fall of Jerusalem (78:1–80:7). He continues:

81:1, 2 'But also hear the word of consolation: For I mourned with
regard to Zion and asked grace from the Most High and said:
3 "Will these things exist for us until the end? And will these evils
4 befall us always?" And the Mighty One did according to the
multitude of his grace, and the Most High according to the
magnitude of his mercy, and he revealed to me a word that
I might be comforted, and showed me visions that I might not be
again sorrowful, and made known to me the mysteries of the
times, and showed me the coming of the periods.

82:1 My brothers, therefore I have written to you that you may find
2 consolation with regard to the multitude of tribulations. But you
ought to know that our Creator will surely avenge us on all our
enemies according to everything that they have done against us and
amongst us. . .

83:5 And we should not look upon the delights of the present
nations, but let us think about that which has been promised to us
regarding the end. . .

84:1 Now, I gave you knowledge, while I still live. For I have said
that you should particularly learn the mighty commandments in
which he has instructed you. And I shall set before you some of
2 the commandments of his judgement before I die. Remember that
once Moses called heaven and earth to witness against you and
said: "If you trespass against the law, you shall be dispersed. And
3 if you keep it, you shall be planted." And also other things he
said to you when you were in the desert as twelve tribes together.
4 And after his death you cast it away from you and, therefore, that
5 which has been said before has come upon you. And now, Moses
spoke to you before it befell you and, behold, it has befallen you
6 for you have forsaken the Law. Also, I, behold, I say to you after
you suffered that if you obey the things which I have said to you,
you shall receive from the Mighty One everything that has been
7 prepared and has been preserved for you. Therefore, let this letter

be a witness between me and you that you may remember the commandments of the Mighty One, and that it also may serve as

8   my defence in the presence of him who has sent me. And remember Zion and the Law and the holy land and your brothers and the covenant and your fathers, and do not forget the festivals and the

9   sabbaths. And give this letter and the traditions of the Law to your children after you as also your fathers handed down to you.

10 And ask always and pray seriously with your whole soul that the Mighty One may accept you in mercy and that he may not reckon the multitude of your sinners, but remember the integrity

11 of your fathers. For if he judges us not according to the multitude of his grace, woe to all of us who are born.

85:1 Further, know that our fathers in former times and former

2   generations had helpers, righteous prophets and holy men. But we were also in our country, and they helped us when we sinned, and they intervened for us with him who has created us since they trusted in their works. And the Mighty One heard them and

3   purged us from our sins. But now, the righteous have been assembled, and the prophets are sleeping. Also we have left our land, and Zion has been taken away from us, and we have nothing

9   apart from the Mighty One and his Law... Therefore, before his judgement exacts its own, and truth that which is its due, let us prepare ourselves that we may possess and not be possessed and that we may hope and not be put to shame, and that we may rest with our fathers and not be punished with those who hate us.

10 For the youth of this world has passed away, and the power of creation is already exhausted, and the coming of times is very near and has passed by. And the pitcher is near to the well, and the ship to the harbour, and the journey to the city, and life to its end...

12 For behold, the Most High will cause all these things to come.

14 There will not be an opportunity to repent any more... Therefore, there is one Law by One, one world and an end for all those who

15 exist. Then he will make alive those whom he has found, and he will purge them from sins, and at the same time he will destroy those that are polluted with sins.

86:1   When you, therefore, receive the letter, read it carefully in your assemblies. And think about it, in particular, however, on the days of your fasts. And remember me by means of this letter in the same way as I remember you by means of this – always.'

87:1   And it happened when I had finished all the words of this letter and had written it carefully until the end, I folded it, sealed it cautiously, and bound it to the neck of an eagle. And I let it go and sent it away.

The end of the letter of Baruch,
the son of Neriah.

84:2. Cp. Deut. 30:19–20.
84:8. *the festivals and the sabbaths*: cp. Col. 2:16.
86:1. *read it carefully in your assemblies*: cp. Col. 4:16.

Paraleipomena Jeremiou

J. RIAUD

Textual witnesses

The long form of the *Paraleipomena Jeremiou* (PJ) was first published in
1868 by A.-M. Ceriani, who discovered the text in a manuscript of the
fifteenth century, preserved in the Brera Museum of Milan.

Some years later, in 1889, J. Rendel Harris brought out the same long
version in a critical edition. But to the manuscripts of Ceriani he added
five new witnesses: the Ethiopic version according to the edition of
A. Dillmann and the German translations of F. Prätorius and E. König,
and four Greek manuscripts preserved in Jerusalem. (For biblio-
graphical details see below.)

Since the publication of Harris's critical edition a great number of
manuscripts has been discovered. In the provisional eclectic edition
published in 1972, Robert A. Kraft and Ann-Elizabeth Purintun counted
no fewer than twenty-three Greek texts of this category, to which they
added, apart from the Rumanian, Armenian and Ethiopic versions, the
numerous manuscripts of the rewritten or short version of the *Paraleipomena* (pp. 4–5). Clearly, a new critical edition of the *Paraleipomena
Jeremiou* is called for. Since this has as yet not been realized, the translation of the fragments given here is based on the edition of J. Rendel
Harris. The important variants of the Kraft–Purintun edition are
indicated in the notes accompanying the translation, which follows
theirs as closely as possible.

Title and main theme

Harris named his edition after the Ethiopic version: *The Rest of the
Words of Baruch* (4Bar). Nowadays, what is commonly being used is
the title of the Greek version (*Paraleipomena Jeremiou*, i.e. 'The Things
Omitted from Jeremiah'); and with good reason: Jeremiah is of foremost importance in this captivating work. His name is mentioned
repeatedly – eighty times in all – and the titles bestowed upon him are
among the most prestigious: 'chosen of God' (1:4; 2:4, 5; 7:15),
'servant' (*païs*) (6:22), 'father' (2:2, 4, 6, 8; 5:5; 9:8), 'priest' (5:18).

But Jeremiah himself merely lays claim to being a 'servant' (*doũlos*)
(1:4; 3:9). He comes forth as the privileged intermediary between man
and God (1:3; 8:1–3), with whom he unceasingly intercedes for the
benefit of his people (cp. 1; 3; 9:3–6). By God's command (3:11) he
accompanies his compatriots into exile, after having committed the
sacred vessels 'to the earth and to the altar' (3:8, 14), and after having
cast away the keys of the temple in the direction of the sun (4:3–4).
When in Babylon, following God's commands, he announces to his
wretched companions the consolation that lies in the prophecies and
teaches them the word (3:11; 5:21); and, like Moses with Pharaoh, he
negotiates with Nebuchadnezzar (7:14). When the moment of the
return to Jerusalem draws near, God commands him to organize this
(8:1–3), as in former days he had instructed Moses to lead the exodus
from Egypt. But, and this is something Moses had not done, he makes
the exiles cross the Jordan (8:3–4; cp. Josh. 3), and allows those who
have listened to him to enter Jerusalem, where together they offer
sacrifices for nine days. On the tenth day Jeremiah is the only one to
make a sacrifice – probably that of Yōm Kippur (Day of Atonement),
exclusive prerogative of the High Priest – and he pronounces a procedure of liturgical thanksgiving. At its conclusion, Jeremiah 'becomes
like one of those who have expired' (9: 1–7). Incontestably, the author
of the *Paraleipomena* made Jeremiah the focal point of his work: in his
eyes Jeremiah was 'the prophet', the 'super-Moses', whose coming had
been predicted by Deuteronomy (18:15).

The *Paraleipomena Jeremiou* are a 'continuous written haggadah,
completing in its own way that which is narrated in the Bible' (J. Licht,
in the article mentioned in the bibliography, p. 67). The central episode
of this haggadah, 'intermediary between the apocalyptic literature and
the midrashim of the ancient rabbis' (J. Licht, art. cit., p. 68), is the
prolongued sleep of the Ethiopian Abimelech (5:1–34). God, keeping
his promise to Jeremiah (3:10), protects Abimelech: he prevents his
witnessing the devastation of Jerusalem and the deportation of its
inhabitants by making him sleep for sixty-six years; sixty-six years
which, as Abimelech persistently repeats, seemed to him to last 'but a
brief moment' (5:2). But not only for this 'righteous man' (5:30) did
all those years pass like a flash of lightning; the same happened to all the
'righteous ones for whose souls the Lord, God of heaven and earth, is
the repose in every place' (5:32), and thus for all exiles whose return
could not be delayed since God had promised Jeremiah to protect
Abimelech until the very moment of this return (cp. 3:10). This
salvation, to be bestowed upon the exiles by God, is symbolized by the

figs which, though out of season and picked sixty-six years earlier, did not shrink or rot and are still juicy (5:3, 26, 28; 6:5); as, by the same token, they are the symbol of that salvation from which Abimelech benefits. The exiled people, purged from its foreign elements (6:13–14; 8:2–3, 5), will revive. Its exile will be brief, like Abimelech's trance, and will vanish from its consciousness like a nightmare.

So the principal theme of the *Paraleipomena* is the exiles' return from Babylon and the restoration of Jerusalem. Present in the first part of the work (1–4), under the form of reiterated promises immediately before and after the fall of Jerusalem, the theme becomes predominant in the third part (6–9), where lengthy descriptions are given of the announcement of the return, its conditions, its preparation and finally its realization with the public worship in Jerusalem (9:1–6).

Relation to Syriac Baruch

The historical framework of the *Paraleipomena*, namely the capture of Jerusalem and the captivity in Babylon, serves a particular purpose: the author describes the catastrophe of AD 70 using the data of that of 587 BC. We observe the same procedure in other writings ascribed to Jeremiah or to his disciple Baruch, especially in the Syriac Apocalypse of Baruch (2Bar). As this work and the *Paraleipomena* present numerous parallels, the question of their interdependence must be considered. Some hold the opinion that the Apocalypse was the earlier work and that the *Paraleipomena* depend on it. Others are inclined to the opposite view. A more balanced hypothesis has been proposed: the Apocalypse could have used an earlier form of the *Paraleipomena*; the *Paraleipomena* as we know them at present would in their turn have used the Syriac Apocalypse of Baruch. It seems difficult to give preference to any one of these theories. The most plausible viewpoint might be that the author of the Syriac Apocalypse of Baruch drew on a source which was also used by the author of the Paraleipomena. See also p. 194 above.

Origin and date

The author of this consolatory writing, which was probably drawn up in Hebrew, was very probably a Jew from Jerusalem; he was well acquainted with the topography of this city, and his Judaism is notably manifest in the prohibition of marriages to foreign women (8:5–8). It is far from easy to determine the date of its composition. The one proposed by Harris, *viz.* AD 136 (that is to say: the year 70, plus the

66 years of Abimelech's sleep), is, perhaps, too precise. It is, moreover, one of the arguments for his hypothesis on the composition: namely that, after Hadrian's edict expelling the Jews from Jerusalem (AD 132), a Jewish-Christian would have wanted to make the banned Jews elude the edict by becoming Christians. Yet Harris' explanation should not be rejected entirely: it would seem that the *Paraleipomena* were written during the period of that generation which lived in the expectation of a speedy reconstruction of the temple, destroyed in 70, and which could reasonably hope that the second exile would not outlast the first, because the span of sixty-six years was approaching (cp. J. Licht, art. cit., p. 70).

The young Jewish-Christian communities which used the great tradition of their predecessors as a basis for their own religious literature, did not neglect the opportunity to appropriate a work that glorified the prophet Jeremiah. The Christian author of its conclusion (9:11–32) had no need whatever to modify the *Paraleipomena*. It sufficed him to 'resuscitate' Jeremiah *three days* after his death (9:13) in order to make him glorify 'the Son of God who awakens us, Jesus Christ' (9:13), and to announce his return on the Mount of Olives. Thus he added to the portrait of Jeremiah a vital element: that of the herald of the Messiah, whose suffering and death he prefigures by the persecutions and death he himself underwent (9:19–32).

Bibliography

I. EDITIONS

A. *Greek text:* A.-M. Ceriani, *Monumenta Sacra et Profana*, Vol. V, 1, Milan, 1868; J. Rendel Harris, *The Rest of the Words of Baruch: A Christian Apocalypse of the year 136 A.D.*, London, 1889; Robert A. Kraft and Ann-Elizabeth Purintun, *Paraleipomena Jeremiou*, (SBL. Text and Translations 1, Pseudepigrapha Series 1), Missoula, 1972.
B. *Ethiopic version:* A. Dillmann, 'Reliqua Verborum Baruchi', *Chrestomathia Aethiopica*, Leipzig, 1886 (re-edited by E. Littmann, Berlin, 1950).
C. *Armenian version:* S. Josepheanz, *Treasury of Old and New Fathers*, vol. I, 'Non-Canonical Writings of the Old Testament', Venice, 1896 (in Armenian).
D. *Rumanian and Slavic versions:* E. Turdeanu, *Apocryphes slaves et roumains de l'Ancien Testament*, (StVTPs 5), Leiden, 1981, pp. 306–63 and 442.

II. TRANSLATIONS

A. *Greek text:* P. Riessler, *Altjüdisches Schrifttum ausserhalb der Bibel*, Augsburg, 1928 (reprinted Darmstadt, 1966), pp. 903–19; notes, p. 1323; Robert

A. Kraft and Ann-Elizabeth Purintun, *Paraleipomena Jeremiou*, Missoula, 1972; J. Licht, 'The Apocryphal Book of the Acts of Jeremiah', *Annual of Bar-Ilan University: Studies in Judaica and the Humanities = Pinkhos Ghurgin Memorial Volume*, Jerusalem, 1963 (translation into Hebrew), pp. 62–72 and XXI–XXII. A new German translation will be given by B. Schaller in vol. 1 of JSHRZ.

B. *Ethiopic version:* F. Prätorius, 'Das Apokryphische Buch Baruch im Aethiopischen', *Zeitschrift für Wissenschaftliche Theologie* 15 (1972), pp. 230–47; E. König, 'Die Reste der Worte Baruchs', *Theologische Studien und Kritiken* 50 (1877), pp. 318–38; R. Basset, *Les Apocryphes éthiopiens – traduits en français*, vol. 1 'Le Livre de Baruch et la Légende de Jérémie', Paris, 1893.

C. *Slavic versions:* Ch. Wolf, *Jeremia in Frühjudentum und Urchristentum* (TU 118), Berlin, 1976.

D. *Armenian version:* J. Issaverdens, *The Uncanonical Writings of the O.T.*, Venice, 1901 (reprinted 1934), pp. 217–32.

III. FURTHER LITERATURE

G. Delling, *Jüdische Lehre und Frömmigheit in den Paralipomena Jeremiae*, Berlin, 1967.

P. Bogaert, *Apocalypse de Baruch. Introduction, Traduction du Syriaque et Commentaire*, vols. I and II, Paris, 1969 (SC. 144–5).

Jean Riaud, 'La Figure de Jérémie dans les *Paralipomena Jeremiae*', in *Mélanges bibliques et orientaux offerts à M. Henri Cazelles*, AOAT 212, 1981, pp. 372–85.

An annotated chronological bibliography up to 1971 can be found in the edition by R. Kraft and A.-E. Purintun, pp. 7–10.

1:1   It came to pass, when the children of Israel were taken captive by the king of the Chaldeans, that God spoke to Jeremiah: 'Jeremiah, my chosen one, arise and depart from this city, you and Baruch, since I am going to destroy it because of the multitude of the sins of

2   those who dwell in it. For your prayers are like a solid pillar in its

3   midst, and like an indestructible wall surrounding it. Now, arise

4   and depart before the host of the Chaldeans surrounds it.' And Jeremiah answered, saying: 'I beseech you, Lord, permit me, your servant, to speak in your presence.' And the Lord said to

5   him: 'Speak, my chosen one, Jeremiah.' And Jeremiah spoke, saying: 'Lord Almighty, would you deliver the chosen city into the hands of the Chaldeans, so that the king with the multitude of his people might boast and say "I have prevailed over the holy city

6   of God"? No, my Lord, but if it is your will, let it be destroyed

7   by your hands.' And the Lord said to Jeremiah: 'Since you are my
     chosen one, arise and depart from this city, you and Baruch, for
     I am going to destroy it because of the multitude of the sins of
8   those who dwell in it. For neither the king nor his host will be able
9   to enter it unless I first open its gates. Arise, then, and go to
10   Baruch, and tell him these words. And when you have arisen at the
     sixth hour of the night, go out on the city walls and I will show
11   you that unless I first destroy the city, they cannot enter it.' When
     the Lord had said this, he departed from Jeremiah.

1. Allusion to the deportation of 587 BC. This is a chronological
fiction: the author describes the catastrophe of AD 70, using elements of
that of 587 BC. This event has been used as a fictitious historical framework by other pseudepigraphers also: 2Bar; 4Ezra; History of the
Captivity in Babylon; 3Bar. 'My chosen one': cp. 1:1, 4, 7; 3:4, 5;
7:15. This title, given to Jacob (Isa. 45:4), Moses (Ps. 106:23), Joshua
(Num 11:28 LXX), Saul (2 Sam. 21:6), David (Ecclus. 47:22), to the
servant of YHWH (Isa. 42:1), is to be found again in the apocalyptic
writings, where it is borne by persons who have played an eminent
role in the history of salvation (ApAB 20:6; TJob 4:11; TIsaac 1:2).
Baruch ('Blessed') appears in Jer. 32:12, 16; 36:4, 10, 32; 43:3, 6; 45
as secretary and confidant of the prophet. In pre-christian Judaism
Baruch is the hero and the patron of several literary works, out of
which only one has found its way into the Septuagint: 'The Apocryphal' Baruch. Attributed to Baruch are: 2Bar; PJ; 3Bar.
2. Allusion to Jer. 1:18. On the righteous who, by their prayers and
their deeds, constitute a protection for their people, see 2Bar 2:2; 63:3;
85:1–2; ApEl 3: 76–7; Philo, Migr Abr 124; Bereshith R. 14:6;
Shemot R. 2:16; A.R.N. 25; P.Targ on Num 20:29; 1 Tim. 3:15.
4. The psalms of supplication start thus (Ps. 5:2–3; 64:2; 141:1). By
declaring himself to be the 'servant of God', the supplicant aims at
drawing attention to himself (cp. 1 Kings 8:30). Jeremiah appears here
as an intercessor (cp. 2:3; 3:6–9; 9:3–6). He holds this function in the
book which is named after him (Jer. 7:16; 11:14; 14:7–9, 11, 19–22;
15:1; 18–20). See also 2 Macc. 15:14.
5. Jeremiah's supplication relies on God's honour. See Num.
14:13–19; Ezek. 36: 16–23. The title 'almighty' is frequently given to
God in the LXX; mostly it is to be translated as 'God of hosts' or
'Shaddaï'.
10. the sixth hour, i.e. midnight.

2:1–3:3. At the sixth hour Jeremiah and Baruch, after their meeting in
the Temple (2:1–9), come up together on the walls of Jerusalem. At the
very moment the destruction of the city is about to begin, Jeremiah
intervenes:

3:4 Jeremiah besought the angels, saying: 'I beseech you, do not
   destroy the city yet, until I say something to the Lord.' And the
   Lord spoke to the angels, saying: 'Do not destroy the city until
   I speak to my chosen one, Jeremiah.' Then Jeremiah spoke, saying:
5 'I beg you, Lord, bid me to speak in your presence.' And the Lord
6 said: 'Speak, my chosen one, Jeremiah.' And Jeremiah said:
   'Behold, Lord, now we know that you are delivering your city
   into the hands of its enemies, and that they will take the people
7 away to Babylon. What shall we do with the holy vessels of
8 your temple service, what do you want us to do with them?' And
   the Lord said to him: 'Take them and consign them to the earth
   and to the altar, saying: "Hear, earth, the voice of your creator
   who formed you in the abundance of waters, who sealed you with
   seven seals in seven epochs, and after this you will receive your
   ornaments. Guard the vessels of the temple service until the
9 gathering of the beloved."' And Jeremiah said: 'I beseech you, Lord,
   show me what I should do for Abimelech the Ethiopian, for he
   has done many kindnesses to the people and to your servant
   Jeremiah; for he pulled me out of the miry pit; and I do not wish
   that he should see the destruction and desolation of this city, but
   that you should be merciful to him and that he should not be
10 grieved.' And the Lord said to Jeremiah: 'Send him to the vineyard of Agrippa by way of the mountain, and I will hide him in its
   shadow until I cause the people to return to the city.' And the
11 Lord said to Jeremiah: 'Go with your people to Babylon and stay
   with them, preaching to them the good news, until I cause them
12–13 to return to the city. But leave Baruch here until I speak with
   him.' When he had said these things, the Lord left Jeremiah and
   ascended into heaven.

2. The sound of the trumpets accompanies the theophanies
(Exod. 19:16; 20:18), and announces the day of YHWH (Joel 2:1;

Zeph 1:16). Here, it is the judgement of Jerusalem that is being announced.

7. Kraft-Purintun (henceforth KP) = verse 9: What do you want *me* to do with the holy vessels of the temple service? – They omit: What do you want *us* to do with them? – According to 2 Kings 25:13–17; Jer. 52:17–23; 2 Chron. 36:18–19; Dan. 1:2, the sacred vessels were taken to Babylon. Ezra 1:6–11 mentions their return to Jerusalem. According to *PJ*, they have been hidden. Other narratives report the safekeeping of the sacred objects of the temple. 2 Macc. 2:4–5 alludes to earlier narratives, which imply that Jeremiah disposed of the precious objects in a cave in the mountain of Horeb. In 2Bar 6:7–10 it is an angel who takes charge of the sacred vessels and addresses the earth.

8. *to the earth and to the altar* (KP: no mention of the altar). This may be a hendiadys: 'to the earth on which the altar is erected'. The points at issue are: an entrustment of the sacred vessels to heaven, a sanctification and an expiatory sacrifice. Jeremiah buries the vessels in the sacred soil under the altar, or leaves them on the altar, charging a divine power to take them to heaven. In his address to the earth there may be an allusion to the work of creation; *the abundance of waters* would then be the 'humid chaos'; *who sealed you with seven seals in seven epochs* would refer to the week of the creation; *your ornaments* could be understood as appertaining to the holy land or the temple.

the gathering of the beloved can hardly mean anything but the people, because, in 4:6, Israel receives the title 'beloved people'. It should be noted that this expression is also found in 2Bar 21:21, and that Israel is often called 'well-beloved' in the LXX: Deut. 32:15; 33:5, 26 (all in LXX); Isa. 44.2; Baruch 3:37; Ps. 60:5 (59:7); 108:7 (107:7); 127:2. (126)

9. KP = verse 12: omit 'to the people'. Abimelech the Ethiopian is no other than Ebed-Melech who, in the Book of Jeremiah, rescues the prophet from the miry pit into which he had been thrown (Jer. 38:6–13; LXX 45:6–13) and who, in return, is promised the safekeeping of his life during the imminent destruction of Jerusalem (Jer. 39:16–18; LXX 46:15–18). In the Masoretic text Ebed-Melech is probably a functional name, i.e. 'the king's servant'. In the LXX it is a proper name, rendered as Abdemelech; the form Abimelech occurs only very rarely in the LXX.

that you should be merciful to him and added with mss. *ab* (and KP).

10. Of all the sites proposed for the vineyard (3:10) or the property of Agrippa (3:15; 5:25; 3Bar (prologue 2)), the most likely one geographically would be Deir Senneh on the south-west slope of the

Mount of Offence. But it is quite possible that the author of the *PJ*, by linking no matter which 'vineyard' or 'property' to the name of Agrippa, wanted to suggest a historical indication.

in its shadow i.e. in the shadow of the mountain added with mss. *ab* (and KP).

11. KP = verse 15, 'And you, Jeremiah'. According to Jer. 40, Jeremiah, though treated with respect by the conquerors, preferred to stay in Jerusalem with those who had not been deported. After the murder of Gedaliah he is forced by a group of Judaeans, who feared reprisals by the occupying forces, to accompany them to Egypt. The *PJ* lean essentially on a tradition of the Babylonian ministry of Jeremiah, which we also find in 2Bar 10:2. The midrash *Ekha Rabbati*, Introduction, 34 gives precise details on the nature of the support given by Jeremiah to his exiled compatriots.

3:14–4:11. As soon as Abimelech has left for Agrippa's vineyard (3:15–16) the host of the Chaldeans, summoned by the 'great angel', invades Jerusalem and takes all the people captive. Jeremiah leaves the city, taking with him the keys of the temple and throwing them away in the direction of the sun. He is taken to Babylon. Baruch, after having uttered a lamentation (4:1–12), retreats into a tomb. As for Abimelech, he is given the promised protection:

5:1 But Abimelech took the figs in the burning heat; and coming upon a tree, he sat under its shade to rest a little. And leaning his head on the basket of figs, he fell asleep and slept for sixty–six

2 years; and he was not awakened from his slumber. And afterward, when he awoke from his sleep, he said: 'I slept sweetly for a little while, but my head is heavy because I did not get enough sleep.'

3 Then he uncovered the basket of figs and found them dripping

4 juice. And he said: 'I would like to sleep a little longer, because my

5 head is heavy. But I am afraid that I might fall asleep and be late in awakening and my father Jeremiah would think badly of me. For if he were not in a hurry, he would not have sent me today at

6 daybreak. So I will get up, and proceed in the burning heat; for is

7 there not heat, is there not toil every day?' So he got up and took the basket of figs and placed it on his shoulders, and he entered into Jerusalem and did not recognize it; neither his (own) house,

8 nor the place, nor did he find his own family. And he said: 'The

Lord be blessed, for a great trance has come over me (today) ! This
9   is not the city (Jerusalem). I have lost my way because I came by
10 the mountain road when I arose from my sleep. And since my head
11 was heavy because I did not get enough sleep, I lost my way. It
    will seem incredible to Jeremiah when I tell him that I lost my
12 way,' And he departed from the city; and as he searched he saw the
    landmarks of the city, and said: 'This is, indeed, the city; and all
13 the same I lost my way.' And again he returned to the city and
14 searched, and found no one of his own people. And he said: 'The
15 Lord be blessed, for a great trance has come over me!' And
    again he departed from the city. And he stayed there grieving,
16 not knowing where he should go. And he put down the basket,
    saying: 'I will sit here until the Lord takes this trance from me.'
17 And as he sat, he saw an old man coming from the field; and
    Abimelech said to him: 'I say to you, old man, what city is this?'
18 And he said to him: 'It is Jerusalem.' And Abimelech said to him:
    'Where is Jeremiah the priest, and Baruch the secretary, and all the
19 people of this city, for I could not find them?' And the old man
    said to him: 'Are you, (then,) not from this city, seeing that you
    remember Jeremiah today, and ask about him after such a long
20-1 time? For Jeremiah is in Babylon with the people. For they were
    taken captive by king Nebuchadnezzar, and Jeremiah is with them
    to preach the good news to them and to teach them the word.' As
22-3 soon as Abimelech heard this from the old man, he said: 'If you
    were not an old man, and if it were not for the fact that it is not
    lawful for a man to upbraid one older than himself, I would laugh
    at you and say that you must be out of your mind, since you say
24 that the people have been taken captive into Babylon. Even if the
    heavenly torrents had descended on them, that is still no reason
25 for them to depart for Babylon. For how much time has passed
    since my father Jeremiah sent me to the estate of Agrippa to pick
    some figs, so that I might give them to the sick among the people?
26 And I went and got them, and when I came to a certain tree in the
    burning heat, I sat down to rest a little, and I leaned my head on
    the basket and fell asleep; and when I awoke I uncovered the

basket of figs, supposing that I was late. And I found the figs
27 dripping juice, just as I had collected them. And yet you claim that
the people have been taken captive into Babylon? But that you may
28 know, take the figs and see.' And he uncovered the basket of figs
29–30 for the old man. And he saw them, dripping juice. And when
the old man saw them, he said: 'O my son, you are a righteous
man, and God did not want you to see the desolation of the city:
God brought this trance upon you. For behold, it is sixty-six years
31 today since the people were taken captive into Babylon. And that
you may know, my child, that it is true (what I tell you), look into
the field and see: the ripening of the crops has not (yet) appeared.
32 And notice that the figs are not in season, and be enlightened.' Then
Abimelech cried out in a loud voice, saying: 'I bless you, Lord,
God of heaven and earth, the Rest of the souls of the righteous in
33 every place!' Then he said to the old man: 'What month is this?'
34 He said: 'Nisan, and it is the twelfth (day).' And taking some of
the figs, he gave them to the old man and said to him: 'May God
illumine your way to the city above, Jerusalem'.

1. *and slept for sixty-six years*: this is also the duration of the exile (cp.
5:30; 7:24), according to the PJ who always give this number. In the
Bible the exile lasts seventy years: Jer. 25:12; 29:10; Zech. 1:12; 7:15;
Dan. 9:2. See also Josephus, *Ant.* x.9.7 (184); xi.1.1 (2); xx. 10.1(233);
War v.9.4 (389); *Apion* 1.19 (132). This number, seventy, is without
doubt to be understood as standing for a long period in general: that
of the life of man (cp. Ps. 90:10). The symbolic number can be applied
historically from 2 Chron. 36:21 onwards. The number sixty-six of the
PJ is probably a round figure, as in the case of the announcement of an
exile of about seventy-seven years in AsMos 3:14. The story of
Abimelech's sleep can be compared with Josephus, *Ant.* xiv.2 (21–4);
Ta'anit 3:8; y.Ta'anit iii.9 (8), 66*d*; b.Ta'anit 23*a*. The narrative of a
long sleep of sixty six years is used by the two Talmuds as midrashic
exegesis of Ps. 126:1. See also Qu'ran, ii.261.
2. We adopt the text established by KP.
3. The figs are symbolical of the return, in Jer. 24:5–6. They play an
important part in the PJ. They are mentioned in connection with the
sleep of Abimelech; it is in order to pick them that Jeremiah sends him
to Agrippa's vineyard (3:15–16); it is the figs that stress the very long

duration of the sleep (5:23–35; 6:3); the eagle takes fifteen of them to Babylon where Jeremiah hands them out to those of the people who are ill (7:8, 32). The expression 'the sick of the people' may have a symbolic meaning: those who suffer because of the exile. On the healing power of figs, see Isa. 38:21; 2 Kings 20:7. In the *PJ*, the figs are certainly the symbol of the life the exiled people will be able to lead again. By the same token this symbol stands, in 6:4–7, for the eternal life.

5. Like Baruch, Abimelech calls Jeremiah *'father'* (cp. 5:25; 9:8). The prophets receive this title: 2 Kings 2:12; 6:21; 13:14.

6. We adopt the variant of mss. *ab*; cp. KP. Harris has: 'and I shall proceed to where there is no heat, no daily toil.'

7. KP add: 'or any of his acquaintances'.

8. ms. *c*: 'today'. *trance*: this might be translated as 'torpor' (5:8, 14, 16, 30). The LXX uses the Greek word corresponding with 'trance' in connection with the sleep of Adam (Gen. 2:21). See also Gen. 15:12; 1 Sam. 26:12; Job 4:13; 33:15.

17. *from the field*: analogous wording in Mark 15:21.

18. *the priest*: see Jer. 1:1. The manuscript *c* reads 'High Priest', which agrees more with the fact that in 9:2 Jeremiah performs singlehandedly the tenth-day-sacrifice, probably that of Yôm Kippur. In 2Bar 33:1 Jeremiah is described as the prophet. *Baruch, the secretary*: thus the mss. *ab*; the Ethiopian reads 'Levite'; *c* gives nothing. Esdras is equally called 'reader, secretary' in 1 Esdras 8:8, 9; 9:39, 42, 49.

21. This verse specifies the task of Jeremiah as the leader in exile for his compatriots (cp. 3:11). Compare this with 2Bar 10:2, where Jeremiah is summoned to 'strengthen the people in captivity', and with 33:2, where the people remind Baruch in the same terms of the assignment Jeremiah had given him. It is within this framework of reference that we should understand this verse of the *PJ*. The Greek term, translated as *teach*, is not in the LXX; it occurs in the New Testament: Luke 1:4; Acts 18:25; 21:21; Rom. 2:18; 1 Cor. 14:19; Gal. 6:6, where it often refers to instruction in the faith.

23 As for the respect due to old men, see Lev. 19:32; Ecclus. 8:6.

31. *the ripening of the crops has not (yet) appeared*. We adopt the text established by KP.

32. *God of heaven and earth*: the same formula in Judith 9:12; 2 Esdras 5:11; Matt. 11:25; *Rest of the souls of the righteous*: analogous formula in Wisd. of Sol. 3:3; 4:7.

33. KP = verse 34: 'Nisan which is Abib'. *a* and *b* read 'Nisan which

is the twelfth'. *c* is corrupt. Nisan is never a twelfth month. The number twelve relates to the day, not the month, as the Ethiopic version well understood it, translating: 'The twelfth of the month of Nisan, which corresponds with that of Miyazia'. The miracle lies in the fact that the figs are ripe out of season, in Nisan. It is to be noted that the episode of the cursed fig tree, told in Mark 11:12-14, 20-2 equally takes place shortly before Easter, i.e. in Nisan.

34. This wish expressed by Abimelech alludes to the heavenly Jerusalem which will descend on earth in the end of time (Ezek. 40-3; Isa. 54:11-14; 60; 62; 1En 63:6; 90:28-30; 2Bar 32:2-6; 4Ezra 7:26; 10:27, 54f; 13:6, 36; cp. Gal. 4:26; Heb. 12:22; Rev. 21:2-22), or she stays in heaven and designates the celestial paradise (1En 25:5; 2En 55:2; 2Bar 4:2-7).

6:1-7:12. An angel takes Abimelech to Baruch, who, filled with amazement, contemplates the figs, still succulent sixty-six years after having been picked. He offers a prayer of thanks to God, and asks the Lord to tell him how to inform Jeremiah of the protection bestowed upon Abimelech. The angel of the Lord appears to Baruch, and announces that an eagle will come to him and will serve him as a messenger. He also reveals to him the conditions for the return of the exiles: all strangers should be set apart within fifteen days; thereafter the return will be effected. Baruch puts this message in writing, modifying it as he sees fit (6:1-23). An eagle appears before him and carries to Babylon Baruch's letter and fifteen figs (7:1-12).

7:13 Then the eagle took flight with the letter, and went away to Babylon. He rested on a post outside the city in a desert place.

14 And he kept silent until Jeremiah came along, for he and some of the people were coming out to bury a corpse. For Jeremiah had petitioned Nebuchadnezzar, saying: 'Give me a place where I may

15 bury those of my people who have died.' And he had given it to him. And as they were coming out with the body, and weeping, they came to where the eagle was. And the eagle cried out in a loud voice, saying: 'I say to you, Jeremiah the chosen one of God, go, and gather together all of your people, that they come here in order to hear the good message that I have brought to you from

16 Baruch and Abimelech.' And when Jeremiah heard this, he glorified God; and he went and gathered together the people along with

their wives and children, and he came to where the eagle was. And
17 the eagle came down on the corpse, and it revived. Now this took
18 place so that they might believe. All the people were astounded at
what had happened, and said: 'Is not this the God who appeared
to our fathers in the wilderness through Moses, and who assumed
the form of an eagle and appeared to us through this great eagle?'
19 And the eagle said to Jeremiah: 'Come, untie this letter and read
20 it to the people.' So he untied the letter and read it to the people.
And when the people heard it, they wept and put dust on their
21 heads. And they said to Jeremiah: 'Deliver us and tell us what to
22 do that we may once again enter our city.' And Jeremiah answered
and said to them: 'Do whatever you heard from the letter, and the
Lord will lead us into our city.'

13. KP = verse 12: 'having the letter tied to his neck; ...and when
he arrived (he rested)'. In the Bible, the eagle is admired for his majestic
and rapid flight and for the vertiginous altitude at which he makes his
nest (2 Sam. 1:23; Jer. 49:16); sometimes he symbolizes God (Exod.
19:4; Deut. 32:11). Here, he is represented as a messenger from God,
and the Israelites see in him a manifestation of God (7:18). The eagle
also symbolizes the celestial beings (Ezek. 1:10; 10:14; Rev. 4:7; 8:13;
12:14), and eternal youth (Ps. 103:5; Isa. 40:31). He is mentioned in
rabbinical literature: Qoheleth R. 2:27 (Solomon is taken away to
Tadmor (Palmyra) by an eagle). In the literature related to 2Bar and to
PJ, see AsMos 10:8–9.
14. KP = verse 13: '(a corpse) outside the city'.
KP = verse 14:'king' (Neb.).
Jeremiah here appears as the leader of the exiles; he negotiates with
Nebuchadnezzer, just like Moses with Pharaoh, and stays close to his
compatriots (verses 14-15), with whom he shares the hardships of
existence in exile (cp. 7:23–9).
15. KP = verse 16: omit: 'all of your people' and read 'come',
instead of 'that they come'. Also: 'a letter' instead of 'the good
message'.
17. Affirmation of the belief in the resurrection. The eagle is the
symbol of regeneration: Isa. 40:31; Ps. 103:5. *that they might believe*:
cp. Exod. 4:1–9, 30.
18. KP = verse 20: omit 'and who assumed the form of an eagle' and
'great'. We also see this astonishment at the occurrence of miraculous

events when Jesus performs his miracles: Matt. 8:27; 9:33; Luke 7:16, etc. *God who appeared to our fathers in the wilderness*: see Exod. 3:10; 19:9; 20:18–21.

19. KP = verse 21: 'I say to you, Jeremiah.'

22. *the Lord will lead us into our city*: cp. Jer. 3:14; Baruch 5:6.

7:23–8:4. Through the medium of the eagle Jeremiah sends a letter to Baruch, describing the hardships and afflictions of life in exile. Then he goes on giving to his compatriots instructions to be followed until the day of the return to Jerusalem (7:23–32). When that day has come, God orders Jeremiah to organize the return of the exiles, and to communicate to them the requirements pertaining to the crossing of the Jordan and the separation of those married couples of whom one has Babylonian nationality. Those who are not willing to obey these commands, are forbidden to enter Jerusalem (8:1–5).

8:5   So they crossed the Jordan and came to Jerusalem. And Jeremiah and Baruch and Abimelech stood up and said: 'No man joined
6   with Babylonians shall enter this city.' And they said to one another 'Let us arise and return to Babylon to our place.' And they
7   departed. But when they were coming to Babylon, the Babylonians came out to meet them, saying: 'You shall not enter our city, for you hated us and left us in secret; therefore you cannot come in with us. For we have taken a solemn oath together in the name of our god to receive neither you nor your children, since you left us in secret.'
8   And when they heard this, they returned and came to a desert place some distance from Jerusalem and built a city for themselves and
9   named it Samaria. And Jeremiah sent them a message saying: 'Repent, for the angel of righteousness is coming and will lead you to your exalted place.'

5. On the occasion of the first return from exile, Ezra (see Ezra 9:1–10:44) had exacted the separation from the non-Jewish wives (cp. Neh. 13:23–7). There is no reason to impose a Jewish-Christian origin on the demands formulated in this verse (cp. verses 1–3). What we find here in chapter 8 may be a myth of Jewish origin, expressing contempt for the Samaritans.

8. According to 2 Kings 17:24–41 the towns of Samaria had been repopulated by peoples of different races and religions, transferred to these places by the king of Babylon. This tradition had imprinted a

vivid contempt for the Samaritans on the minds of the Jews (cp. Ecclus. 50:25–6; TLevi 7:2; Luke 9:52–3; John 4:9; 8:48; Josephus, *Ant.* XVIII.2.2 (30); XX.6.1 (118–24). This contempt is condemned by the gospels: Luke 10:33–6; 17:11–19; John 4:7–29, etc. In chapter 8 of the *PJ*, the contempt with regard to the Samaritans is mitigated by verse 9.

9:1–7. Those who have remained with Jeremiah offer sacrifices on behalf of the people for nine days. On the tenth day, Jeremiah is the only one to offer a sacrifice and to pray a prayer of thanksgiving. And he becomes 'like one of those whose soul has departed'.

9:8 And Baruch and Abimelech stood there, weeping and crying out in a loud voice: 'Our father Jeremiah has left us – the priest of God

9 has departed!' And all the people heard their weeping and they all ran to them and saw Jeremiah lying on the ground as if dead. And they tore their garments and scattered dust on their heads and

10 wept bitterly. And after this they prepared to bury him. And

11 behold, there came a voice saying: 'Do not bury the one who yet

12 lives, for his soul is going to return again to his body.' Having heard this voice they did not bury him, but stayed around his tabernacle for three days, saying in their incertitude: 'When will

13 he arise?' And after three days his soul came back into his body, and he raised his voice in the midst of them all and said: 'Glorify God, all of you glorify God and the Son of God who awakens us, Jesus Christ, the light of all the ages, the inextinguishable lamp, the life of the faith.'

8. KP = verse 8: 'Woe to us'.

11. Compare Mark 9:7; John 12:28. *His soul is going to return again to his body.* Death is seen as the separation of soul and body, cp. verses 12–13. The second part of chapter 9, the verses 11–32 which deal with the second death of Jeremiah, can only have been composed by a Christian writer; Jeremiah rises from the dead three days after his death (verse 13); he glorifies the Son of God, Jesus Christ, light of the world, life of the faith. In verse 13, we again find the notions of faith and life rejoined (cp. 6:4). Light and life are Johannine themes; these themes appear in the *PJ*: that of the light (6:9, 12; 9:3, 13, 16, 25); that of the life (4:8; 6:4; 9:3, 13–14).

12. KP = verse 13: omit 'in their incertitude'.

13. KP = verse 14: add 'with one voice' after 'glorify God'.

9:14–18. This glorification of Jesus Christ provokes the fury of the people.

9:19 When Jeremiah was saying this concerning the Son of God – that he is coming into the world – the people flew into a rage and said:

20 'These words are a repetition of those spoken by Isaiah son of

21 Amoz, when he said: "I saw God and the Son of God." Come, then, and let us not kill him by the same sort of death with which

22 we killed Isaiah, but let us stone him with stones.' And Baruch and Abimelech were greatly grieved because of this deranged behaviour, and also because they wanted to hear in full the mysteries that he had seen.

23 But Jeremiah said to them: 'Be silent and weep not, for they cannot kill me until I have described for you everything I saw.'

24 And he said to them: 'Bring me a stone.' And he set it up and said:

25 'Light of the ages, make this stone to become like me in appear-

26 ance.' Then the stone took on the appearance of Jeremiah. And

27 they were stoning the stone, supposing that it was Jeremiah. But Jeremiah delivered to Baruch and to Abimelech all the mysteries

29 he had seen. And forthwith he stood in the midst of the people,

30 desiring to complete his ministry. Then the stone cried out, saying: 'O foolish children of Israel, why do you stone me, supposing that

31 I am Jeremiah? Behold, Jeremiah is standing in your midst!' And when they saw him, they immediately rushed upon him with

32 many stones. And his ministry was fulfilled. And when Baruch and Abimelech came, they buried him, and taking the stone they placed it on his tomb and inscribed it thus: 'This is the stone that was the ally of Jeremiah.'

20. AscenIs 3:13–18; 9:12–16; 11:2–32.

21. According to MartIs 5:1, Isaiah was sawn asunder. See also Heb. 11:37.

22. KP = verse 23: omit 'because of this deranged behaviour'.

23. KP = verse 26: 'until I have described to Baruch and Abimelech everything I saw'. 'Light of the ages': see John 1:9.

26. KP = verse 27: 'by God's command'.

28–31. The addition of this second death of Jeremiah might be explained as being prompted by the wish to bring heterogeneous data into agreement with each other: Jeremiah's flight to Egypt (Jer. 43:6, 8; his being stoned (*Vitae Prophetarum*, Jeremiah, 1), and his exile in Babylon (2Bar; *PJ*; Seder ʿOlam Rabbah xxvi). We also find again in these verses 28–31 the theme of the persecution of the prophets (2 Chron. 24:19–22; 36:15–16; 1 Kings 18:4; 19:10, 14; Jer. 2:30). After the exile, this theme recurs in discussions by sectarian groups (e.g. in connection with the persecution of the Teacher of Righteousness). The remarks by Josephus (*Ant.* ix. 13.2 (265); x. 3.1 (38)) testify to the importance this theme (see also Neh. 9:26) had in popular imagination. In the time of Christ 'sanctuaries' or 'chapels' were erected in places where several prophets were supposed to have been martyred.

On this topic of the persecution of prophets, see – apart from the *Vitae Prophetarum* very popular with the Jews at the beginning of the Christian era – Matt. 5:12; 21:35–6; 23:29–37; Mark 12:2–5; Luke 6:23; 11:47–51; Acts 7:52; Rom. 11:2–3; 1 Thess. 2:15; Jub 1:12; 4Ezra 1:32.

32. The wording of the inscription is comparable to that of certain inscriptions found in Palestine and elsewhere. See 1 Sam. 7:12.

The Testament of Job
RUSSELL P. SPITTLER

Genre, purpose, features

Beyond the biblical book which bears his name, Job is remembered both in the Old Testament (Ezek. 14:14, 20) and in the New (Jas. 5:11). Little wonder, then, that the fame of the heroic sufferer led to a Testament of Job, since the times abounded in 'testaments' attributed to a wide range of patriarchal worthies. As with other testaments of the hellenistic era, a particular trait of character is praised – patience, predictably, in Job's case.

Unlike many testaments, the TJob shows little interest in the future, though at times the vocabulary of apocalyptic surfaces. Nor is there found in the TJob that pessimism over the present state of the world which is so often characteristic of apocalyptic.

What does occur, however, is a high regard for the upper world such as later came to characterize Gnosticism – a blend of oriental mysticism with Christian thought, which thrived about the second to the sixth centuries. To this higher cosmic realm Job avows allegiance in spite of his woes. His three daughters enter the same upper world when they don charismatic sashes made from their father's belt-like 'phylactery', which had brought about his recovery from illness. By means of the magical sashes, the daughters speak in the tongues of angels.

In one place Job asserts that his kingdom 'and its splendour and majesty are in the chariots of the Father' (TJob 33:9). Such an assertion shows kinship with Merkabah mysticism, a hellenistic Jewish speculative mysticism focused on the 'chariots' (*merkabōt*) of God.

A striking prominence is given to women by the TJob. Job's present and former wives are given names. He is the patron of needy widows. Fully a half-dozen distinct terms are used for female slaves. Job's daughters figure prominently in the closing section of the book. Given Jewish values at the time, it is a wonder the daughters are given any inheritance at all, to say nothing of the quasi-magical sashes they were bequeathed.

More traditional Jewish interests apparent in the TJob include a ban on foreign marriages, concern for proper burial, developed notions of angels and Satan. Laments abound too, for the living as well as for the dead.

The TJob thus curiously blends standard Jewish propaganda against idolatry, Jewish Merkabah mysticism, female prophecy, Gnostic-like disregard for the future coupled with an existentially focused spiritual idealism, and even – as the phylactery seems to require – serious religious magic. All this makes for a decidedly singular 'testament'.

Contents and structure

Following the title and setting (chapter 1), Job first encounters a revealing angel, who foretells calamities if Job persists in his intent to destroy an idol's shrine (2–5).

Once the shrine is destroyed, Job and Satan occupy the TJob (6–27). Job's piety and generosity are celebrated (9–15) then contrasted with his losses (16–26). Opening (6–8) with Satan's masqueraded approach to Job, this section closes (27) with a direct confrontation in which Satan concedes defeat by patient Job.

Sitting at the dump outside the city, Job receives his friends – who (in language similar to the LXX, Job 2:11) come as kings with armies (28–45). They test Job's sanity, but Job gives insoluble riddles of his own. In the end, they are rescued by Job's intercession. By the marvellous belt with which Job 'girded himself', God brings recovery to Job, which leads to the death-bed scene. Job distributes his property to his sons.

Then Job bequeaths charismatic sashes to his three daughters (46–53). When each in turn puts on the sash, she loses interest in worldly affairs and begins to praise God in an angelic dialect. Finally (51–3), Nereus – Job's brother – describes the whisking-off of Job's soul in a chariot, his death and burial.

Overall narrative progress in the TJob emerges in the sequence of Job's relations with the angel (2–5), with Satan (6–27), with his friends the kings (28–45), and finally with his daughters (46–53). TJob 1, 51–3, fit the tale into the form of the testament genre.

Origin and date

The judgement of scholars is divided on whether the apocryphon was Jewish or Christian in origin. As it stands, the TJob does not show much obvious Christian editing. Yet its distance from orthodox Jewish concerns is clear. One line of assessment has traced the origin of the work to sectarian Jews – such as the Essenes, the Qumran sect at the Dead Sea community, or the Egyptian Jewish sect known as the Therapeutae described by Philo in Vit Cont.

Women, who figure largely in the TJob, had little place at Qumran; but they enjoyed a much more prominent role among the Therapeutae in Egypt. Hymn composition, mentioned in the TJob, was described as an activity of that community by Philo. A fascination among them for the number 50 may account for Job's '50 bakeries' (TJob 10:7), which has no Septuagintal source.

These and other considerations suggest an origin of the TJob among the Therapeutae about the first century AD, although the century prior or the one following are also possible. The document may have urged endurance as a response to impending persecution – mild or severe. It served, no doubt, as a polemic against idolatry and may well have filled missionary propaganda purposes.

A suggestion has been made that the Montanists, a second-century pneumatic-prophetic Christian group, may be responsible for the final section of the document (TJob 46–53), where praise of patient endurance gives way to the daughters of Job speaking the language of the angels and the Cherubim. In their contest with the Montanists, the orthodox Christians demanded biblical precedent for prophets who spoke in ecstasy (Eusebius, *Ecclesiastical History* v.17.1–3). Though proof is not possible, it is an attractive possibility to think that the TJob in its present form was furnished by the Montanists as a rigged pseudo-canonical precedent to legitimate their own ecstatic, and largely female, prophecy.

In any case, the TJob is an essentially Jewish work composed in Greek close to the times of Jesus and Paul, Philo and Josephus.

Relation to the LXX

Proposals for a Hebrew or Aramaic origin lack conclusive evidence. The obvious relation of the TJob to the LXX book of Job makes original composition in Jewish Greek nearly certain. The TJob agrees often with the LXX (which is twenty per cent shorter than the Hebrew text) in places where both considerably differ from the Hebrew text yet resemble each other.

It is the narrative framework of the biblical book of Job, Job 1–2 and 42 (particularly as these are given in the LXX), which furnishes much of the story in the TJob. But the LXX form of Job 29–31 also drew the interest of the author of the TJob.

Given the complicated development of the LXX textual tradition, it is even possible that the TJob – having used some early form of the LXX text – may have influenced the eventual form of the LXX text itself.

Text and translations

The principal witnesses to the TJob are three mediaeval Greek manuscripts. The best of these, in many ways – and the text largely followed in the selections given below – is labelled P. Located in the Bibliothèque Nationale in Paris, this ms. dates from the eleventh century. A sixteenth-century copy exists in the same library.

A ms. known as S is in Messina, Sicily, and it dates to AD 1307/8. Though highly irregular spellings frequently appear, it seems to reflect a separate textual tradition of the TJob.

V is held at the Vatican libraries at Rome. Written in AD 1195 over an erased earlier work, this ms. reflects conscious editorial improvements and chronological harmonizations. It also shows a penchant for abbreviations. As a witness to the text of the TJob, it is clearly secondary – although it apparently shares with S a common text form differing from P.

A few representative variant readings of P, S and V are given in the notes to the selections.

A tenth-century version in Old Church Slavonic is known from three mss., only one complete. Since 1968, existence of a fifth-century manuscript (incomplete) of a Coptic translation has been known. Its publication will facilitate the eventual development of a critical edition of the text of the TJob.

Modern translations have appeared in French, English, German, Hebrew and (in part) Serbo-Croatian. Plans exist for translations into Spanish and Japanese.

Bibliography

A convenient and inexpensive edition of the TJob with the SV text and facing English translation is R. Kraft (ed.), *The Testament of Job* (SBL Texts and Translations 5, Pseudepigrapha Series 4), Missoula, 1974. Pp. 17–20 contain an extensive annotated bibliography up to 1971.

S. Brock has produced a careful edition of the Greek text according to P, with the variants of S, V and the Slavonic versions noted in the apparatus: *Testamentum Iobi* (PsVTGr 2), Leiden, 1967.

Two important studies appear in volume one of the *SBL Seminar Papers 1974* ed. G. MacRae, Cambridge, Mass., 1974: (1) J. Collins, 'Structure and Meaning in the Testament of Job', pp. 35–52; and H. C. Kee, 'Satan, Magic, and Salvation in the Testament of Job', pp. 53–76.

The complete English translation, from which the extracts below have been adapted, appears in J. H. Charlesworth (ed.), *The Old Testament Pseudepigrapha*, vol. 1, pp. 829–68.

The most recent German translation is that by B. Schaller, 'Das Testament Hiobs' in JSHRZ III/3, pp. 301–87.

The selections chosen summarize the TJob, sample its literary variety, and typify its theological interests.

PROLOGUE: TITLE AND SETTING

1:1 The Book of the Words of Job, the one called Jobab.

2   One day, when Job fell ill and began to put his affairs in order,

3   he called his seven sons and three daughters. Their names are Tersi, Choros, Hyon, Nike, Phoros, Phiphe, Phrouon, Hemera, Kasia and

4   Amaltheia's Horn. And when he had called them he said, 'Gather round, my children. Gather round me so that I may show you what the Lord did with me, all the things which have happened to me.

5   I am your father Job, fully given to endurance.'

1. The title, *The Book of the Words of Job*, follows a frequent usage (e.g., 1 Kings 14:19, Tobit 1:1, Luke 3:4). Identification of Job as *the one called Jobab* – the name of the second king of Edom (Gen. 36:33f) – places Job among the Patriarchs as a descendant of Abraham (as also does the LXX, Job 42:17c) and strengthens his portrayal as a king.

2. The *seven sons* and *three daughters* are the second set of children referred to at Job 42:13, since Job's first family died in the tornado described in the canonical story (Job 1:18–19). The names of the sons appear in P only, while the names of the daughters are the same as those used by the LXX in translating the Hebrew text (Job 42:14).

3. *Hemera*, 'Day'; *Kasia*, 'Incense'; *Amaltheia's Horn*, the legendary cornucopia of Greek Mythology – the three daughters.

5. *endurance*, or patience, is the celebrated virtue of the TJob and the reason for the sole mention of him in the New Testament: 'You have all heard how Job stood firm, and you have seen how the Lord treated him in the end' (Jas. 5:11).

TJob 2–5 recount the interview of Job with the angel: if Job will oppose the idol worship (a common object of contemporary Jewish opposition

in the literature of the time), he will in fact oppose the devil who inspires
such worship. Job destroys the shrine, and the devil devastates Job, who
nevertheless patiently endures and at last triumphs.

THE ANGEL'S PROMISE

4:3, 4   Again the angel said, 'Thus says the Lord: If you try to purge
Satan's place, he will rise up against you angry for battle. But he
will be unable to bring death on you. He will bring on you many
5   plagues, he will take your goods for himself, he will carry off your
children.
6   But if you are patient, I will make your name famous in all
7   generations of the earth till the end of the age. And I will return
8   again your goods. You will get back twice as much, so you will
know that the Lord is impartial – he treats well anyone who obeys.
9   And you shall be raised up in the resurrection. For you will be
10   like a sparring athlete, both enduring the pains and winning the
11   crown. Then you will know that the Lord is just, true, and strong –
giving strength to his elect.'

4. That Satan *will be unable to bring death* to Job corresponds to a
similar limit set by God in the canonical account (Job 2:6). The biblical
Job at first suffers loss of property and kin, his own person exempt.
Later he undergoes personal illness, but his life is assured. In the TJob
such gradualism drops out: illness, bankruptcy and bereavement arrive
at once. In common with its canonical forbear, the TJob attributes to
Satan the immediate cause of the calamities. In the canonical book,
only Job's righteousness and piety occasion his troubles: in the TJob,
it is his militant opposition to idolatrous worship that leads Satan's
attack. Thus, the TJob – like *Bel and the Snake* in the Apocrypha – was
a tract against idolatry.

6. *if you are patient*, reflects the patience motif of the TJob: no such
line appears in Job 1–2.

9. No promise of *resurrection* is made in the canonical book of Job.
But the LXX adds to the end of the Hebrew book these words: 'It is
written that he will rise again with those whom the Lord raises up'
(Job 42:17a LXX; cp. also Job 14:14 LXX). This LXX addition is
converted to the past tense in V's distinctive ending at TJob 53:8: 'he
was raised up with those whom the Lord raised up'. Cp. Matt. 27:52.

Affinities of the TJob with the LXX as against the Hebrew text are undeniable, though the precise sequence of the textual interrelations is complicated.

10. Athletic imagery for the disciplined race of piety appear in the canon (1 Cor. 9:24–7) and beyond it (4 Macc. 6:10). Early church fathers wrote often of the 'athletes of God', including martyrs. Greek sports were still popular in hellenistic times.

Till now, Job and the angel have dominated the story. In 6–27 Job and Satan become the protagonists. The encounter begins indirectly (6–8), with Job secluding himself from Satan – who seeks entry disguised as a beggar. It ends with Job's confrontation with Satan who, like a defeated athletic competitor, concedes the match (27). What occurs between is mainly a recital of Job's piety, wealth and generosity (9–15) followed by a poignant (and at times poetic) recital of his losses (16–26).

SATAN ATTACKS JOB

6:1, 2 Listen, children, and marvel. As soon as I went in the house and
3 secured the doors, I gave my doormen this order. 'If anyone seeks me today, permit no entry. Say instead, "He has no free time; he is inside concerned with an urgent matter."'

4 While I was inside, Satan knocked at the door – having disguised
5 himself as a beggar. And he said to the doormaid, 'Tell Job I want
6 to see him.' When the doormaid came and told me this, I told her to say I was not available.

7:1 When he heard that, Satan left and put a yoke on his shoulders.
2 And when he got back, he said to the doormaid, "Say to Job, 'Give
3 me a loaf of bread from your own hands, so I may eat.'" So I gave a burnt loaf of bread to the girl to give to him along with this
4 message, 'No longer will you eat my bread, for you are a stranger to me.'

12 When he heard this, Satan sent the girl back to me and said, 'As this loaf of bread is completely burnt, so I shall do to your body also. Within the hour, when I am gone I will destroy you.'
13 And I said back to him, 'Do as you please. If you try to do me in, I am prepared to endure whatever you inflict.'

6:4. Satan, who here *disguised himself as a beggar*, elsewhere in the TJob appears as 'King of the Persians' (17:2) and a 'bread-seller' (23:1). The Apostle Paul knew that 'Satan himself masquerades as an angel of light' (2 Cor. 11:14).

7:1. Because the Greek word translated *yoke* (*assalion*) appears nowhere else in Greek of any period, its precise meaning is uncertain. Since it goes on the shoulders, it is something worn or borne – perhaps a shawl (*sali* in modern Greek) or wallet, perhaps a basket in which to carry the bread. Satan comes to Job disguised as one of the many indigents he regularly aided.

7:3. The *burnt loaf*, a touch of humour on the part of the author.

7:13. It is Job, the paragon of patience, who utters '*I am prepared to endure whatever you inflict.*'

JOB'S PHILANTHROPY

9:1 Listen, I will show you the things that have befallen me, my
2 losses. I used to have 130,000 sheep: of them I designated 7,000 to
3 be sheared for the clothing of orphans and widows, the poor and the
  helpless. And I had a pack of 80 dogs guarding my flocks. I also had
4 200 more dogs guarding the house. And I used to have 9,000 camels:
5 from them I chose 3,000 to work in every city. After I loaded them
  with good things, I sent them away into the cities and villages,
  ordering them to go and distribute to the helpless, to the destitute,
  and to all the widows.

2–5. The riches of Job listed at Job 1:3 include 7,000 sheep and 3,000 camels. The TJob vastly enlarges these figures, but ends up with a precisely corresponding 7,000 sheep and 3,000 camels as the numbers of animals specifically designated for charitable services.

5. In addition to Job's own philanthropy, he underwrote the charitable ventures of others.

JOB AT THE DUMP

20:7 In great trouble and distress I left the city and sat at the dump,
8 worm-ridden in body. Discharges from my body soaked the ground.
9 There were many worms in my body. If a worm ever sprang off,
  I would pick it up and return it to its original place saying, 'Stay in

the very place where you were put until you are directed otherwise by your commander.'

7. That Job *left the city* is said also in the LXX (Job 2:8), but not in the Hebrew text. *worm-ridden*. cp. Job 7:5: 'My body is infested with worms.' Cp. 2 Macc. 9:9; Acts 12:23.

9. The capture and replacement of the fleeing worms exceed a resigned stoicism: it fulfils the motto of Job 2:10, 'If we accept good from God, shall we not accept evil?' Tertullian, writing about AD 200, also mentioned Job's return of departing worms (*De patientia*, 14:5): he may have used the TJob or a common source. The *commander* is God, even though Satan has brought on the illness.

Among Job's losses was his (first) wife, who is given the name Sitis in the TJob. Unnamed and only briefly mentioned in the biblical book (Job 2:9f), her speech is elaborated by the LXX. An extensive and imaginative description of her decline is portrayed in the TJob (21–6). Impoverished because of Job's woes, Sitis at first works for slave wages. Eventually, she is forced to sell her hair for a few loaves of bread. Finally she dies ignominiously in a manger and is buried – Job's losses completed. In the following selection, Job's wife speaks:

JOB'S WIFE SELLS HER HAIR FOR BREAD

24:7, 8 'So I ventured boldly into the marketplace, even though I was heartsick to do so. The breadseller said, "Pay money, and you can
9   have some." But I also showed him our straits and then heard him say, "If you have no money, Woman, pay with the hair of your head and take three loaves. Perhaps you will live for three more
10 days." Remiss, I said to him, "Go ahead, cut my hair." So he arose and cut my hair disgracefully in the marketplace, while the crowd stood by and marvelled.'

8. The *breadseller* is Satan in disguise.

11. By saying '*Go ahead, cut my hair*', Sitis agrees to the shame accorded shorn females in antiquity. A lengthy and skilful poetic lament for her is inserted at this point. Only a portion of it follows:

A LAMENT FOR SITIS

25:1 Who is not amazed that this is Sitis, the wife of Job?
2   Who used to have fourteen draperies sheltering her chamber and

doors within doors, so that anyone was considered quite worthy
merely to gain admission to her presence –

3   Now she exchanges her hair for loaves of bread!

4   Whose camels, laden with goods, used to go off into the poor
districts –

Now she gives her hair in return for loaves of bread!

Chapter 25. This *Lament for Sitis* parallels the prophetic mocking song,
a sample of which appears at Rev. 18, where a refrain of doom for
Babylon appears three times (Rev. 18:10, 16–17*a*, 19).

   1. *Sitis*, from the name of Job's city, Ausitis (given only in S at
TJob 28:7 but found also at Job 32:2 LXX) – which in turn probably
derives from the canonical Uz (Job 1:1).

   4. As did her husband, Sitis also had *camels, laden with goods,* commissioned for the service of the poor.

The climax comes in 27:1–7 when Job challenges Satan to show himself.
Doing so, Satan confesses he has been bested by the underdog, whose
triumph was achieved by patient endurance.

JOB'S TRIUMPH AND SATAN'S DEFEAT

27:1   Turning again to Satan, who was behind my wife, I said 'Come
up front! Stop hiding yourself! Does a lion show his strength in a
cage? Does a young bird take flight when it is held in a basket?
Come out and fight!'

2   He then came out from behind my wife. As he stood, he wept
and said, 'Look, Job, I am weary and I quit, even though you are
flesh and I am a spirit. You suffer physically, but I am in deep

3   trouble. I have become like a wrestling athlete who has pinned
his competitor. The one on top silenced the one below by filling his

4   mouth with sand and bruising his limbs. But because the underdog
showed endurance and did not give up, in the end the upper one

5   cried out in defeat. You, Job, were the stricken underdog. But you
overcame my wrestling tactics.'

6, 7   Ashamed, Satan left me for three years. Well then my children,
you also must be patient in everything that happens to you. For
patience is better than anything.

1. Job invites Satan to show his full strength, like an uncaged lion and a released bird.

3–5. The athletic imagery recalls and fulfils the earlier words of the angel to Job, 'For you will be like a sparring athlete, both enduring pains and winning the crown' (TJob 4:10).

7. The sentence *For patience is better than anything* is the climax and theme of the TJob.

With Satan defeated and departed, Job's friends – described as kings with separate armies in the TJob – arrive to console him. TJob 28–45 focuses on the friends, all of whom have something to say. Job triumphs over them as well, receiving from God the healing of his illness mediated by a remarkable 'phylactery'. Following thus Job's encounter with Satan (TJob 9–27), Job's dialogue with his friends (TJob 28–45) constitutes the second major section of the work.

JOB VISITED BY THE KINGS

28:1 After I had spent twenty years under the plague, the kings also
2 heard about what happened to me. They arose and came to me, each from his own country, so that they might encourage me by a
3 visit. But as they approached from a distance, they did not recognize me. And they cried out and wept, tearing their clothes and throwing
4 dust. Then they sat beside me for seven days and nights, and not
5 one of them said a word. It was not due to their patience that they were silent. Instead, it was because they had known me before these evils, when I lived in lavish wealth.

1. Chronological details vary in the different texts of the TJob. The biblical book states only that Job lived 140 years (twice threescore and ten) after his restoration. The LXX makes that 170 years and gives as a total life span 240 (or 248) years, an appropriate longevity for a patriarchal figure. P has Job at the dump for 48 years: after 11 years his food is reduced, after 17 years Sitis sells her hair for bread, after *twenty years* the three royal friends arrive to spend 27 days reviewing Job's case. P gives no final age for Job. S follows P in this scheme, but in an added ending gives Job's total years as 248. V limits Job's testing period to 7 years, but agrees with the 170 added years and the 248 total.
2. Job's friends were called *kings* already in the LXX. The royal friends appear in the same order as in the canonical book: Eliphas, Baldad, Sophar, Elihu (minor variant spellings occur).

3. *throwing dust* was a customary way of expressing grief. Job himself does the same elsewhere in TJob (29:4).

4. *seven days and nights* agrees with Job 2:13. But the visit lasted at least twenty-seven days (TJob 41:2).

5. *their patience*, of course, was no match for Job's endurance.

ELIPHAS CONFIRMS JOB'S IDENTITY

31:1 After seven days of such considerations, Eliphas spoke out and said to his fellow-kings, 'Let us approach him and question him carefully to see if it is really he himself or not.'

2 Since they were about a half-stadion distant from me because of the stench of my body, they got up and approached me with per-
3 fumes in their hands, while their soldiers accompanied them scat-
4 tering incense around me so they would be able to get near me. It took them three days to furnish the incense.

5 When they had come close, Eliphas spoke up and said to me:

> Are you Jobab, our fellow-king?
> Are you the one who once had vast splendour?
> Are you the one who was like the sun by day in
>   all the land?
> Are you the one who was like the moon and the
>   stars that shine at midnight?

6 And I said to him, 'Yes, I am indeed.'

1. *Eliphas* is Elious in P, S and V. Textual confusion exists.

2. A *half-stadion*, about 300 feet. The canonical book of Job says nothing about *the stench* arising from Job's illness nor about the incense and perfume used to overcome the odour. The terminal illness of Antiochus IV was accompanied by such an odour (2 Macc. 9:9–12).

4. The *three days* are reduced to three hours in V, which characteristically smooths the text.

5. These queries of *Eliphas* anticipate the longer 'royal lament' to follow.

6. '*Yes, I am indeed*' translates the Greek expression *ego eimi* widely used for the repeated revelatory 'I am' of Jesus occurring in the Fourth Gospel.

THE LAMENT OF ELIPHAS FOR JOB

32:1 Now listen to the lament of Eliphas as he recounts all the wealth
of Job:

2   Are you the one who commissioned 7,000 sheep for
        the clothing of the poor?
          Then where is the splendour of your throne now?
        Are you the one who designated 3,000 camels for the
        transport of goods to the needy?
          Then where is the splendour of your throne now?
3   Are you the one who appointed a thousand cattle for the
        needy to use when they plough?
          Then where is the splendour of your throne now?
4   Are you the one who had golden couches, but now
        you sit at the dump?
          Then where is the splendour of your throne now?

1–2. This *Lament of Eliphas* for Job is one of several poetic sections of
the TJob (25, 32, 33, 43), and they disclose no small literary skill. This
form of lament utilizes temporal contrast to mark the tragedy. The
refrain *Then where is the splendour of your throne now?* appears regularly
throughout the poem.

3. The *thousand cattle* restate the five hundred yoke of oxen mentioned earlier (TJob 10:5; 16:4; cp. Job 1:3).

JOB'S RESTORATION

44:1 When Eliphas ended the hymn, while all were singing in
response to him and encircling the altar, we got up and entered the
city where we now make our home. There we held great festivities
2 in the delight of the Lord. Once again I sought to do good works
for the poor.
3   All my friends and those who had known me as a benefactor
4 came to me. And they queried me saying, 'What do you ask of us
now?' Remembering the poor again to do them good, I suggested,
'Let each one give me a lamb for the clothing of the poor who are

5   naked.' Every single one then brought a lamb and a gold coin. And
the Lord blessed all the goods I owned. He doubled my estate.
45:1   So, my children, now I am dying. Above all, do not forget
2   the Lord. Do good to the poor. Do not overlook the helpless.
3,4   Do not take to yourselves wives from strangers. Look, my children.
I am dividing among you everything that is mine, so each of you
may have unrestricted control over his own share.

44:1. Philo describes (Vit Cont 80) hymn composition and use of
antiphonal response as characteristic of the Therapeutae.
44:2. By resuming *good works for the poor*, Job is fully reclaimed.
44:5. V makes the *gold coin* an alloy – one 'of gold and silver'.
As the angel had promised (TJob 4:7), God *doubled* Job's estate.
45:3. Characteristically Jewish is the admonition not to *take to yourselves wives from strangers* (cp. Gen. 24:3, 37; Ezra 10:10; Tobit 1:9;
Jub 20:4; TLevi 9:10).

Merely named earlier (TJob 1:3), the daughters of Job dominate this
final section (46–53) of the TJob. Job has just made legal disposition of
his property – but to the sons alone. The daughters, complaining, are
told their father has saved the best for them. Their share consists in
marvellous sashes for each of them, having magical capacities – good
for this world and the next. These charismatic sashes permit the
daughters to see Job's soul carried off by the guardian death angel. Job's
brother, Nereus, completes the narrative with an account of Job's
death and burial (TJob 51–3).

THE INHERITANCE OF JOB'S DAUGHTERS

46:5   When Job called his daughter who was named Hemera, he said
to her, 'Take the signet ring. Go to the vault, and bring here the
three golden boxes so I can give you your inheritance.' So she left
6   and brought them back.
7   And he opened them and brought out three multicoloured cords
whose appearance was such that nobody could describe – since they
were not from earth but from heaven, shimmering with fiery sparks
9   like the rays of the sun. To each one he gave a cord saying, 'Wear
these around you so it will go well with you as long as you live.'

5. The *signet ring* may have functioned as a key. For *three golden boxes*, P reads 'one golden box'.

7. The *three multicoloured cords* derive from a tri-stranded girdle or belt by which Job is later (TJob 47:5f) said to have been cured. V speaks of 'three cord-like aprons'. The customary Greek words for 'belt, girdle' (*zone, kestos*) are not used.

8. That the cords *were not from earth but from heaven* and are *shimmering with fiery sparks* reflects the vocabulary of apocalyptic. Angels whose person emanates *fiery sparks* are mentioned at 3En 29:2.

9. Because worn *around* ('lit. about your breast',)and possessing the ability to introduce heightened religious states, the cords can be seen as charismatic sashes.

THE CHARISMATIC SASHES

47:5   'Calling me, God furnished me with these three cords and said, "Arise, gird your loins like a man. I shall question you: you answer me."

6   So I took them and put them on. From that very time on the worms disappeared from my body and the plagues too. Then my

7   body drew strength from the Lord actually as if I had not suffered

8, 9   a thing. I also forgot the pains in my heart. And the Lord spoke to me in power, showing me things present and things to come.

10   Now then, my children, since you have these cords you will never have to face the enemy. Neither will you worry about him

11   in your mind, since these came from your father's protective amulet. Rise then, gird yourselves with them before I die so you can see those who are coming for my soul and marvel over the creatures of God.'

48:1   Then the daughter named Hemera stood up and wrapped her own cord about her as her father said. And she took on another

2   heart, no longer minded toward earthly things. And then she spoke

3   ecstatically in the angelic dialect, giving out with a hymn to God in accordance with the hymnic style of the angels. And as she spoke ecstatically, she allowed 'The Spirit' to be inscribed on her garment.

47:5–9. '*Arise, gird your loins*' was demanded of Job by God (Job 38:3, 40:7). This challenge climaxes the biblical story: Job, who has asked hard and relentless questions of God must now answer God's questions to him. It was with this triple-corded sash that Job girded himself for the divine interrogation. Literary restraint marks the TJob, for the actual recovery episode is not detailed. We are told only that Job's *body drew strength from the Lord* and that he *forgot the pains* of his *heart.* Thus the triple-stranded sash by which Job had been healed becomes the inheritance of the daughters.

47:10. One effect of the sashes is to fend off evil: the daughters *will never have to face the enemy,* as did both their father and mother in the story.

47:11. *protective amulet,* lit. phylactery. Probably from the realm of Jewish magic rather than the practice of encasing biblical quotations in small leather boxes strapped to one's wrist, forearm, or forehead. Females were in fact not permitted to wear phylacteries (Tefillin 3). Job's reference to *those who are coming for my soul* reflects the Greek myth of the psychopomps – celestial guides who accompany the soul upon its release from the body.

48:1–3. The effects of donning the sash are similar for each daughter. They lose earthly ties, speak *in the angelic dialect* (various angelic groups are named), and precipitate certain writings as the apparent work curiously titled 'The Spirit' suggests. This reference to angelic glossolalia forms a close parallel to Paul's reference to speaking 'in tongues of men or of angels' (1 Cor. 13:1).

JOB'S DEATH AND BURIAL

52:1 Three days after Job fell ill on his bed (without suffering or pain, however, since suffering could no longer touch him on account of
2 the omen of the sash he wore), he saw those who had come for his
3 soul. Standing up, he immediately took a lyre and gave it to his
4 daughter Hemera. To Kasia he gave an incense-censer. To Amal-
5 theia's Horn he gave a kettle-drum, so that they might bless those
6 who had come for his soul. And when they took up the instruments,
7 they saw the gleaming chariots which had come for his soul. And
they blessed and glorified God each in her own distinctive dialect.
53:5   When they brought the body to the tomb, all the widows
6 and orphans circled about, forbidding it to be placed into the tomb.

7 But after three days they laid him in the tomb in a beautiful sleep,
8 since he received a name famous in all generations for ever. Amen.

52:1. Although in life Job underwent lasting pain, in death he is
without suffering or pain – all a consequence of the glorious charismatic
phylactery which God had given Job to effect his healing.

52:3. Job himself also used the *lyre* (TJob 14:1f).

52:6. *gleaming chariots* also carried off Enoch (Gen. 5:24; 3En 6:1).
and Elijah (2 Kings 2:11).

53:5. The soul carried off, *the body* now is taken *to the tomb.*

53:6. With the *Amen*, P ends. The other witnesses to the text each
add a different conclusion.

Index

Compiled by Th. C. C. M. Heesterman-Visser and M. de Jonge

146; *PJ* as continuous written haggadah completing biblical narratives
214
righteous: judgement of 30, 33, 51;
reward of 36; Noah as r. individual
37; Enoch as righteous man 41;
blood of r. 49; prayer of r. 49;
appointed number of r. reached 49,
50; intercession by angels for r. 50;
r. and holy 50; r. will conquer in the
name of the Lord of Spirits, r. in
judgement 53; Abraham as r. and
hospitable man 58, 60; r. man prefers
death to breaking the law 147; r.
(pious) versus sinners 160, 162–5, 167,
168, 170
righteousness: plant of r. and truth 36;
Enoch, scribe of r. 41; spring of 50,
51; secrets of 52; spirit of those who
sleep in r. 52–3; sun of r. 89, 90; rod
of r. 91
romance(s) 93, 96
Rome 44, 204
Ruth 93

sabbath 113, 114, 118, 119, 133, 144, 211,
212
Sabinus 153
sacred objects in temple: removed by
angel 198; swallowed by earth 198,
199, 214; buried by Jeremiah 219, 220
sacrifice(s) 13; of Isaac 16–18, 130; s. and
wonders 22; s. and holocausts of
Manoah 22, 23, 24; laws about s. in
Jub 113, 123, 132; s. could not be
offered with frequency in exile 149,
151
saints, robes and transformation of 182
Samaria: fall of 187, 188; built by foreign
spouses 227, 228
Samaritan Pentateuch 129
Samaritans 7, 227, 228
Sammael (= Malkira) 181; will serve
Manasseh 183; leader of the Satans
after the Fall 184; dwelt in Manasseh
185
Samnas, secretary of Hezekiah 182;
= Shebna 184
Samsiel 31
Samson, announcement of his birth 8,
20–4; genealogy 20
Samuel 151
sanctuary, measurements of 13, 15
Sarah/Sarai 23, 115; barren, mother of
Isaac 61; womb opened 61, 62;

sorrow for Abraham's death 69;
death of S. 130
Sariel 34
Sartael 31
Satan 126–7; no Satan any more in period
of peace in future 134; his active role
in MartIs 179–80, 185–6; S. Job's
adversary in TJob 232, 236, approaches
Job in many disguises 237, 239, stands
under God's command 239, is de-
feated by the patient Job 240
Saul (king), death of 7; exorcised by
David's hymn 24, 25
Saul (Paul), Christ's appearance to 101
Scriptures, study of 160
'sealed' until the end of days, apocalyptic
writings 3
secret tradition in apocalyptic writings 3
Seleucids 153
Semyaza, leader of the angels 30, 32, 33,
34, 35, 37, 38
Septuagint 72, 75, 93, 233, 234
Seriah 197
Servant of God (Jeremiah) 213, 214, 217,
218
Seth 131
seventy: generations 36, 38; s. years of
exile 38
sexual purity 72
Shalmaneser, king of Assyria, captured
Samaria and took the nine tribes into
captivity 187–90
Shechem/Shechemites 92, 136–7, 140,
141
Shem 125, 126, 131
Sheol (Hell), returns its deposit 10, 20; 54;
Abaddon 55
Shiloh 141, 142
shortening, of times 14; s. of days of
suffering 16
signs, of zodiac to interpret heaven 13, 15;
s. and wonders 2
Simeon 71, 107, 136
simplicity/'singleness' (of heart) main
virtue in T12P 72, 75–83; description
of 'simple' person 79–81
Sin 13; s. and punishment 7; s. as cause
of sterility 21; s. as just 30; sins
committed in the world 63; s. and
sinners 61–7; punishment for sinners
157; sinners versus righteous 160,
162–5, 170
Sin–Exile–Return pattern 73, 82, 146
Sitis, Job's wife, her sufferings and death
239, 240